S0-DHW-508

CHRISTIAN FAITH
AND SOCIAL ACTION

Edited, and with an Introdu

JOHN A. HUTCI

CHRISTIAN FAITH
AND
SOCIAL ACTION

A SYMPOSIUM BY

JOHN A. HUTCHISON

ROGER L. SHINN

CHARLES D. KEAN

CLIFFORD L. STANLEY

JOHN C. BENNETT

PAUL L. LEHMANN

ALEXANDER MILLER

PAUL TILLICH

EDUARD HEIMANN

VERNON H. HOLLOWAY

WILL HERBERG

LISTON POPE

REINHOLD NIEBUHR

Christian Faith and Social Action

EDITED BY JOHN A. HUTCHISON

CHARLES SCRIBNER'S SONS

NEW YORK   LONDON

1953

GOSHEN COLLEGE LIBRARY
GOSHEN, INDIANA

COPYRIGHT, 1953, *by* CHARLES SCRIBNER'S SONS

All rights reserved. No part of this book
may be reproduced in any form without
the permission of Charles Scribner's Sons

PRINTED IN THE UNITED STATES OF AMERICA

[A]

261.8
H97c

HN
31
H8.5

102229

TO REINHOLD NIEBUHR

CHRISTIAN, THEOLOGIAN, PROPHET, STATESMAN

————————❋————————

With the grateful affection
of his fellow-workers and friends,
this book is dedicated without his knowledge

A10329

Preface

———— * ————

WHAT is the relation of Christianity to society, of Christian faith to the complex problems of social policy? On this question there has been a growing interest in recent years. However, it will also not be far wrong to say that confusion has kept pace with interest. The writers of this volume disclaim any panacea for these vexing problems; indeed, it is an important aspect of the viewpoint which draws us together to assert that there are no such panaceas. But perhaps we may be permitted to express the hope that the essays we have written will make a modest contribution to the clarification of some of the urgent and complicated problems in this field.

This book of essays was first suggested at a meeting of the Frontier Fellowship in the spring of 1950. As the project went ahead, it was suggested that the essays be dedicated to Reinhold Niebuhr. Not only were many of us his students, and all of us his friends and associates, but at almost every step of writing we found ourselves face to face with his work, extensive and penetrating, in the field. Our thinking was inescapably oriented to him; why should not our book be dedicated to him? Unanimously we decided it should be. His own essay was written without the knowledge that the book was to be dedicated to him.

As it was written, each of the essays was circulated among other contributors for criticism and suggestions. The process has been stimulating to us; we can only hope that it has clarified our writing. The work of the editor has been greatly facilitated by financial assistance from the Class of 1900 Fund of Williams College, for which hearty thanks are tendered.

JOHN A. HUTCHISON

Williamstown, Massachusetts
March, 1953

Contents

———————*———————

Two Decades of Social Christianity

JOHN A. HUTCHISON

-- ✳ --

JOHN A. HUTCHISON *teaches religion at Williams College. He is a graduate of Lafayette College, Union Theological Seminary, and Columbia University, and has taught at the College of Wooster. He is the author of* WE ARE NOT DIVIDED, *and (with J. A. Martin)* WAYS OF FAITH, *and is a Kent Fellow of the National Council on Religion in Higher Education.*

I. PERSONS AND EVENTS

BIBLICAL religion involves the paradox of being on the one hand irreducibly moral and social in nature, yet never being reducible completely and without remainder to any code or system of ethics. Thus, when it has been taken seriously, it has created in its adherents a distinctive combination of high moral idealism and what is really a transmoral quality, namely, humility or contrition. This combination of moral and religious qualities has, however, never been easy to maintain and has always been subject to errors and distortions.

In contemporary society many forms of liberalism have made the mistake of attempting to construe biblical faith simply and solely as ethics. However, within the religious community the opposite attempt to deprive religion of any social relevance has been the more pervasive and dangerous tendency.

In such a situation it is extremely hard—and extremely necessary—to maintain the ethical and social relevance of biblical faith without neglecting its trans-moral aspects—in other words, to do justice to both religion and ethics in the Christian faith. It is this enterprise which gives unity and significance to the essays in this volume. All of them deal, in one way or another, with this common theme.

It is also this theme that imparts interest to the organization which

I

inspired the writing of this book of essays. This organization, founded in 1930 as the Fellowship of Socialist Christians, was known from 1947 to 1951 as the Frontier Fellowship. In 1951 the Frontier Fellowship was incorporated in a more comprehensive organization known as Christian Action. The historical sketch of the Frontier Fellowship, which follows here, claims interest not through the importance of the organization, but as the record of a project of corporate thinking about the relation of Christian faith and social ethics in contemporary America.

In the Frontier Fellowship from beginning to end, no person was more influential than Reinhold Niebuhr. His voice and pen commanded an attention which led some observers to call the organization not so much a fellowship as a discipleship. Taken seriously, this is a charge which Niebuhr would have been the first to repudiate. If he spoke and wrote often and vigorously, he never appealed to any authority other than the facts of human existence as men encounter those facts in active daily life. If he was listened to with serious attention, it was because others believed that he had something extremely important to say. In any event, Niebuhr's influence on the organization and its members and friends was profound from first to last. It is therefore appropriate that these essays be dedicated to him as a token of gratitude for his leadership in thought and action.

The reader will note that the concluding essay in the volume is by Niebuhr. Since it is an unconventional procedure for a man to contribute to his own *Festschrift*, we hasten to add that Niebuhr's essay was written without his knowledge that the volume was to be dedicated to him. However, readers who are acquainted with him will agree that it is appropriate on such an occasion to give Niebuhr the opportunity to say a few words.

And characteristic words they are. One of the perplexing things about Niebuhr's thought is its many facets. Or, to change the figure of speech, he is like a juggler who bewilders his audience by keeping many balls in the air at once. His fundamental task (which was also the main concern of the Frontier Fellowship) through more than two decades has been the development of a Christian social ethic adequate on the one hand to the deepest insights of the Christian faith, and adequate on the other hand as a guide to social action in the upheaval and turmoil of twentieth-century history.

This is an enterprise which does not fit neatly into any conventional category, whether theology, ethics, politics, economics, or sociology, but embraces material from all of them. One of the stimulating aspects of Niebuhr's work is the way in which he has transgressed intellectual boundaries, doing significant work in different fields. His thinking is as timely as the daily newspaper or the current session of Congress or the United Nations, but it has also involved wide reading and study of literature, philosophy and theology as well. But always the unity of the task has been the effort to relate biblical categories of understanding to the ever-changing facts of the human situation.

This is a highly controversial enterprise in which Niebuhr has made enemies both among the theologians and the social scientists. He is himself a polemical thinker who likes nothing better than to point out the inadequacy of some conventional idea. For this he has been called everything from Communist to Fundamentalist. High among the charges has been that of unreason or irrationality. However, if we may define reason as the persistent appeal to the facts of human existence as men encounter those facts in active daily life, then Niebuhr is the most factual and reasonable of thinkers.

By implication Niebuhr's work may be termed Christian apologetic—but by implication only. There is a notable and admirable absence of any defense or hortatory recommendation of Christian ideas or values in Niebuhr's thought. He is rather concerned to understand the human situation and act in it. His writing is apologetic in the sense of seeking to show that Christian categories are more adequate for thought and action than are the competing categories of Marxism, secular liberalism, and other faiths and faith-substitutes.

Niebuhr is also a great teacher. Most of the writers in this book have been his students. All of us have been stimulated alike by his vigorous mind as well as by the vigorous and friendly personality. We join with countless others throughout the world in expressing gratitude to a great Christian thinker and teacher.

The Fellowship of Socialist Christians was founded in 1930 by a small group of people, including Reinhold Niebuhr, John Bennett, Frances Perry, Bedros Apelian, Ralph Reed, Herman Reissig, Norman

Sibley, and others. Their immediate and professed aim was to explore and express a form of social Christianity independent of both Marxism and pacifism. To an outside observer they must have looked very much like the Social Gospel organizations and fellowships common to many Protestant denominations in the early decades of the twentieth century, or like some of the Christian socialist organizations of the same period. As we shall see, the Fellowship of Socialist Christians did share some of the characteristics of both groups, but it was the differences rather than the similarities which proved to be more important.

For one thing, these people declared themselves to be Socialist Christians rather than Christian Socialists, thus deliberately asserting the primacy of their religious foundations, their social views being an attempt to discover relevant and adequate social applications for these religious premises. In the course of twenty-one years, their Socialism, never completely orthodox in its outlook, was to grow into a social philosophy for which the term *Socialist* was no longer appropriate. This development was symbolized by a change of the name in 1947 from the Fellowship of Socialist Christians to the Frontier Fellowship. The change, discussed for several years before it was actually made, was motivated by the desire for a name more accurately descriptive of the social views of the organization. However, it most emphatically did not mean that its members had made the journey, so popular during those years, from radicalism to reaction. They had not ceased to be radically critical of existing social institutions, but they had come to the conclusion that Socialism in any precise sense of the word was no real cure for the ills of society. The way in which they had come to conceive of remedies is discussed in several of the chapters which follow, notably those of Tillich, Heimann, and Holloway.

Practically, the Frontier Fellowship never sought to be a mass movement or to lead the forces of a Christian social revolution. While it always earnestly sought for more members and for a wider hearing for its views, it was throughout its two decades of existence primarily a meeting of kindred spirits for mutual stimulation and clarification. Its range of interest was from the theological basis of social action to the specific forms of action which best express religious principles.

While not primarily an 'action' group, it did incidentally carry on some noteworthy projects. Publication of a quarterly journal began in 1935. From 1935 to 1940 it was called *Radical Religion,* and since that time *Christianity and Society.* Since 1951 this publication has been taken over by Christian Action. Reinhold Niebuhr has been its editor during the entire period. Other activities of the Fellowship included the support, for several years during the 1930's, of the Delta Cooperative Farm in Hillhouse, Mississippi, support for a lay German theological institute at Bad Boll during the years after World War II, and more recently, support of the East Harlem Protestant Parish in New York City. Individual members have been active and often prominent in causes ranging from Americans for Democratic Action to the World Council of Churches.

What were the basic convictions which drew the original group together and maintained its identity from 1930 to 1951? This book is an attempt to articulate some of these common convictions. However, the reader should be warned that common convictions do not preclude differences and disagreements. The common convictions of the Frontier Fellowship never constituted a party line or an imposed dogma. There were always sharply varying emphases and interests in its membership, some of which have found their way into the pages of this book. Also there was a significant development of thought between 1930 and 1951, which is described in Niebuhr's essay. We never thought it a vice to change our minds when facts showed our previous ideas wrong or inadequate, or when new occasions demanded new duties and new ideas.

In this introductory essay we shall attempt only an outline sketch of a few of the ideas developed in more detail in succeeding chapters. As we have said, the Frontier Fellowship sought to understand and interpret Christian faith in ways relevant to contemporary society and its problems. This brought it into active controversy with at least four different groups or tendencies in contemporary American thought: (1) conventional religion, (2) the Social Gospel, (3) Marxism, and (4) secular liberalism. Here we shall indicate the line of thought the Fellowship followed in each of these arguments.

II. RADICAL CRITICISM OF CONVENTIONAL RELIGION

Toward conventional religion—the religion of the radio programs, of the church page of the newspaper, of the Main Street church—

the Frontier Fellowship maintained an attitude consistently radical and prophetic, in the original sense of those much abused words. It was radical in the sense of going to the roots of the issues involved. It was prophetic in the sense in which Amos criticized Amaziah (Amos 7:10-17) and Isaiah pilloried the popular religion of his day (Isaiah 1:10-17).

This aspect of prophetic religion is so little understood and so often misunderstood that it calls for explanation. It was Karl Marx who once remarked that the criticism of religion is the beginning of all criticism. The Frontier Fellowship would agree with that judgment—with the significant addition that the criticism of religion is itself a religious task. This is, of course, a view which Marx and his followers would neither understand nor agree with. However, one of the essential features of prophetic religion is that all human things stand under the judgment of God. The prophet regards it as his God-given or God-demanded mission to speak this word of judgment from God. Such an attitude implies a radical criticism of every aspect of human life and society. Prophetic religion has, thus, a kind of built-in principle of social criticism.

Now one of the aspects of human culture most difficult to keep under this judgment is religion. Religious institutions are prone in every age and society to claim exemption from criticism for the reason that they claim to speak for God. But what clergymen and Churches so often fail to see is that this function can easily become a process of investing some partial human interest or perspective with divine sanction. It can become the illicit process of deifying some human thing. The Frontier Fellowship saw this process from the first in such obvious cases as the tacit deification of national values (whether American, Russian, German, or any other!) or of the economic values of Capitalism or Communism. What we did not see at first—or what at first we did not see so clearly, and what we learned slowly and painfully through two decades of observation and study—is that this principle applied with equal force and truth to our own values. As Niebuhr puts it in his essay, there can be ideologies of conscience. Perhaps the crucial task of any man's personal religion is to keep his own values under the judgment of God, thus enabling him to see their partiality and his consequent need for the mercy of God.

That this self-critical role of religion has been so largely forgotten by modern man is doubly tragic, for it has meant that religious institutions and persons under criticism have tended not to regard the criticism as a prophetic word from God, but as a critical attack upon God. And they have responded accordingly. Even more important, it has meant that the critics, by and large, have not understood the genuinely religious significance of their work. Thus they have interpreted it in secular rather than religious terms.

The Frontier Fellowship's criticism of conventional religion in America emphasized the close alliance between American Protestantism with conservative and sometimes reactionary politics. In a day of Spiritual Mobilization, Christian Economics, and other movements which identify the will of God with American destiny and *laissez-faire* Capitalism with Christian freedom of spirit, this point need not be labored.

Conventional religion in America inherited from later Calvinism and from pietism an attitude of individualism. The proper business of religion, it teaches, is not to offer guidance to society but to save individual souls. But behind the façade of individual piety, this attitude has frequently given a religious sanction to the interests and values of American culture, thus converting the Christian religion into a culture religion in which the myths, rites, and values of the American tribe are celebrated and deified. This involves a two-fold tragedy. The religious tragedy is that such religion fails utterly to bring any of our life, individual or social, under the perspectives of biblical religion. To put it bluntly, there is nothing essentially Christian in such a faith whatever the label it bears. The moral tragedy is that it affords no principle of social judgment whereby American interests or values may be realistically appraised and evaluated. Our social policies and attitudes are thus deprived of the wisdom and perspective which the Christian tradition might give them.

Conventional religion in America has also frequently been guilty of sentimentality in the precise sense of emotion unrelated to the facts. Such attitudes have a perennial human quality for the good reason that the world has never lacked foolish people whose emotions live an unreal compensatory life, apart from the facts of real life. But in the American scene these attitudes have derived from the additional source of a demonstrably inadequate philosophical and theological orientation. We will return presently to this theme. Meanwhile we may note that this inadequacy has contributed to the sentimentality as well as the irrelevance of much conventional religion. In the present volume, Holloway's essay illustrates this criticism in its application to international policy. Here as elsewhere the Frontier Fellowship was concerned to evaluate current religious practice in the light of biblical faith on the one hand, and urgent social problems, on the other.

III. THE SOCIAL GOSPEL—PRO AND CON

The Social Gospel movement raised other issues for the Frontier Fellowship. The term *Social Gospel* refers to a type of social Christianity which grew up in the last half of the nineteenth century and the early decades of the twentieth century. It involved a mixture of social and theological liberalism. While it had roots in earlier, religiously inspired reform movements such as abolition and the temperance movement, the Social Gospel may be characterized as the response of morally sensitive Christians to the vast new problems of industrial America. It was an effort to bring what was conceived to be Christian morality to bear upon social problems ranging from corruption in government and business to immigration, housing, labor organization, etc. From the first, the Social Gospel was not a unified creed or movement, but a wide range of tendencies. Projects varied from prayer meetings for working men to the institutional church to blue prints for a Christian socialist state. Among its leaders have been such differing and varying figures as Walter Rauschenbusch, Washington Gladden, Frank Mason North, Francis McConnell, Harry F. Ward, and G. Bromley Oxnam, to mention only a few.

It is the enduring achievement of the Social Gospel to have recaptured the social nature of the Christian faith and to have expressed it in new and challenging terms. Later nineteenth-century American Protestantism had, as we have seen, construed religion largely as a matter of saving individual souls. Salvation was often expressed in naïvely and exclusively other-worldly or next-worldly terms, with the result that religion had little or no relation to the problems of human society. This individualism and other-worldliness were so widely assumed that any vigorous assertion of a religious concern for society was regarded as subversive of both religion and society. In such a climate of opinion the Social Gospel reasserted and reclaimed the social nature of the Christian religion. While its proponents were not primarily theologians, this must be regarded as an important theological as well as social achievement. Socially it had the force of challenging if not breaking the close alliance between Protestantism and the American business class.

In these respects—and they are important respects—the Frontier Fellowship continued the Social Gospel tradition. Like the Social Gospel, the Frontier Fellowship sought a social interpretation of Christianity. Its discussions and writings were never far from the most urgent problems and needs of society; and its members were in the thick of many struggles for social justice. If they "went theological," it was to find categories adequate to guide social action. This concern, which defined the Frontier Fellowship, also finds expression in this volume. Whatever differences of opinion and emphasis may be discovered in the essays which follow, they have in common this important characteristic: they seek an interpretation of Christian faith relevant to contemporary social action.

But in other respects the Frontier Fellowship carried on an unceasing and unsparing criticism of the Social Gospel, embracing both its theological presuppositions and its social conclusions. We have already noted that the Social Gospel was related to the rising theological and social liberalism of the nineteenth and early twentieth centuries. This liberalism derived from two principal sources: (1) an older tradition of American liberal thought expressed in such figures as Channing, Emerson, Theodore Parker, and others, and (2) German theological thought of the nineteenth century, notably the thought of Albrecht Ritschl. Within a wide spectrum of ideas the Social Gospel exhibited certain themes or emphases which continually recurred. One such theme was the immanence of God within nature and society. God was conceived to manifest himself in the harmonious order of nature and in the humanitarian progress of society. Echoing the controversy over organic evolution, this theology emphasized God's presence in natural law. But what in nature was evolution was conceived in human social history as progress. It was thus a loving, indeed a friendly and genial God who manifested himself in the upward and onward march of humanity. Here veritably was a God without wrath! For anyone living in the troubled mid-twentieth century, it is hard to comprehend the widespread acceptance of so blandly hopeful a faith a brief fifty years ago.

This theology also included an equally genial conception of man. Some formulations went to the extreme of asserting that God had distinguished himself chiefly by creating so excellent a being as man. Others contented themselves with an emphasis on the dignity and goodness of man with little reference to his evil or sin. True, evils were clearly apparent in society, but man with the help of his genial father in heaven had the capacity to effect their progressive solution. With the ever-kindly but often vague help of God, man could make his way by continuous progress into that ideal society which the Social Gospel called the Kingdom of God.

Into this picture Jesus fitted as the supreme teacher and exemplar. Rebelling against the sterility and rigidity of theological conservatism, liberal thought sought to move back from the 'Christ of the creeds' to the 'Jesus of history,' with his teachings of the fatherhood of God and the brotherhood of man. Obviously, such thoughts fitted in well with the mood and temper of the Social Gospel.

Upon such ideas the Frontier Fellowship levelled its fire. Its criticisms derived both from a mid-twentieth-century conception of social tragedy and evil, and from the apparent disparity between the Social Gospel and biblical views of God and man. The two lines of thought mutually re-enforced each other. Sobered and saddened by the storms of the times, men were more willing and more able to understand the Bible. Conversely, the Bible illuminated man's understanding of his contemporary plight. The Social Gospel's over-estimate of man's capacity for goodness and consequent under-estimate of his sin led alike to bad theology and bad social policy. Theologically it may be said that until man understands the desperate nature of his sin, he can have little comprehension of the God who is Judge and Savior. Until he recognizes his need for a Savior, he is not likely to recognize his Savior. Socially, the optimism of the Social Gospel led to forms of social action irrelevant to social fact. As we have noted, Holloway's essay offers detailed documentation of this tendency in

American thought about international relations. A more realistic philosophy might have kept men closer to the relevant social facts.

This conception of man led also to an excessive, sometimes exclusive reliance upon reason and education as factors in social change. This point was made effectively by Niebuhr in *Moral Man and Immoral Society* in 1932. Since man's best efforts at rationality and altruism are tainted with self-interest, he argued,—since men are never so reasonable or generous as liberal thought had imagined, or as they imagine themselves—any policy which places excessive reliance upon such forces is very likely to be self-defeating.

This is a point frequently misconstrued by intellectual opponents who regard it as an advocacy of unreason and force in social relations. Nothing could be further from the truth. It is a factual observation—an empirical generalization—that men are seldom as reasonable or as generous as they like to suppose themselves. Now reason and altruism are extremely valuable instruments for social organization, but we will be able to use them better if we have some realistic notion of their limits. It is surely a part of reason's task to ask quite factually and critically how reasonable men are, and so to discover the limits of reason. Dogmatically to postulate the omnicompetence of reason is surely a quite unreasonable act! Similarly, it is of the greatest importance, both theoretically and practically to discover both the possibilities and limitations of altruism in human action.

From such general considerations more specific criticisms follow. From the first, the Frontier Fellowship sought to draw a clear line between justice and charity in social policies. The Social Gospel frequently maintained that if in obedience to the teachings of Jesus men would only love one another sufficiently, justice and law would become unnecessary. Such a view is not only theologically shallow, overlooking both the towering heights of the New Testament ideal of love and the abysmal depths of human evil; it is socially unrealistic. There is small likelihood that capital and labor, for example, will soon love each other and the whole community enough to dispense with the pursuit of laws which relate them to each other and to the whole community in some tolerable degree of justice. There is equally small likelihood that white men will soon love black men enough to dispense with the campaign

for laws aiming at inter-racial justice. This is not to say that love is
socially irrelevant, but simply that apart from hardheaded applications
in just laws and social structures it is meaningless.

Holding such views, the Frontier Fellowship did not hesitate to
align itself with individuals and groups who were the victims of injustice, as, for example, labor, especially when it was denied the right
to organize, and also the American Negro.

Another example of the Frontier Fellowship's criticism of the
Social Gospel was its view of pacifism. Many advocates of social Christianity have identified Christian love with an unequivocal opposition
to all war. To the Frontier Fellowship, this identification was suspect
for several reasons. Theologically, it was often based upon the very
questionable assumption that the Christian religion is simply a matter
of following Jesus, or practising the way of love. Ethically the infinite
demands of Jesus' law of love were scaled down to an avoidance of
violent coercion, often oblivious to the insidious evils of non-violent
coercion. The Frontier Fellowship argued in Niebuhr's phrase that
"love is always relevant but never a simple possibility." To seek simply
to love one's neighbor as oneself is to seek the impossible. Nevertheless,
love is the ultimate ideal by which we judge all our approximations.
It is not only the yardstick and goal of human progress, it is an incen-
tive to seek whatever approximations are possible.

Pacifism has frequently been blind to the operations of egotism
in human life, believing that men will presently come to love one
another so much that war can be abolished. The Frontier Fellowship
argued that such reasoning frequently betrayed its adherents into
irresponsible social policies. A more realistic approach would admit
the possibility of coercion, and hence of violence in all social organization. From this it follows that the practical or possible aim is not
to seek to eliminate it altogether but to minimize it. But to minimize
it may conceivably involve its expedient use.

The Frontier Fellowship did not hesitate to apply such propositions
to both domestic and international problems. Thus, for example, the
pursuit of peace apart from other aims is delusive and irresponsible.
A better aim of international policy is the far-sighted and responsible
use of American power to further justice and oppose injustice in the

world. Similarly in domestic policy, the ideal of peace unrelated to justice is hardly a defensible social goal.

While opposed to a pacifism which aims at reforming or reorganizing society on the basis of love, the Frontier Fellowship has expounded and some of its members have exemplified a pacifism of witness or vocation. Renouncing any specific aim to 'win friends or influence people,' they have believed that love is the ultimately valid rule of human life and have found an individual vocation in reminding their fellowmen by precept and practice of this truth. It is a fact which men involved in the struggles and conflicts of social life are apt to forget. As Socrates found it to be his vocation to be a gadfly to his fellow-Athenians, so such a pacifism is a perennially appropriate vocation for individual persons who feel called to it.

What emerges from this evaluation of the Social Gospel is a chastened and sobered version of social Christianity. Opponents have called it lame, half-hearted, and defeatist. Proponents reply that it is a serious attempt to learn from the Bible and from two decades of tragic social history.

IV. MARXISM EVALUATED

From the beginning, the Frontier Fellowship undertook an appraisal of Marxist thought, as a task of religious as well as social importance. Several of the essays in this book illustrate this interest. The first issue of *Radical Religion* stated editorially that one objective of the new quarterly was to "clarify the affinities and divergences of Marxian and Christian thought." This is a subject on which there have been both real differences of opinion, and also real development of thought during the past two decades of Frontier Fellowship existence. While the Fellowship was never orthodox or fellow-travelling in its attitude toward Marxism, there was at first a considerable amount of unconscious Marxism in its social analysis. There was a sufficient residue of Marxism as late as 1942 to enable the Statement of Principles to speak of the "expanding and contracting periods of capitalism." But in the years which followed, this residue of unconscious dogma was distilled out and discarded.

It is important to distinguish between the Frontier Fellowship's approach to Marxism and that of two other religious groups, (1) Christian fellow-travellers who put Christian labels on what are essentially Marxist ideas, undertaking no real criticism or evaluation, and (2) Roman Catholicism and fundamentalist Protestantism, which have been content to label Marxian as the anti-Christ, thus from the opposite viewpoint avoiding the necessity for critical discernment. In the Frontier Fellowship we always honestly sought for what was valid in Marxism. Tillich's conception of the dehumanization of man in technical society and Miller's treatment of vocation in this volume both show the influence of Marxist thought.

But if we learned anything in our study of Marxism, it was that the present form of communist thought is a tragically evil thing which free men must oppose and resist—and also try to understand. Our attempt at understanding began with a distinction between Marxist theology and Marxist social analysis. At the present time it is a threadbare cliché to call Marxism a religion or a religious substitute, but this was by no means so generally understood two decades ago. The Frontier Fellowship may fairly claim to have seen this fact from the beginning and to have spent much time and effort seeking to understand it.

The essential quality of a religious object is its capacity to evoke and sustain from its adherents an absolute or unqualified allegiance, thus constituting for them the meaning of existence. On such a basis the religious character of both Nazism and Communism becomes apparent. But these two political faiths or religions have a very different religious quality. Nazism is a recrudescent form of primitive tribalism. Communism is, by contrast, a Hebrew-Christian heresy. This can be seen, as Shinn points out in his essay on history, from the fact that Marxism shares the biblical view of history as a dynamic and meaningful movement. For both the Bible and Marxism, history is a great drama with a beginning, a climax and an end. Parallel to the Garden of Eden story is the communist tale of primitive Communism. The fall of man takes place in the Christian story due to man's desire to be as God, while in Marxism the fall is constituted by the introduction of private property with its attendant acquisitiveness and exploitation. The coming of Marx is a climax in the Marxist drama of history, similar to the coming of Christ for Christianity. Communism like Christianity has its version of the Church and of the new age. It has also been remarked that the Marxist dialectic of history acts in a way similar to the biblical God who casts the mighty from their thrones and exalts those of low degree.

From a Christian viewpoint, Marxism is to be judged not as simply false, but what is much more dangerous because more plausible, a mixture of truth with explosively dangerous falsehood. Thus the refusal of Marxism to recognize God makes it an easy prey for the idolatrous worship of the communist cause and subsequently of the Russian state. Again, in its conception of man and human history Marxism differs from other forms of modern thought by what at first appears to be a greater realism regarding evil. It sees the hard facts of injustice and misery with clearer eye than many alternative philosophies. But it makes the fatal mistake of identifying all human evil with acquisitiveness, or lust for private property, thus drawing the utterly false conclusion that when the system of private property is destroyed evil will be abolished. It is ironical to observe, in passing, that this view of evil is a close relative of the economic man of Adam Smith. From a biblical viewpoint, it is easy enough to see that sin or evil is deeper and more pervasive than any system of property. For the Bible, sin is that infinite self-centeredness in which man confuses himself with God as the center about which all things move. In social relations, sin assumes the character not so much of acquisitiveness as the will to power and dominion. We may confirm this view by noting the unchecked power impulses of the Russian commissar.

The Frontier Fellowship was also particularly concerned to evaluate the Marxist charge that religion is the 'opiate of the people,' *i.e.*, a compensatory illusion employed for socially reactionary purposes. The view that religion is a compensatory illusion, is to be sure, not limited to Marx and his followers. A widespread view in the modern world, it involves at least three fallacies which it is sufficient simply to state. First, it confuses the psychological genesis of an idea with logical disproof of it. To term an idea 'wishful' is not necessarily to disprove it; truth is a matter of logical evidence not psychological genesis. Second, it seems to suppose an exclusively empirical conception of truth. Whatever cannot be tested by strictly empirical methods is regarded as illusory. Third, it assumes that religion always does function as an opiate in human life, while in point of actual fact and experience we had found it, at best, a stimulant.

But we did not dodge or duck the hard, plain fact that religion is sometimes socially reactionary, counselling acquiescence or resignation where rebellion would be more appropriate, telling men that their miseries are divinely ordained. And we sought for a rule by which we might distinguish alterable from inalterable evils. We also observed that religion is not the only human interest used as an opiate. Indeed, Marxism has here mistaken a truth about man for a truth about religion.

Where perhaps we differed most deeply from Marxism was our belief that religion is a perennial human thing, which, shut out the front door, will force an entrance into the back door of men's lives. The wise course is thus not to seek its abolition as a pre-scientific superstition, but rather to make it as wise and socially creative as humanly possible.

V. SECULAR LIBERALISM EXAMINED

In contrast to the monolithic nature of Marxism, secular liberalism appears protean. This type of thought, widely prevalent through contemporary America, may be described as the attitude which, unable honestly to affirm belief in the traditional God or religion, transfers belief to man and the possibilities of human life. Its attitude toward traditional religion is overwhelmingly critical, ranging from agnosticism to dogmatic rejection. Positively, it places great emphasis on the role of intelligence as embodied in science and popular education. If only men would apply scientific method to their urgent human concerns, and then propagate the results by an improved education, a progressively better life would be assured for all men. This creed also places great emphasis upon democratic values and the democratic way of life.

The impact of this philosophy is so widespread that no man or idea in the western world has been uninfluenced by it. In this book, Miller describes the corrosive or erosive effect of secularism upon the traditional religious view of vocation. Shinn depicts more positive aspects in his treatment of progress. Since its influence upon the academic mind has been particularly great, it is natural that Herberg's essay, entitled *Faith and Secular Learning,* should deal with it systematically and in detail. As Herberg points out, much of the plausibility of humanism as a faith derives from its criticism of follies and excesses of traditional religion. It is predominantly a critical faith; and in many of its specific criticisms the Frontier Fellowship joined. However, we never felt it necessary to convert our criticism into a metaphysic.

It is fair also to point out the close resemblance between many of the social values espoused by humanism and those which the Frontier Fellowship espoused as Christian. Often we found ourselves standing shoulder to shoulder with secular liberals on some issue such as racial or industrial justice. The irony of such situations was frequently heightened by finding traditional religious persons and forces on the other side of the battle lines. To a faith like ours, which held the end of man to be action and not contemplation, such facts as these engendered a respect and humility in our dealings with humanism.

Frontier Fellowship criticism of humanism and secularism was concerned to emphasize the fact, which is vigorously denied by many adherents of the view, that humanism is a religion or religious-substitute. Many humanists regard its secular or non-religious character as altogether basic to the position. But as noted in the case of Marxism, religion shut out the front door, forces an entrance through the back door of men's lives. The humanist by his denial of any absolutes does not avoid encounter with an absolute. He simply drives it underground, thus depriving men of any responsible criterion for dealing with the issues involved in this type of experience. As Herberg states it, human autonomy is not a consistently possible or tolerable ideal for contemporary man.

We have already noted the similarity between many of the ethical values of humanism and those of traditional Christianity. This similarity has led many traditionally religious observers to speak of humanism as a 'cut-flower' religion, or to charge that it has borrowed or stolen its ethical values from Christianity. Put more practically and less dogmatically, the test is to see whether this faith can recreate these values, passing them on in new forms to successive generations of adherents. In this sense, humanism constitutes an experiment in new forms of religion which should be watched with great interest by all students of the subject. The Frontier Fellowship watched for two decades with interest and with considerable skepticism concerning the creativity and stability of humanism as a faith.

In one further respect humanism seemed to us hopelessly inadequate, namely its extremely optimistic view of man and human evil. Committed *a priori* to a faith in the possibilities of human life, it is poorly equipped for an adequate understanding of human tragedy and sin. Perhaps, indeed, it is true that only a faith whose final object is above or beyond man can fully take in the tragically evil character of much of human experience. Having high hopes for man, humanism has aroused utopian hopes. Whatever its plausibility for the earlier years of the present century, it can afford men little guidance for the present time of troubles. Humanism has tended to regard evil as ignorance—inadequate thought or education—which might thus be overcome progressively by men's growing capacity for scientific intelligence. To the Frontier Fellowship these ideas seemed refuted by the facts of daily life.

VI. BIBLICAL FOUNDATIONS

We must turn briefly now to the Frontier Fellowship's own position, sketching briefly some of its main emphases in relation to the essays which follow in this book. As we have said, the Fellowship was an attempt to rediscover biblical faith in ways relevant to contemporary social action. But to say "biblical faith" raises a flock of questions. What is biblical faith? What is the nature of biblical authority and inspiration? Why the Bible rather than the *Bhagavad Gita* or *Das Kapital?*

As Niebuhr put it, we sought to take the Bible seriously but not literally. Despite occasional charges to that effect, we were not Fundamentalists seeking to uphold a literal conception of biblical inspiration. Whatever else and whatever more it might be, the Bible was for us a literary and historical document which must be studied with all the rigor and candor of literary and historical scholarship. But neither could we have classified ourselves as modernists. For all its gains, that viewpoint had thrown the baby out with the bath. With its talk of the Bible as a record of man's search for God and of abiding experiences in passing categories, it simply did not seem to take the Bible seriously.

Rejecting both Modernism and Fundamentalism, we found ourselves, along with many others at the same time, feeling our way toward a third position. There was nothing sacred about the words or the text of the Bible; it is not so much the revelation of God to man as it is a record of that revelation. When we approached the Bible in this way, we found there a distinctive view of man's nature and destiny. Thus we could agree with Barth that what the Bible contains is not the correct human thoughts about God but the correct divine thoughts about man. The biblical view of life found verification in thought and life for us.

This is not to say that biblical faith can be logically derived or demonstrated in any facile way. Like any major philosophy or faith, there is an element of mystery which prevents a slide-rule derivation. Rather this faith must be regarded as the gift of God's grace. But once attained, it is man's privilege and duty, if he is to remain a rational creature, to test his faith by all the facts of experience. This task of relating faith critically to experience in all its many aspects is what Christianity has traditionally called apologetics. Our specific field in the Frontier Fellowship was the relating of Christian faith to the problems of social understanding and social action. Our testimony was that we could understand the problems of society and act upon them more adequately in Christian terms than any alternative terms we could find.

But what is the biblical view of life? In its unity and diversity, it may be compared to a great symphony. Here we can barely mention the major themes as they bear upon the argument of this book. The primary theme of the Bible is that God is sovereign Lord so that men as his creatures may find fulfillment of life in his service, and only there. As Roger Shinn states it, God is Lord of history. The metaphors of sovereignty and lordship emphasize the essential biblical truth that God is, to use other spatial metaphors, *above* history and culture, and also *in* them. Or, to use the opaque (but still metaphorical) terms of the theology textbooks, he is both transcendent and immanent.

From this biblical view of God emerge some of the distinctive biblical truths about man and his history and culture. From the sovereignty of God emerges the biblical view of human history. As Shinn argues, history has meaning. Biblical religion is thus to be set in sharp contrast to those faiths and philosophies which regard man's life in time as illusory. But also, as Shinn argues, it is not a meaning which can be exhaustively stated or embodied in any finite constellation of events.

This conception of God and history has its bearing upon individual life in the notion of vocation or calling. The sovereign Lord calls men into his service. But if we state this truth from the human side, regarding man's work as his response to the call of God, we come directly to the doctrine of vocation. This traditional Protestant doctrine, which has received increasing attention in recent thought, is expounded in Miller's essay.

While the traditional Christian God is both above history and within it, the attitude of Christianity toward culture has frequently depended upon which of these metaphors receives the greater emphasis. It is an important fact of contemporary religious thought that after a century or more of immanence theology, the transcendence of God has lately received the greater emphasis. This view is notably expressed in Kean's paper on the crisis of contemporary culture, which the author sees principally in its vertical reference to the God who stands above all cultures. Other writers in the volume, while agreeing in this emphasis, go on to sketch man's efforts to work out his destiny under God in conformity to God's will.

The dialectic of God's transcendence and immanence is also to be seen in Stanley's paper on the Church. The Church is in but not of the world. On the one hand, it is an association of altogether human beings, but its reason for being is to serve a purpose above or beyond the world.

From the biblical view of life may be derived important truths about morality or ethics. Since the Frontier Fellowship was a social action group, this was close to our central concern. We always understood biblical religion as fundamentally an ethical religion, unlike the faiths or philosophies which profess to go 'beyond' ethics. Conversely we never undertook the popular but futile task of separating ethics from religion. Faith and works always seemed to us two sides of a single reality.

But what principles of morality does biblical faith yield? We were never tempted by a fundamentalist concern for literal obedience to the words of the Bible, whether the Ten Commandments, the Sermon on the Mount, or the letters of Paul. Nor were we tempted by natural law theories of ethics, which in their way seemed as rigid as Fundamentalism.

Our ideas on this problem underwent considerable development in the course of two decades. At first we were content to regard Socialism as an application of fundamental religious ideas to the specific problems of contemporary society. But as Socialism appeared increasingly obsolete, we sought for a different principle. More and more our ethical principle came to be respect for, affirmation of, personality. The problem of ethics, so conceived, was to oppose social structures and arrangements which degrade personality, and to promote those which fulfil personality. The ethical task is the humanization of man. It is this important proposition which is the theme of Tillich's paper on *The Person in a Technical Society*.

But personality does not occur in isolation. Rather the notion of persons-in-community expresses the truth about man. It is this truth which is dealt with in Lehmann's essay on the Christian community as living context for the Christian ethic.

In the conception of man as a person, freedom assumes an altogether basic significance. Man's essence, namely personality, is not a gift of nature, but rather something which in responsible freedom he must achieve. Man must freely become a person. Therefore any system which strikes at man's self-determination, as does modern totalitarianism, strikes at the very roots of his humanity. This momentous current issue is discussed by Heimann. Also significant in his essay is the historical connection which he establishes between Christianity and man's freedom.

But the notion of men as persons-in-community needs concrete application and implementation if it is to guide social action. What kind of society best embodies this ethical ideal? And conversely, what kinds of social structures frustrate them? While we gave up the attempt to construe Socialism as such an implementation, we did not cease to be interested in Socialist analyses of concrete problems and in Socialist criticism of Capitalism. The experience of Great Britain under the Labour Party seemed to us an extremely valuable social experiment. If some parts of the experiment yielded negative results, that did not vitiate the entire experiment. And in social thought as well as natural science, negative results have real value. Again, we did not cease to be critical of aspects of Capitalism which seemed to us to frustrate personality. In short, in order to implement our ethical ideas we found ourselves moving pragmatically toward what is often termed a 'mixed system,' namely an economic system involving elements of both public and private enterprise.

The search for good (that is to say, for better rather than worse) social arrangements involves a large measure of pragmatic judgment and testing among existing and possible arrangements and systems. There is often no way of judging before the fact whether a given structure will be humanly good or evil. But while such judgments are pragmatic, they are momentously significant for human weal and woe. This kind of pragmatic, factual search for the genuinely better course of action is superbly illustrated in Bennett's paper on the *The Church Between East and West*. Of just such pragmatic but supremely important discrimination the life of Christian men consists. We serve a God who is absolute, but our service, like everything else about us, is relative. It is not therefore unimportant. It is important as a relative response to the absolute, as a human response to God.

The Christian Gospel and History

ROGER L. SHINN

———————————————— ✳ ————————————————

Roger L. Shinn *is Professor of Philosophy and Religion at Heidelberg College. Educated at Heidelberg College, Union Theological Seminary, and Columbia University, he served with distinction in the United States Army during World War II. He is the author of* BEYOND THIS DARKNESS *and* CHRISTIANITY AND THE PROBLEM OF HISTORY *and is a frequent contributor to religious periodicals. He is a Kent Fellow of the National Council on Religion in Higher Education.*

It is not unusual for men to believe that they live in turbulent times. History generates enough turbulence to vindicate the belief repeatedly. Even so, perhaps the twentieth century has the right to think that it is going through a time of more-than-ordinary troubles.

Along with revolution, *blitzkrieg,* and destruction of empires have gone violent upheavals of ideas and faiths. We have seen an amazing procession of repentant communists, disillusioned idealists, remorseful Nazis, conscientious traitors and spies, fifth columnists, pacifists turned militarists and militarists turned pacifists, renegades from democracy or socialism, wretched apostates and noble converts of all sorts. Only the stupid or ignorant have escaped intellectual and spiritual tempests. Whatever his beliefs about the universe, the observer is tempted to say of the world of culture and ideas, "Whirl is King."

The causes of the confusion are numerous, but surely one important cause is the mistaken philosophies of history with which the twentieth century has met its crises. It is customary in these days to stress economic and sociological theories of historical causation and to smile at the idea that philosophies might cause anything, good or bad, in history. But those who are least concerned about philosophy

23

are most likely to be the unconscious victims of inept philosophies. And nowhere does philosophy come closer to men's everyday thinking than in the philosophy of history.

Hence it is easy to illustrate recent ideas about history, without turning to scholarly writings, by looking at some of their journalistic expressions. With an ironical look at the half-century just completed, the first 1950 edition of *Time*, under the caption, "The View from 1900," said:

> [The world] looked forward to the 20th Century with a degree of confidence unequaled by any previous age and unregained since. Paced fast or slow, progress was sure, limitless, irreversible. Virtue walked with progress; they fed each other . . . the mood of the hour seemed to wipe out the black misery of preceding centuries. The worst was over; man was out of the woods.

In a similar mood of retrospect the British *Economist* of January 6, 1951, reprinted a paragraph from its issue of January 4, 1851, leaving comment up to the reader:

> When we refer to a few only of the extraordinary improvements of the half century just elapsed—such as the 35 years' peace, so far as morals are concerned; such as the philanthropic and just conviction that the welfare of the multitude, not of one or two classes, is the proper object of social solicitude; . . . the advances in religious toleration, and in forbearing one with another . . . the extended application of machinery to all the arts of life . . . :—when we refer to a few events of this kind, we become convinced that the half century just elapsed is more full of wonders than any other on record. . . . All who have read, and can think, must now have full confidence that the 'endless progression' ever increasing in rapidity, of which the poet sung, is the destined lot of the human race.

If we consider, not the academic philosophies of history, but the political and economic attitudes which guided most of the general thinking of the past century, we find two pervasive viewpoints. Although they differ strikingly, they are similarly optimistic. One, the *laissez-faire* attitude, assumed that without any human guidance history offers mankind a destiny of increasing progress. The outlook is especially characteristic of classical Capitalism, but its extent is much broader. The second, the revolutionary attitude, sees serious evils barring progress and advocates a radical change to bring in the better age. It is best illustrated by Marxism, but it, too, includes many types of thought.

I. THE GODS OF ADAM SMITH AND HERBERT SPENCER

Few ideas about history could be so comfortable as those implied in the classical capitalistic theories of Adam Smith. Has any god ever demanded so little or promised so much as the providential power of *The Wealth of Nations?* Man is required only to follow his self-interest; as he does so, he is "led by an invisible hand"[1] to promote the general welfare. The god of the *laissez-faire* philosophy encouraged men to sow selfishness with the expectation of reaping social good.

Nor is this philosophy of history entirely forgotten today. True, every important nation finds it necessary deliberately to help providence guide its economy; but to the stalwarts of *laissez-faire* these actions show only a shameful loss of faith. An ex-congressman, writing in the self-styled *Christian Economics,* quotes Adam Smith to support his belief in providence. "The ethical result," he writes with perfectly straight face, "is inherent in the competitive, private property system regardless of the motives of its managers. . . . Yes, 'God works in wondrous ways His marvels to perform.' "[2]

The understanding of history implicit in Adam Smith was spelled out explicitly and sometimes modified by his followers. Herbert Spencer performed the paradoxical feat of stressing both the ruthlessness and the beneficence of history's deity in far stronger terms than Adam Smith had done. Spencer rejoiced in the brutalities of life. Starvation, disease, death of the poor and weak are "the decrees of a large, far-seeing benevolence," which prescribes the survival of the fittest and the consequent improvement of the human race. Spencer's soaring optimism reaches out to the most confident philosophy of history imaginable: "Evolution can end only in the establishment of the

---

[1] *The Wealth of Nations,* Bk. IV, Ch. 2. In justice to Adam Smith it should be remembered that he was less hidebound than many who invoke his name to this day. He insisted that the advantage of the lower classes and wage-earners coincided with the advantage of society, whereas the advantage of those who lived by "profit" often did not. And he said that any government intervention should be on the side of labor. (See Bk. 1, Ch. 8; Ch. 10, Pt. 2; Ch. 11.) Nevertheless, Smith holds the most benign view of a natural or divine providence which turns man's selfishness to good account.

[2] Samuel B. Pettingill, "Only the Free Can Be Strong," *Christian Economics,* April 10, 1951.

greatest perfection and the most complete happiness." And all this is quite apart from any human devising. Man need only keep hands off. "Progress is not . . . a thing within human control, but a beneficent necessity."[3]

Few would be so foolhardy as to echo Spencer's hard-boiled statements today. Yet it is interesting to watch apologists for classical capitalism frequently shuttle between the kindlier mood of Smith and the more brutal cheerfulness of Spencer. In either case the assumptions about history and society are similar. Conscious direction of the economic and social process only interferes with history's progress. Individuals should, of course, plan for their personal welfare and advantage, but general social planning is harmful. The gracious workings of gods, or nature, or chance—all are about the same—are more favorable. For history, rightly understood, is kindly indeed.

The gods of Smith and Spencer have dealt deceitfully with their worshippers. Events have gone far to shatter what Tawney calls "the smiling illusion of progress won from the mastery of the material environment by a race too selfish and superficial to determine the purpose to which its triumphs should be applied."[4] And events have been harder to meet because the misplaced faith left men so unprepared.

II. MARXISM AND PROVIDENCE

If classical capitalism has furnished the most widely prevalent notions of history in the modern world, Marxist influence has probably had the second greatest impact. The Marxist and capitalist, though bitter foes, agree remarkably often. Thus the Marxist interpretation of history merely modifies many of the illusions of its supposed opposite.

Adam Smith's implied philosophy of history may be likened to a gradually ascending escalator, on which the occasional jostling of the riders does little serious harm and actually helps to move the escalator upward. In Spencer's version the crowding, struggling riders often shove each other off; but those who hang on move still more swiftly and certainly to a goal of perfection. Marx (who, although a slightly older contemporary of Spencer, represents a newer set of ideas) depicts

---

[3] The citations from Spencer come successively from: *Social Statics*, 1850 ed., Ch. 25. *First Principles* (New York: Appleton, 1880), p. 517. *Illustrations of Universal Progress* (New York: Appleton, 1864), p. 58.

[4] *Religion and the Rise of Capitalism* (New York: Harcourt Brace, 1926), p. 283.

the escalator as moving through a series of jarring zig-zags. Revolution, usually violent, marks each shift in direction. But the over-all motion is nonetheless forward and upward.

So confident was Marx of the progressive character of history that he could write:

> Therefore, mankind always takes up only such problems as it can solve; since, looking at the matter more closely, we will always find that the problem itself arises only when the material conditions necessary for its solution already exist or are at least in the process of formation.[5]

Such hopefulness might inspire envy from even the most energetic Marx-haters of this baffled twentieth century, which has taken up problems (including some bestowed upon it by Marx) that may go tragically beyond the powers of mankind to solve.

Sometimes with discerning realism, sometimes with blind cynicism Marx cut through much of the superficial optimism of his time. But in his total philosophy this despiser of utopianism was as utopian as any he criticized. His repetitious insistence upon the scientific character of historical materialism veils, without hiding, a sort of "providential dialectic" as romantic as any of the providential views he rejects. In the dialectical process of history, as he saw it, every movement contributed something to the over-all progress. Even the hated bourgeoisie, said the *Communist Manifesto,* had accomplished wonders in production, drawn barbarian nations into civilization, broken down nationalism, and made the world an interdependent whole. Capitalism had transformed both the system of production and social relations so as to prepare man and history for the coming utopia—the synthesis growing out of all previous theses and antitheses.

For beyond the tortuous, often violent progress of past and present, there was to be the classless society following the revolution and temporary dictatorship of the proletariat. Here the very nature of human motivation was to be changed. Violence and coercion—even the state—would disappear. In a co-operative society the "free development of each" was to be the condition for the "free development of all."

The "providential dialectic" of Marx attracted many an idealistic

---

[5] Preface to *A Contribution to the Critique of Political Economy* (Chicago: Kerr, 1904), pp. 12-13.

believer, often to disillusion him sadly. This secularized religion was fitted to sustain ardent hope and fanatical courage during difficult days. But history has given little support to the faith that a sweeping revolution can set the world right.

III. PRESENT PERPLEXITIES AND NEW VISIONS

A generation nurtured on fraudulent hopes for history has found itself unfitted to meet brutal realities. The two traps set by previous generations have caught countless victims. The first—baited by Smith, Spencer, or other evolutionary optimists to their left—tempted all hopeful souls who were content to overlook the malignant evil within history and hope that things would turn out all right in the end. The second—baited by the revolutionaries, whether Marxists or anti-Marxist—caught those who thought that one great victory over evil would set the world on the right track. The traps were deceptively camouflaged. Many who were proudly convinced that they saw through *laissez-faire* economics were captured by its more pervasive cultural hopefulness. And many who had no desire to overthrow the bourgeoisie were sure that peace and prosperity would graciously follow the conquest of Hitler, or Stalin, or someone else.

In the early days of the fighting in Korea a perceptive press dispatch reported on the psychological unpreparedness of soldiers who had been "thrust with all haste from the soft comforts of garrison duty in Japan, Okinawa, and Hawaii or the peaceful atmosphere of the United States into the filth and violence of the battlefield."[6] Men accustomed to swimming on the beach at Waikiki were embittered by the mud-holes of Korea. Given the exigencies of military life, such sudden shifts are perhaps unavoidable. More serious is the problem of a whole culture which has grown up in the Waikiki mood and must suddenly learn the facts of life about mud and blood. Or of a culture which, when it does face evil, promises its warriors—literally or figuratively—that they will be home by Christmas, then sends them into years of bitter fighting.

In this situation some traditional Christian ideas about history, rooted in the Bible and developed by St. Augustine and a long succession of thinkers, have come alive after long neglect. Thus historian

---

[6] See report by Richard J. H. Johnston in the *New York Times*, Aug. 13, 1950.

Arthur Schlesinger, Jr., writes: "A culture which staked too much on illusions of optimism finds itself impotent before an age dominated by totalitarianism and war; history, in a sense, has betrayed its votaries." While not himself claiming any "decisive faith in the supernatural," Schlesinger says: "The Christian account of human motivation is massive, subtle and intricate, and it throws light on certain present dilemmas which baffle liberalism or Marxism. Whatever you may say about Augustine, he would not have been much surprised by the outcome of the Russian Revolution."[7]

As a historical (rather than a mystical or philosophical) religion, Christianity grapples directly with the problems which threaten to wreck modern culture. It conveys its conceptions about history through a mighty drama with the universe and the whole of time as its setting. The story starts with God's creation of the world and man. With man's defiance of God sin enters the world. History then is the struggle between divine and demonic forces, in which evil is always active and God's purpose is always a demand and a reality for the faithful. God never forsakes history. His eternal Kingdom impinges upon history, stands at the goal and end of history, and repeatedly penetrates history. Most decisively it invades history when God comes, in the person of His Son, for the salvation of men and history. The Son is crucified—evil demonstrates its cruel and mighty historical power. But faith responds to a resurrection. It recognizes a victory over evil and takes the Cross for its symbol of triumph. Still sin ceaselessly exerts its force in the world. But those in whom Christ has evoked trust and loyalty can live in the confidence of the Kingdom of God which has won a victory in history and which promises final victory yet to come.

This account is sometimes dismissed on the grounds that it is an interpretation depending upon faith rather than a strictly factual reading of history. And so it is. But so are all human understandings of history. The word history may, of course, refer to the bare sequence of events in human societies. But just as often the word refers to the selection of recorded and remembered events. It is in the latter form that history enters into human consciousness. The process of recording

---

[7] See review of Reinhold Niebuhr's *Faith and History* in *Christianity and Society*, XIV, No. 3 (Summer, 1949), pp. 26-27; "Niebuhr's Vision of Our Time," *Nation*, CLXII (1946), 754.

and remembering inevitably involves selectivity and interpretation. As the remembered events are related to each other, some loom large as the unifying events which bring coherence into the tangled sum of details.

The Christian finds his historical understanding illumined by the remembered history of God's dealings with Israel and God's revelation in Christ. Clearly he cannot prove by universally accepted criteria that this reading of history is better than another. But he can show that this remembered history, which frankly sees the facts in the light of faith, can illumine human problems as other schemes (like those discussed above) cannot. That is why this Christian account of history, too disturbing for the modern taste, has recently been rediscovered and proclaimed by many a penetrating thinker.

IV. CRITICAL ASPECTS OF CHRISTIAN THOUGHT

The Christian message is a Gospel, a declaration of good news. Thus it may seem strange that its impact upon the contemporary world has so often been critical. Especially in the most energetic of its recent theological formulations it has gained a reputation for puncturing illusions and undercutting optimism.

But in its critical character Christianity is not untrue to itself. For biblical faith both demands and makes possible a searching criticism of the hopes of culture. The demand is real because the God of Israel and the Christian community has always refused to tolerate idolatry; prophets and apostles had ruthlessly to criticize false faiths and values which tempted men's allegiance. The possibility exists because Christian confidence gives a degree of independence from deceptive ideologies which often buoy up human hopes.

Of course, Christian thinkers themselves can claim no infallibility or immunity from the errors and sins of society. They need both to acknowledge their part in the follies of their time and simultaneously to realize that the culture which they criticize may liberate them from some of the errors of their own ecclesiastical tradition. Only then may they find in the Christian Gospel the perspective for illuminating criticism.

This criticism may be brought against both of the prevalent forms of modern confidence which have been sketched above. Against the *laissez-faire* assurance biblical faith must assert the power of evil in history. The battle is not only against "flesh and blood," but also against "the spiritual hosts of wickedness in the heavenly places" (Eph. 6:12). When things are allowed to take their course, they do not inevitably improve. Whatever the varied forms of the Christian belief in Providence, it has never asserted that the world will automatically get better or that private selfishness many times multiplied insures public good. It has frequently asserted that the wages of sin is death.

Against the revolutionary confidence—whether it be proclaimed in the name of Marxism, reaction, nationalism, world government, or any of numerous others—the Christian criticism applies similarly. Some of these movements may have their valid aspects. Like revolutions of the past some might be beneficial, some harmful. But none is *the* answer to history's problems. None represents *the* triumph over evil. Sin is more persistent than any of its particular manifestations. The clamoring promises of utopia, whether in the twentieth century or in centuries past, show treacherous misunderstanding of history.

It is sometimes asked why the sort of Christian thought represented by this volume is so critical of utopianism. Even if utopias are unattainable, are they not valuable goals? Should not the Christian be more friendly to noble aspirations than to cynical acceptance of evil?

The questions are right in their implication that Christian faith recognizes evil in order to fight it, not to acquiesce in it. Sin, not faith, has prompted the indolent philosophies which discourage action on the pretext that the world cannot be improved.

But inherent in biblical faith is the understanding that man's final trust and confidence belong only in God. There is no final salvation of history in social organization, for before Him "the nations are as a drop of a bucket." No historical rearrangement can promise that security—all but baffling the best of Christian insight—which is able to "take no thought for the morrow." As Augustine explained it to his generation, the peace achieved by political measures is "not to be lightly esteemed," for it is a gift of God, but it is not to be confused with the only secure and eternal peace—the peace of the City of God.[8]

---

[8] *The City of God,* XIX, 26; XV, 4.

If utopianism thus borders on sacrilege, it also has its very specific practical dangers. Although it may inspire temporarily greater efforts than historical realism, it is ill suited to the persisting struggle against evils which are never finally rooted out of history. A nation roused to the vision of a "war to end war" sees its dream fade and turns to isolationism. Awakened tardily to far greater dangers, it makes a tremendous effort to defeat a particular incarnation of evil in a Second World War; then, with a victory won, it hastens to relax, dissipate its strength, get its economy back to normal. When still further dangers threaten, it alternates dizzily between grandiose dreams of having its own way with the world and the despairing chill of actualities.

Again, utopianism may hinder accurate historical analysis. It often tempts men to cry peace when there is no peace. It has blinded men to the power of evil in their enemies and in themselves. It has, on occasion, drained off idealistic emotion in grandiose dreams; thus in the second quarter of the twentieth century there were times when concrete useful proposals of workaday politicians were sometimes dying by a few votes while utopians, not deigning to support anything so ordinary, pursued their fancies. (As one example among many earlier and later ones, there was the refusal of certain devotees of the Kellogg-Briand Peace Pact to support any measures for collective security.)

A final disastrous outcome of the utopian dream is likely to be fanaticism. The dedicated servant of the utopian movement too often forgets the pervasiveness of historical evil, localizes it in particular institutions, and aims to crush it out. So he falls victim to what the British historian Herbert Butterfield calls "that mythical messianism—that messianic hoax—of the twentieth century which comes perilously near to the thesis: 'Just one little war more against the last remaining enemies of righteousness, and then the world will be cleansed, and we can start building Paradise.' "[9]

Thus it was that Arthur Koestler's old Bolshevik, Rubashov, tortuously sought to justify the crimes the Party committed, until near the end of the trail he looked back two decades and thought: "Nobody foresaw the new mass movements, the great political landslides, nor the twisted roads, the bewildering stages which the Revolutionary State

[9] *Christianity and History* (New York: Scribners, 1950), p. 41.

was to go through; at that time one believed that the gates of Utopia stood open, and that mankind stood on its threshold."[10]

V. CHRISTIAN AFFIRMATIONS

Against the background of recognition of evil the Christian Gospel proclaims confidence. The Christian hope has rich meanings for personality and for the community of faith which is the church—meanings which are being rediscovered in this century as they have frequently been in the past. But here we shall consider only three affirmations which have direct bearing upon the social-historical analysis and efforts of the Christian.

The *first* is the affirmation that God is Lord of history.[11] This biblical doctrine differs from two frequent conceptions of history. (1) Many philosophies and religions, including perhaps the greatest Hellenistic and Oriental ones, have considered history unimportant. They have taught that history is a vain cyclical repetition, perhaps even an illusion. They have offered salvation in a mystical escape from the physical, historical world. They have emphasized eternal, timeless truth and depreciated the transitory and temporal. Or they have, whether in primitive fertility cults or in great pantheistic systems, found "Nature" more important than history. (2) Other philosophies, particularly the prevalent naturalisms of the Western world, have stressed the importance of time, denying or neglecting eternity. They have said that history has its own importance, that it needs no supernatural or super-historical, that man's acts and destiny are meaningful only for the history in which he lives.

By contrast to both of these tendencies, biblical thought affirms that history is important but that it derives its importance from God. The Divine Creator has a purpose for history; He gives it its impor-

---

[10] *Darkness at Noon* (Signet Edition), p. 95.

[11] There are great variations in Christian thought on this theme. This essay follows the direction of a considerable consensus of writers in the Ecumenical Church, a consensus generally typical of the Frontier Fellowship and Christian Action and made famous in America by Reinhold Niebuhr. It differs from two brilliant recent works: Karl Löwith's *Meaning in History* (Chicago University Press, 1949), with its anti-historical interpretation of the New Testament; and John Baillie's *The Belief in Progress* (New York: Scribners, 1951), with its attempt to establish a belief in religious progress on New Testament grounds. These same two tendencies, with several other variations, may be found throughout the history of Christian thought.

tance and its meaning. History is not self-sufficient and does not provide its own meaning. "All flesh is grass. . . . The grass withereth, the flower fadeth; but the word of our God shall stand forever." Yet against this realization of the transitory character of history is the affirmation—by the same Second Isaiah—that God governs history and works His judgment and redemption in it. "Why sayest thou, O Jacob, and speakest, O Israel, My way is hid from the Lord, and my judgment is passed over from my God?"

The New Testament emphasizes even more the passing character of history, its evil, and its emptiness. But in the midst of all tendencies to other-worldliness is its central affirmation that the Holy God has entered into time for the salvation of history. "The Word became flesh and dwelt among us, full of grace and truth." It happened, not in some remote heaven, but in Palestine "under Pontius Pilate."

Thus history has divinely given meaning, purpose, direction. The Bible does not assert that all historical events are clear clues to God's nature, or that by accumulating enough historical information any disinterested observer can learn how God goes about ruling the universe. God is a "hidden God," a mysterious God, and His Lordship is opposed by the demonic challenges which make up so much of the record of history. Short of the final judgment, the final redemption, history remains a confusing picture. There are intimations of God's judgment in the defeat of evil historical powers, experiences of His grace in social creativity and renewal. Amid these fragmentary revelations of judgment and grace the Christian lives by the faith that the God who created man and gave a measure of historical freedom is concerned for history and will redeem it. Upon human darkness a light has shined, a light which enables the Christian to see upon Calvary the abiding symbol both of the might of evil and of the power of redemptive grace.

The *second* affirmation concerns the Kingdom of God. In Christ's teaching the Kingdom of God is "at hand." It is the promise which brings hope and eager expectation into a history where evil produces suffering and frustration. But it is also in some sense a present reality whose power is evident in the conquest of disease and evil. It is the goal of history—a goal which has come into history with Christ but which awaits the future (often described as the return of Christ and the Judgment of the world) for full realization. It comes among men now; yet men live less in satisfaction than in hope.

The Kingdom of God has appeared in varying aspects to Christians involved in the problems of history. To Walter Rauschenbusch and the Social Gospel, the Kingdom of God was a historical goal of "humanity organized according to the will of God."[12] To many a European Christian more recently the Kingdom of God has been an eschatological hope, not only unattainable in terms of historical organization but so utterly transcendent as to give almost no guidance for historical, political decisions.[13]

Each of these interpretations grasps part of the significance of the Kingdom of God and misses part. The Social Gospel brought some truly creative attempts to put faith into practice and to realize some of the teachings of Jesus in social organization. Strikingly contrasting theologies in Europe today have brought courageous defiance of tyrannical governments which sought to usurp the place of Christ in men's loyalties. More inclusive understandings than either of these have seen God's Kingdom as both a continual divine judgment upon all historical hopes and as a constant power driving men to historical activity in God's service.

Religious hopefulness is constantly tempted to take the form either of a utopia (the this-worldly heresy) or of an opiate (the other-worldly heresy). The Kingdom of God is not a utopia, because it implies God's judgment upon all historical attainments. It is not an opiate, because it calls men to responsible action. God's Kingdom is rather a hope and a powerful reality in historical life.

The *third* affirmation concerns human responsibilities in history. On this issue there have been both honest variations in Christian thinking and hypocritical perversions of Christian doctrine. But the main thread of biblical thought can be separated from its distortions.

The belief in the divine lordship over history reminds men that they are not all-knowing and all-powerful. It checks the Messianic

---

[12] *A Theology for the Social Gospel* (New York: Macmillan, 1917), p. 142.
[13] Karl Barth, addressing the World Council of Churches assembly at Amsterdam, 1948, proclaimed that "God's design" is the Kingdom established in Christ and does not mean the work of the church "for the amelioration of human life" or for establishing world peace and justice. The address is printed in *The Christian Century*, LXV (1948), p. 1330ff. *Cf.* Reinhold Niebuhr's answer, pp. 1138-40.

complexes of frantic revolutionaries and egotists with their reckless confidence in their ability to control the future. It offers a measure of confidence to conscientious men worried that their limited foresight must settle historical questions of vast moment.

But faith does not relieve men of their responsibility in history. Perhaps paradoxically, the most radical declarations of divine sovereignty (e.g., Calvin's) have gone with the strongest emphases on human responsibility, decision, and loyalty. Christianity rejects any sort of historical determinism which makes man a cog in an impersonal historical mechanism. Likewise it rejects beliefs that divine sovereignty means that everything is all right or that everything is getting better.

Thus, at its best, the faith in divine Providence can mean, as John Baillie says, "the tranquillity of the Stoic and Yogi without their apathy, and the zeal of the revolutionary without his restless fever and fret."[14]

It is sometimes claimed that the strongest motivation for historical activity is the hope of visible accomplishment. Christian conceptions of history do not deny men such hope. The critique of utopianism, with its insistence that historical achievements offer no final security, does not deny the possibility or worth of such achievements. No rigid barriers are set up to halt social advances at any given point. The faith in the Kingdom of God as a power in history means the faith that history offers countless opportunities for realization and redemption.

But in the end motivation for responsible activity may be the stronger because it does not depend utterly upon questionable promises of historical success. Often in the twentieth century, as in ages past, faith in God has stirred men to action when all ordinary human hopes had failed.

No correctness of doctrine can assure faithfulness in life. Man's sinful rationalizations can make any doctrine an occasion for egotism or complacency. But *faith*, guided by doctrine, can win its victories. Christian doctrine is that God so loved the world that He acted in history for the salvation of men. Christian faith, then, will express its love for God and neighbor through faithful activity in history.

---

[14] *The Belief in Progress*, p. 73. For an illuminating discussion by a professional historian of the meaning of Providence for the statesman and historian, see Herbert Butterfield, *Christianity and History*, Ch. 5.

The Contemporary Cultural Crisis

CHARLES D. KEAN

———————————————— ✳ ————————————————

CHARLES D. KEAN is Rector of Grace Episcopal Church, Kirkwood, Missouri. Following graduation from Brown University, he entered journalism. Turning to theology, he studied at General Theological Seminary, graduating in 1937. He is the author of many articles and books, among them, CHRISTIANITY AND THE CULTURAL CRISIS, THE MEANING OF EXISTENCE, and THE INWARD CROSS.

I. THE SYMPTOMS OF THE CRISIS

AN APPARENT contradiction exists in the modern world between political peace and economic stability. The result is the turning of normal social expectancies upside down, as war seems to bring chaos. One of the two major symptoms of the cultural crisis of our time is the seeming inability of modern nations to conceive practically of peace and economic stability at the same time.

The observation about this contradiction is certainly an over-simplification of the real situation, but noticeable symptoms tend to be such exaggerated phenomena. It can be argued that the order brought to the economic scene by war, both "hot" and "cold," is illusory, and that the chaos brought by peace is largely the result of readjustment in a world which has never had a working peace long enough for the process to be completed. But even with recognition given to the partial truth of such comments, the general impression of contradiction remains as a terribly confusing cultural force in our day.

The contradiction has existed since before 1914, so that a majority of today's adults have never known anything else. The problem has grown more acute year after year. It is not that a majority of people do not desire simultaneously both peace and prosperity, but rather that

37

when it comes to formulating public policy, they are unable to see their political and economic problems in such a perspective that both peace and stability appear to be simultaneously possible.

The background of this contradiction can be worked out easily in terms of simple cause and effect. But there is a more basic interpretation which must be made. This is illustrated by the fact that peace without general economic stability soon ceases to be peaceful because internal political tensions in the various nations become accentuated and international rivalries are increased, while, on the other hand, economic stability without a general atmosphere of political peace is only speciously prosperous.

The antithesis between peace and economic stability is the first major symptom of the cultural crisis of our times. It does not require very much perspicacity to recognize its existence. The other major symptom is equally serious but a little more subtle. It lacks dramatic manifestations. But it is just as real and presents just as serious a dilemma.

This second symptom is that freedom and an adequate standard of living likewise appear to be antithetical in our day. At first glance this does not appear to be so. But freedom to be an understandable concept must be explored beneath the surface of political configurations, so that in some real sense it can describe man's relative mastery of his own historical destiny. In this context it can be easily seen that modern man is becoming more and more the prisoner of his own technological enterprise.

While legitimate and important distinctions may be drawn between the various political economies of our day, the fact remains that collectivization as an engineering process—rather than as a political philosophy—is the concomitant of that standard of living which western man has come to regard as desirable. Transportation, communications, the production and marketing of all the necessities of life require a high organization both of capital and personnel. Therefore, the ability of any individual to affect the process, or even to handle his own affairs with any real independence of the process, becomes relatively impossible.

In the western world, man has paid the price of becoming an interchangeable part in the technological structure for the high standard of living he enjoys. Yet the observation must be made that collectivization in itself does not produce a high standard of living. Nazi Germany was one proof of that fact, and Soviet Russia today is an even more tragic example of what happens when the logic of the contradiction is reversed. But on the other hand, the result in the western world of relatively cheap and available automobiles, telephones in most homes, standard brands of clothing, food, and equipment has been to cause a standardization and regimentation of human as well as material resources. One has only to remember the "Great Depression" to have the truth of this contradiction brought home.

Since freedom and economic well-being are apparently opposed to each other, neither has any practical meaning by itself. Freedom at the expense of economic security and the appurtenances of what *Life* magazine calls "modern living," loses its glamor for the average western man; while a high standard of living without any real control over individual destiny leaves the individual, as Karen Horney has put it, likely to acquire "the neurotic personality of our time."

Here are the two symptoms of cultural crisis—the contradiction between peace and prosperity, and the contradiction between freedom and an adequate standard of living. When these are explained simply in terms of sociological or economic causation, their real significance is lost. They are symptoms of a breakdown in western culture. Modern man in the western world—for that matter in the communist-dominated countries, too—is unable to visualize and interpret his predicament, so that he can never attempt with general confidence a creative approach to the problems which beset him.

Individuals may propose attacks upon the results of these two contradictions. Indeed, fascism was in large measure a general reaction to this crisis situation by means of widespread group psychosis. Communism is a demonic attempt to cancel out the contradictions by an all-embracing political and economic program which is supposed to remove every possibility of unpredictable variations from the social scene, as well as to eliminate political and economic tensions. Fascism might be compared culturally to a paranoid lashing out at all and sundry in destructive frenzy, while Communism appears to be a reaction to the cultural crisis in which man turns to eating himself and forcing his neighbors to do likewise.

The fact remains that men are unable to account for the very pressures with which they must contend by the categories they are accustomed to use, and this means that western culture itself is called in question.

II. THE MEANING OF CULTURAL CRISIS

We live in an age of cultural crisis. This expression is used to describe a pervasive anxiety which makes many people feel that not only are they unable to deal adequately with their immediate problems, but even more seriously, they are uncertain as to the actual nature of what disturbs them. Therefore, they are continually prone to vent their hostility on groups and things which cannot be regarded in reality as fully responsible for the threatened nature of their existence.

Whatever political reality there may be to the threat of Communism in America, the widespread fear of Communism appears to be rather a matter of attempting to nail a free-floating general anxiety to a concrete object, rather than a serious attempt to deal with a political problem. Because world Communism is a deliberate attack upon the results of the cultural crisis without an adequate facing of the underlying nature of the problems of our age, it must be opposed. It cannot be regarded as the cause of our difficulties, but rather as one of the more serious results of our failure to appreciate the real causes.

To say we live in an age of cultural crisis does not mean that there are not analyses and proposed solutions being offered. We know the contrary to be true. It does not refer to the wide differences of opinion as to what we ought to do—except as these differences reveal a fundamental moral uncertainty. On the tactical level, differences of opinion may indicate cultural health rather than sickness.

Again, to say that we live in an age of cultural crisis does not mean that there is no health at all in western civilization. There is plenty of evidence to the contrary, and one of the most hopeful signs of it is the continued ability of both the United States and England to work out pragmatically mixed approaches to complicated political and economic questions. What cultural crisis does mean in this reference is that it is terribly difficult today to capitalize on the elements of health because the framework within which civilization is understood appears to be either so ambiguous or so inadequate as to make clear decisions in practical affairs impossible.

The threats of a third world war and of widespread economic confusion seem to indicate that our problems cannot be handled simply by the re-adjustment of the political and economic details. When the cultural framework can be taken for granted, men do meet their problems of social change by rearranging the details of their political and economic life. But when the underlying intellectual, emotional and institutional structure itself is involved as part of the problem with which we have to deal, then the situation becomes serious.

Culture is this structure in its totality. It includes not only the explicit intellectual rationale of civilization at particular times, but also the ideological factors which weight most normal decisions by individuals and groups in some specific direction. It includes the whole interlocking pattern of assumptions and both conscious and unconscious premises which men take for granted in seeking to understand an issue, to communicate with each other and to take practical action. Culture is summed up in a general individual and group sense of self-fulfillment.[1]

Cultural stability is the most significant yardstick available for determining the relative health of a civilization. When the culture is fulfilling its functions, men can think, relate themselves to each other, and act with some real confidence that these processes can be congruent with things as they are—even if this is not the case in actual practice. When the culture is shaky, men's thoughts, relationships and actions have no sure foundation of confidence, even though they may appear to be pragmatically satisfactory. The expectancy which focuses social life is blurred, and anxiety inevitably results.

To say that we live in an age of cultural crisis, then, is to recognize that this sense of expectancy, by which the institutions and political and economic fabric of western civilization have been built, is hard to connect meaningfully with the historical decisions we have to make. Whether it is a question of American foreign policy, or of

---

[1] For a fuller exploration of the meaning of culture in relationship to civilization, see Charles D. Kean, *The Meaning of Existence* (New York: Harpers, 1947), Ch. II.

the role of the family in an urban technological society, there is no sufficiently clear perspective to enable men to make accurate decisions and to take purposeful action.

Historical issues continue to arise, but in the absence of an adequate perspective, consistent policies are difficult to make. The result is that there is a wide-spread free-floating anxiety regarding the past and the future, while the present remains confused. Satisfactions tend to become hysterical, while disappointments become either depressing or paranoid.

Western culture for the past two and a half centuries (and indeed for a much longer period if one wishes to go back to the roots) has been built upon two parallel and interlocking sets of presuppositions. These do not appear sufficient today to enable men to interpret their experience adequately. The two presuppositions are, (a) that by an objective relationship to whatever concerns him, man is able to control, manipulate or at least to adjust to, circumstances satisfactorily; and (b) that individual self-fulfillment through economic acquisitiveness is the means whereby a healthy society lives.

These two presuppositions have been analyzed by many writers for a long time. While they may be stated in various ways, and while recognition must be given to shadings of emphasis between the classes in any nation or region, they are still the dominant characteristics of western society. But modern man is losing confidence in them without realizing it. They are not opposed by a live alternative, since even Communism is just a very systematic rationalization of western culture. The problem is that modern man is slipping into a position in which he has not cultural presuppositions which make decisive action meaningful.

The general evolution of western society since the Industrial Revolution—to say nothing of the evolution since the Renaissance—has been a long series of technological and scientific victories at the expense of the structure which made possible the winning of these victories. Three developments illustrate this point: (1) the popularity of what might be called "the peace of mind" school of religious thought; (2) the vogue of literary existentialism; and (3) atomic science. None of these can be explored fully in an essay of this size, but each is important.

The "peace of mind" school, as exemplified by Norman Vincent Peale's *Guide to Confident Living* and Joshua Loth Liebman's *Peace of Mind,* and including work by as widely divergent people as Fulton J. Sheen and Dale Carnegie, is an attempt to enable men to escape the results of the cultural crisis without facing the fact that the crisis arises out of an historical situation where real problems demand solution.

On the one hand, these searches for personal confidence presuppose the continued relevance of both premises and use a popularized version of the depth psychology and a Ritschlian understanding of the function of religion to authenticate it. They proclaim in various ways the possibility of individualistic self-fulfillment in nineteenth-century terms. On the other hand, they suggest that the tensions which threaten men can be eliminated by the use of a proper technique, again derived from a combination of psychiatry with Christianity understood, not as Cross, but as euphoria.

Literary existentialism is another phenomenon which helps to illuminate the crisis of our culture. This is the school of thought associated with the names of Martin Heidigger in philosophy and Jean-Paul Sartre in the field of the novel and the drama, and must be distinguished from "existentialism" as the name for the influence of Soren Kierkegaard upon modern Protestant theology.

Any treatment of literary existentialism in short compass is bound to be inadequate, yet the existence of the school as such has significance for understanding the crisis of our culture. It is important to realize that this school arose during the unstable years of the decade prior to World War II and came to flower during the war itself. There are wide differences of interest and orientation within it, ranking from the attempt to make a synthesis with Roman Catholicism—as with Gabriel Marcel—to the frank nihilism of Sartre.[2]

Literary existentialism on the whole, however, denies the significance of culture at all. It concentrates on knowledge through decisive action. The effect of this is not unlike the grin of the Cheshire Cat, as if decision without content and content without context were possible. As a matter of fact, both Marcel and Jaspers are quite aware of

[2] The quarterly, *Christianity and Society,* devoted its issue of Winter 1949-50 to this subject. Particularly see the articles by Paul Tillich and L. F. Thornton, Jr.

this problem. For our purpose in this essay, this school serves to dramatize by its rejection of western culture the seriousness of the breakdown because no one feels compelled to reject that which he can take for granted in the normal course of living.

The rise of atomic science as the present high point of both western science and technology illuminates still another facet of the cultural problem. A direct corollary of the two presuppositions of our age is the general conviction that science—primarily the physical sciences—and ethics blend with each other as part and parcel of the same thing. The bomb dropped on Hiroshima brought an end to this miscegenation which the modern world had condoned. But it did not relate science and ethics in an alternative way. Instead, it left a question mark, which society only partly recognizes and about which it finds little to do.

These three manifestations of the cultural crisis, each in its own way, illuminates the fact that people do not find it easy to meet their practical problems of home, business, community, and world responsibility in the light of their inherited expectancy. This is because men cannot grasp the full significance of the difficulties they encounter, and when these are not clarified so as to be dealt with, their persistence causes increased confusion. Yet the three illustrations also point to the fact that men are not as yet prepared to analyze their culture critically, but that they either try to continue affirming it, or seek to reject it, or find it a frustrating problem.

At its inception, the communist movement purported to be the creation of a new culture, but its formulators did not go far enough in their analysis of that which they criticized. While the criticism made a positive contribution in its illumination of unfaced evils in western civilization, its own acceptance of the fundamental basis of that which it attacked made it peculiarly dangerous. Its attack on evils which men found hurting them had considerable appeal in spite of its assurance that it alone could provide an adequate foundation for social reconstruction.

As events have worked out in the past half-century, that which was theoretically dangerous in Communism became a terrible destructive force since one of the two greatest national powers in the world became the bearer of the communist promise. The combination of the tendency to cynical self-justification, found in all nations and enhanced in proportion to the actual power at that nation's disposal, with the messianism of a communist theory, which was actually a rationalization of a false alternative to that which it criticized, has made Russian Communism the menace that it is.

While the western world as a whole does not recognize this aspect of Communism for what it is, it is true that the movement as a desirable alternative to the traditional methods of handling political and economic affairs has lost most of its appeal. Its illumination of social injustice has become part of the general heritage, but its program now appears to be a way of embalming rather than reconstructing the culture as a whole.

Communism will not be accepted in the western world except where Russian military interference is sufficient to allow communist minorities to seize political control. In the Far East, it still has the appeal of a creative force. The political and economic ineptitude of the western powers makes the ambiguity of its Far Eastern appeal relatively unnoticeable, even though it appears to combine a blatant nineteenth-century nationalism requiring an individualistic basis with the mechanistic social approach of orthodox Leninism.

Yet the search for some kind of political and economic formula which will annul the tensions which distress us continues. In the United States there is still considerable faith, as evidenced by the right-wing Republican, that the "trickle-down" theory must still be tried. From this point of view to that of the radical anti-communist left, there are a number of differing faiths. But probably the most significant aspect of the cultural crisis is that the vast majority of people seem to have little confidence whatsoever, no awareness of the nature of their difficulties and no hope capable of practical expression, that anything will be done to change the situation.

III. THE CHRISTIAN FAITH AND THE CRISIS

For the Christian faith, here is challenge and judgment. Here also is the grace of God. The crisis of western culture is not by itself redemptive, but it affords a special opportunity for proclaiming the Gospel so that man can hear it and respond.

In one real sense, the very existence of culture is the arch-enemy of Christian faith. While it is impossible for man to live without culture of some kind in that he must have a framework for interpretation for the total setting of his life within history, he is always tempted to place his real confidence in that interpretation. When the current of affairs appears to flow quietly, the culture itself is given the role of God to all practical purposes. When the cultural situation is confused, men still tend to seek for a stable order as if that were an end in itself.

All cultures presuppose the possibility of man constructing an adequate man-centered frame of reference, even though they may use theological verbiage to describe this setting. What is really significant is that within such a frame of reference, men take it for granted that they have an institutional structure within which the problems of life not only can be met but ought to be met. For instance, during the depression of the 1930's, one of the more serious problems to be faced was the tendency of men, even whole families, to devalue themselves as they encountered unemployment, rather than question the rightness of an institutional framework which operated as if men were things.

While every culture, by its inherent tendency to pretension, is the arch-enemy of Christian faith, man cannot live without culture. A New Testament Christianity appraising the predicament of this middle period of the twentieth century cannot be naive enough to suppose that because we are in a period of cultural breakdown—and possibly of radical revision—we can eliminate having to deal with culture as such. Man must devise some generally acceptable set of categories, given concreteness by social institutions, or he cannot deal with life at all.

For Christianity, the challenge is to approach the problem of cultural reconstruction on an understanding that culture must be subordinate to faith. Yet there must also be an awareness, which Roman Catholic thinkers, no matter how profound in other areas, do not understand, that faith itself can become so involved in culture as to cease to be faith in the New Testament sense. This was the tragedy of the Middle Ages, where culture and faith became so identified with each other that the culture itself could not be analyzed and criticized.

The challenge, if it is to be accepted with realism, involves judgment. The Christian Church in its practical operations is as much involved in the culture of our times as any other social institution. It cannot face the problem of cultural crisis as if its organized life were not part of the problem. It cannot really claim to have understood the two great symptomatic contradictions of our day any more accurately, in its official teaching and institutional program, than the rest of the civilization of which it is a part.

A Christianity, which sees the challenge and accepts the judgment as being upon its own corporate life along with the total culture of our times, may make a profound contribution to the way in which men come to terms with their more serious dilemmas. Christianity will not serve in this as if it were a political-economic-social alternative. Christianity, as such, is not a different kind of engineering to be substituted in the world of technology, nor is it another way of organizing cities and handling international affairs. But Christianity can provide the basis for a new hope, as through faith in Christ it gives men a sense of "citizenship in heaven" along with a profound sense of responsibility on earth where they dare to admit their actual sin. And Christianity can make possible a creative attack upon social tensions, as through faith in Christ it gives men an awareness that "we are all one in Christ Jesus," even though the divisions of history are not cancelled.

Western culture understands peace to consist of the elimination of international tension, either through the suppression of all major difficulties or through the achievement of an equilibrium secure enough to withstand all conceivable shocks and strains. The modern cultural problem raises the question as to whether such an understanding of peace is either broad or deep enough to have any long-range significance. Certainly, peace as understood in the New Testament is neither monolithic nor judicial in essence, but rather it is an underlying harmony resting upon faith in Christ Jesus. But this harmony is not to be thought of as a political alternative to the various schemes attempted or proposed in the international scene. Rather, it stands in judgment on all political achievements, yet at the same time it is also a continual inspiration to those seeking more adequate political adjustments.

Western culture understands economic prosperity to consist either of continually full employment or of an ever-expanding productive industry or both. Whether or not prosperity is understood in terms of production or consumption or in some balance between them, the premise that economic prosperity, however conceived, is self-authenticating continues. It is a fundamental good. It is an end in itself. The crisis of modern culture raises the question as to whether economic activity in any form can be regarded as the ultimate index of social health. As understood in the New Testament, the community—which certainly involves political action and economic enterprise—is not to be understood primarily in these terms, but rather as the "colony of heaven." But this is an entirely different thing from the "Christian social order" imagined by the Social Gospel movement of three decades ago. It is both a judgment on all social orders, since one can be the *politeuma* fully, and it is also the inspiration for those who work for better social conditions.

Western culture understands freedom to be the absence either of political coercion or of economic pressures, but in both cases its reference is to the "rights" of individuals to be self-determining. The contemporary crisis cannot but raise the question as to whether this understanding of freedom has the kind of dimensions which make it a meaningful category for the description of human existence. The New Testament sees freedom as the result of adoption into the family of the sons of God.

Western culture understands an adequate standard of living to be measured primarily by its material components. It is in this sense largely that the charges of "materialism" so often levelled against our age have any pertinence. People may vary greatly in what they regard to be necessary—as against simply desirable, but nobody wants to discard the opportunities for easier living made available by technological advance. The cultural crisis raises the question not whether our material accomplishments are in themselves wrong, but whether we understand that an adequate standard of living must have three dimensions: opportunity, environment, and appreciation. In the light of the New Testament, the setting for the good life is to be understood qualitatively not quantitatively, but the quantitative issue is not ignored.

When the historian of the future writes the story of the middle period of the twentieth century, he will be in a position to see more accurately than we can see now the significance of the contradictions between peace and prosperity, between freedom and an adequate standard of living. Certainly he will be able to appreciate more fully the various causes of that general lack of sureness with which we face our various political, economic, and social issues, which is the most distinctive characteristic of our age. But while we cannot have the advantages of afterthought in the course of dealing with immediacies, the Christian faith is rooted in an appreciation of the grace of God which frees us for creative action now.

Every age has its problems, and while those of this mid-century period are very serious indeed in their own right, our confused relationship to them is even more significant than the problems themselves. It is in this particular setting that the Christian doctrine of the grace of God is most important, and we become receptive to it as we make our own the Psalmist's insight, "The Lord is king, be the people never so impatient; He sitteth between the Cherubim, be the earth never so unquiet"; and likewise Paul's understanding in the Second Epistle to the Corinthians, "My grace is sufficient for thee: for my strength is made perfect in weakness."

The history of Christianity has seen continual attempts to synthesize it with whatever culture was prevailing in order that it might be used as cement for the social structure or as re-inforcement for the particular ethical standards of a society, and above all as the means whereby men may find justification within the social process. The Age of Justinian saw one form of such an attempt and the Middle Ages another. Kierkegaard felt that Gruntvig and Martensen were doing just this kind of thing in the Denmark of their day a century ago. The point is that Christianity is never a means to something else without ceasing to be fully Christian.

In our twentieth-century crisis, the distinctive contribution of a New Testament point of view has not been made very well. This is because the Christian Churches are still seeking to justify themselves in terms of the prevailing social structure. And tragically, the leadership of the Christian Churches co-operates more often than not, as in the various attempts to sell organized Christianity to the American people as a bulwark against Communism.

The general understanding of the relationship of the Christian Church to modern culture has continued to be much the same for a long time, but a peculiar advantage for the proclamation of the Gospel arises from this very fact. Within the increased tempo of social change in the past two centuries, the usefulness of Christianity for these auxiliary purposes has become less and less significant. A large element of modern society has come to believe that it can satisfy the same essential purposes without having to bother with the impedimenta of Christian traditions and statements. Therefore, the Gospel has become relatively useless for secondary purposes auxiliary to aims regarded as more important, and the opportunity exists for its proclamation in a primary sense.

We proclaim the Christian Gospel, not as the means of saving western society nor as the means of building the new order as the old one falls to pieces, but as the will of God for man. There is no such thing, in the New Testament sense, as a Christian culture—a Christian social order. God alone is Lord of history, and all human achievements are weighed in his hand as nothing. The Cross, taken seriously, both affirms and denies what men may accomplish, and this includes all culture.

As long as men have societies, they will have to use presuppositions in doing business with each other. The Cross recognizes this as the way life works since so much of its symbolism is concretely related to first-century Palestinian culture, and through its very congruence with the understandings of its own historical age is also available for the self-interpretation of other ages. But the Cross also denies the perennial titanism of all cultures, and thus enables us to see the pretensions of our inherited presuppositions. Man can never be in a purely subjective relationship to an otherwise objective world (in which other men are also objects) because he exists as the image of God, not as God himself. Man can never use any kind of self-fulfillment, economic or political, individualistic or socialistic, as the basis of society, because fulfillment is the free gift of God alone and is available only by faith and not through human accomplishment.

Yet our practical tasks continue and must be met. And the process of dealing with them requires the formulation of new presuppositions or the modification of the old ones so as to allow people to take into account the realities of life. This means the continuation in some form of culture as the framework in which men deal with their historical problems. The difference, from the Christian point of view, is in the light in which these are faced.

Our expectancy is not in the achievement of a society without tension, a peace in which all conflicts of individuals and groups are annulled, nor a prosperity which is automatic, nor a freedom without demands. Our expectancy is rather that we may continue to seek both political peace and economic prosperity, both individual freedom and an adequate standard of living for everybody, not as ends in themselves, but as practical occasions in which we may see the love of God taking concrete form in human society. We know that the judgment of God must be pronounced on what we achieve as well as on what we oppose, and we pray that we may be given the grace to recognize it and accept it.

The Church, in but not of the World

CLIFFORD L. STANLEY

———————————————— ✻ ————————————————

CLIFFORD L. STANLEY *is Professor of Systematic Theology at Virginia Theological Seminary. Following graduation from the University of Virginia, he studied at Virginia Theological Seminary and Union Theological Seminary. After several years as a parish minister, he returned to Virginia Seminary to assume his present post.*

THE idea of the Church belongs to the inmost circle of great Christian truths. It is a very central and culminating concept. For the sake of the Church both Creation and Redemption were wrought. To the Church all things are given, including a share in the world's judgment. The Church as the "beloved community" opens the springs of tenderness and fires the imagination! It is a privilege to think and write about the Church.

I. FOUR DESCRIPTIVE ANALOGIES

The reality of the Church has been expressed in a number of great analogies. The first and perhaps the best known is the figuring of the Church as the body of Christ.

The words "body of Christ" are apt to suggest a dualism and a hierarchy to us. We begin by sharply differentiating "body" and "soul." Christ is "divine" and he is the "soul" of the Church; we are "human" and are the "body" of the Church. Or, Christ is the "head" in the sense of commander, while we are his body in the sense of obedient instruments. These ideals are not Hebraic nor biblical. Furthermore, they are valid only to the degree that they accord with the biblical idea of the "body of Christ."

Hebraic psychology and anthropology were radically unitary, not

53

dualistic. The words "body" and "soul" were used, but they did not refer to two ingredients or constituents of man. For example, the soul was not thought to survive after death. In Hebrew thought "the body is the basis of personality" (Wheeler Robinson). It is the man himself. A bodiless man would be a monstrosity, yes more, a contradiction in terms. Sometimes a body (*i.e.*, a man) was in an inert state, sometimes in an animated state. This led to the distinction of soul and body. The soul was the 'go' of the body. A body without its 'go' was undesirable; a 'go' without a body was unthinkable.

This analogy, "body of Christ," does not mean to suggest contrast between Christ and Church, as divine is contrasted with human, or as soul and body are contrasted in our thought. It does not mean to suggest a relation of superiority and inferiority, as master is related to servant. It means just the opposite. The analogy of a single life is used to express the relationship between Christ and the Church. They are as it were incorporated in a single life. Viewing this life as body, we can say that Christ is the 'go' of that body, its animation, its life. Viewing this life as 'go,' we can say that the 'go' is real and actual because it has a real body to animate.

The analogy of the "body of Christ" expresses the incredible unity between man and Christ. As Luther said, they are "one cake," one loaf. Together they constitute one life, "the perfect man . . . the stature of the fulness of Christ," Christ is no less than a new mankind; he is in all and all are in him. When we think of the meaning and vitality of this unitary life, we call it *Christ* or *Spirit of Christ*. When we think of the location of this life, its presence in the real world, where it can and does make a difference, we call it *body of Christ* or *Church*.

A second analogy finds Christ and Church related as husband and wife. This is found notably in Ephesians, Chapter 5. This second analogy introduces the idea of the covenant. Husband and wife are related by word and agreement. This contrasts with the nature-like relation between parent and child. The relation between marriage and history, the realm in which shared meaning unites men, is therefore close. The idea of God's covenant relation with His people and the concept of marriage are brought together as early as Hosea's time, perhaps earlier. Thereafter the analogy has a long and continuous history.

In the case of the "body" analogy above, the relation of Christ and his people is the interior access to each other had by parts of one life, the nexus between impulse and organ. Standing by itself, this might suggest the elimination of the personal identities of Christ and of those who are his. The covenant or marriage type of union, however, presupposes the independent existence of the persons. Furthermore, it is a union on the level of understanding and consent and is therefore a true relationship.

In our time marriage suggests a mutual love. In ancient times, while there was mutuality in marriage, there was also a primacy of the husband. This note has disappeared from our sociological pattern (wives no longer promise to "obey"!). As a result, the headship of Christ, formerly suggested by the idea of marriage, has to be suggested by other analogies. In ancient and modern times marriage suggests an interpenetration of persons on the level of meaning, an approach even more intimate than the nexus between the several parts of a single organism because it is subjective as well as objective. The dialogue between Christ and his bride, the Church, is nowhere more wonderfully expressed than by Bach, especially in some of his cantatas.

There is a third analogy, perhaps the most popular of all in our period. Here the Church is regarded as the family of God. Nowadays we understand the unparalleled importance of the family in shaping fundamental attitudes and lifelong patterns of action. Because of its small scale, the family is particularly fitted to be an arena for fully personal life and conduct. In this respect, the family with its warm interrelationships seems even more precious than ordinarily because of the disintegration of personal life in the industrial age.

The family analogy for the Church is based in the Father-son relation of Christian thought. In biblical thought the father is "he who commands." It was the role of the Hebrew father to impart the burden of the Law. The great father-passage in the New Testament is, "O my Father, let this cup pass from me: nevertheless, not as I will, but as thou wilt"; "Our Father . . . thy will be done." The son, conversely, is "he who obeys." The spirit of adoption, whereby we cry "Abba, Father," is a spirit of obedience. The family of God is primarily a structure of law and obedience and not of natural or even affectional interlinkage. (The "descending love" or *agape* of God by which He meets the demands of the *Law* and the response of gratitude or *eucharistia* of man are beyond what we usually mean by affection.)

One strand of modern thought understands this. In some psychological circles it is held that the father is the symbol of demand, whereas the mother is the symbol of repose and comfort. The mother who sheltered in the womb invites back into its unlit securities. The father drives one out into the responsible world, into the life of individual selfhood.

Other lines of thought understand the biblical idea less well. Such ideas as "the infinite value of personality," self-realization," "self-expression," the fear of "repressions," and so on, clash with the idea of command and obedience. This is the "authority problem" of modern autonomous man. If a family is a unit composed of personalities that are a law to themselves, each doing what he likes and the result somehow satisfactory—the very caricature of a Progressive school—then the Church as the family of God is a dangerous idea and must not be used.

The Church is a family not only because of the vertical relation between Father and children but also because of the horizontal relation between the children of God. The divine Law of human relations is reaffirmed and indeed made more stringent, since this is the effect of unveiling the principle within the law. The effective norm is not conventional practice but "be ye perfect as your father in heaven is perfect." Men are to be not just men (!) but the children of their father which is in heaven. "Call no man, on earth, your father." Men are to be sons like the Son; "Love one another as I have loved you." This love is not only a command but, by grace, a reality. The "descending love" of God becomes the only cause and the sole explanation of a similar love of man by man. In I Corinthians 13 we have the description not of an aspiration but of a reality. "We know," says John, "that we have passed out of death into life because we love the brethren."

The analogies of body and of marriage suggest primarily the vertical relation between Christ and the Church. The family analogy, while expressing this, adds to it the horizontal relation of man with man. This is also the case with the fourth analogy, wherein the Church is regarded as the Holy Nation. The Church as the People of God is a richly suggestive idea, marked by a great antiquity. The classical expression of this is in I Peter: "Ye are a chosen generation, a royal priesthood, a holy nation, a peculiar people." Just as the body analogy is personal and physical, and as a marriage and family analogies are domestic, so the nation analogy is unmistakably political and social.

This is wonderfully confirmed by the original name of the Church. This is the Greek word EKKLESIA, reflected by the Latin *Ecclesia*, the Spanish *Iglesia*, the French *Église*. It is only in the Germanic languages that the word *Church* is used. The nearest modern equivalent of the Greek word *ekklesia* is the word *state*. The *ekklesia* was the responsible assembly of those qualified to conduct public business. It served as a symbol of the collective life of the people, which came to self-conscious expression in it.

When the Bible was translated into Greek—the so-called Septuagint version—the word *ekklesia* was used to translate the Hebrew *Qahal*. This latter word expressed the assemblies of the people and the collective life of Israel symbolized by them. Ecclesia was thus a synonym for Israel, the chosen people, the people of God's own possession. The more obvious political connotations of the word *ecclesia* were dropped, but the very usefulness of the word depends finally on its power to suggest a collective life built around some constitutional form. On the other hand, religious overtones were imported into the usage of the word. If we were to translate *ekklesia theou* as "God's nation," we would come about as close to the flavor of the original as it is possible to come. It need be added only that when the Christian folk wanted a name to denominate its existence as a people it chose this word of the Greek Bible—*ekklesia*.

The four figures we have presented—body, marriage, family, nation—are analogies, not fancies. They are used, not because there is too little content in the idea of the Church for factual description, but because there is too much. Behind all the analogies and dictating the selection of just these particular ones is the definite, unalterable truth which is the Church. The analogies suggest that this truth is two-fold. The Church is the name of *a relation of God and man* which is as close as that of the parts of an organism, as intimate as a marriage. Secondly,

there is in the Church *a kind of humanity* which is as strongly marked
as a family, as individualized as a nation.

II. JUSTIFICATION AND SANCTIFICATION CONSTITUTE
THE CHURCH

The new relation with God and the new humanity figured by
these analogies are constituted through Justification and Sanctification.
There are other ways to express the two-fold truth of church life, its
vertical and horizontal dimensions, but this one will serve to disclose
many of its characteristic aspects.

Justification is a Pauline word with a special meaning. It refers to
a way of meeting the demands of the Jewish Law or of by-passing it
altogether (the "righteousness apart from the Law"). Luther used the
word in the sixteenth century when the merit theology of Latin
Christianity received a final intolerable expression in William of
Ockham. Just as Luther could not use the word as Paul did, so our
situation is not that of Luther. But just as Luther did not hesitate to
apply this great idea to his time, so we should feel free to use it if it
proves fruitful.

Behind the Justification idea lie two convictions. First, the problem of existence is insoluble in terms of existence. No action of man
can do more than rearrange factors and accentuate life's problem. In
terms of the Jewish Law, this was the inability to meet its demands,
discerned by Jeremiah and Ezekiel. This was the guilt of sin, a diag-
nosis which rooted the trouble in man's will. The Greek found life to
be self-frustrating too, but he traced this to tragic guilt, a natural taint
which blemished all life and involved its destruction. Tragedian and
prophet agree in pessimism about man, however. The appearance in
our day of historical disillusionment, psychological despair, existentialist "disgust" and "encounter with nothingness," the meaningless-
ness which opened the way for the synthetic meaning of Fascism—
such things as these mark the present-day arrival of the hopelessness
which makes Justification relevant.

The second conviction behind Justification is that reality, actuality
must be maintained. It is impossible to destroy it. Every act is based on
actuality and, like an exercised muscle, strengthens it—even an attempt
to destroy it. Furthermore, actuality is good. Essential being is in it,

and that is good. It is true that actuality contradicts its essence but it also realizes it. It is possible to distinguish between actuality and essential being, but not to separate them. The fall into sin was also a fall upward into reality. "A poor thing, but mine own." To destroy actuality—which is impossible—would destroy all being along with evil. Finally, actuality, the realm of separated, even anarchic, beings, is the precondition of community, which is the union of the separated.

Justification is a solution that meets both of the above needs. It does not solve the insoluble problem of actuality by destroying existence, because reality must be maintained. It does not simply leave existence with its problem, but it is a real solution. It is a solution on the theological level, not the moral level. It is believed and not seen. The solution can be expressed negatively or positively. The negative formulation holds that sin is overcome, overwhelmed. It remains on the moral level, remains as a fact, but its ultimate quality is changed. Its fangs are drawn. Being is cleansed from one bound to another.

The positive formulation finds that essential goodness equates itself with the reality that denies it. Reality is now the good, indeed the only good there is. There is no good above it or apart from it. No law. No condemnation. No sting in death. This is true even if no single sad fact could be changed. This is true before a single sad fact is changed. And it is true because the meaning of all has been changed. The world that we *see means* redemption. This conviction is the very structure of the Christian consciousness. The Church is man in Justification.

Justification is reconciliation on the basis of actual existence; Sanctification is reconciliation on the basis of essential goodness itself. In some almost inexpressible way, man goes back to the original situation, before the Fall. Sanctification means "made holy," and Christians are "saints" or "holy ones." Holiness means divine property, the realm of divinity itself. To be made holy means to be caught up into the divine realm. This new immanence of the divine, this new intimacy between man and God, is the Holy Spirit. The Holy Spirit is God in the Church.

Sanctification means a new access to the creative springs of all things. It is power—to become the sons of God. It is power, as Agape, as love, for human relations; power to overcome the demonic character of existence. It is knowledge that Jesus is Lord, that the Church is the community of the Holy Spirit. It meets the problem of beginning with "the Father, almighty creator"; the problem of the creature's threats to us with "the love of God, which is in Christ Jesus" and the problem of death with the resurrection of the body. While Sanctification makes real changes in the real world, the recognition of them is a further work of the Spirit. "Spiritual things are spiritually discerned." The Holy Spirit can never become a simple psychological energy or illumination.

Sanctification deals with the things that can be changed because man is able and because they are inherently changeable. Christianity brings a new order of possibility into the world. No wrong, however ancient or crystallized, is to be accepted without scrutiny and challenge. But there is a resistant factor present, an objective limit somewhere which cannot be changed without demolishing the structures of actuality itself. In St. Paul's language, the new "Spirit" is conjoined with the "body of death." "The body is dead because of sin (*i.e.* in the past) the spirit is life because of righteousness" (*i.e.* now possible). Just as Justification is a life of holiness in spite of the sinful facts of life, so Sanctification is a life of holiness hampered by and in some sense built upon structures that contradict it. Church life is thus dual, and to expressions of this duality we now turn.

III. THE MIXED CHARACTER OF THE CHURCH

The mixed, dual quality of Church life can be expressed in terms of *time*. The best expression of the temporal description of Church life is in the Epistle to the Hebrews where it is claimed that we live in this age by the power of the age to come. The Greek mind understood what an "age" was, but this present formula would have baffled it. In Greek thought was reflected the ancient, widespread Aryan myth of the four ages—gold, silver, bronze, iron—to which Hesiod had added a fifth or heroic age. The Greek also understood an age (*cosmos*) as one of the world orders that repeated themselves with depressing exactitude in the thought of the Stoics, of Aristotle, and others. The Greek knew an age as an order lower than its predecessor, or exactly like it.

In biblical thought, on the contrary, this age and the one to come are different in quality and the age to come represents a great improvement on the present one. This present age is in the power of the "prince of this age": "the whole age lieth in the evil one," the evidences of whose misrule are apparent in malformed bodies, 'possessed' minds and spiritual disorders of every sort. The age to come is under the rule of God's representative, the Messiah. It is to be a time of health and freedom. The stark contrast between the ages, the superiority of the age to be, are biblical commonplaces. What is new is the presence of both ages in the Christian people at the same time!

They live in the present but by the power of the future. What this means is that the future is now. The quality of the final fulfillment marks our immediate present and we no longer wait. The element of presentness is powerful in the Christian consciousness. Now is the time. On the other hand, the fulfillment does not lose its futurity, its finality by becoming present. There is no adulteration of it, no dusty dimming of its splendors. Nevertheless, the fulfillment occurs in the midst of conditions that do not attain to it, so that it requires imagination to realize that life's water has indeed been transformed into wine. The fulfillment occurs in conditions that contradict it (a famous example being found in Romans, Chapter 7) so that it requires faith to see that deliverance is a present possession.

Christianity is willing to admit the shortcomings of its "brave new world." In the midst of them we "groan" and we "hope" for their removal. Yet we have something of finality even in this unlikely situation. This element of finality is an "earnest." Being an earnest, it is only a part-payment but, just the same, a true part. Being an earnest, it is also an evidence of the further and full payments to come. Consequently, *this very mixed, partial fulfillment means an entire fulfillment,* and we are content.

The mixed quality of Christian life can be expressed in terms of *space* also. Here the classical passage is in Philippians, where St. Paul explains that, while we live on earth, our citizenship is in heaven. One of the remarkable political phenomena of the Roman Empire was the "colony." The inhabitants of a colony were automatically citizens of Rome, a privilege given to no other political subdivision. In view of this, colonials were really Romans who were compelled to live abroad due to circumstances. Their citizenship did not transport them to

Rome forthwith, but their remote residence did not compromise their political status. Philippi was a "colony" and the Philippians would have understood Paul's allusion. Indeed, Moffatt translates the passage in question (Phil. 3:20) by the words, "we are a colony of heaven."

This duality is a gain. Heaven becomes "real." It ceases to be an ideal possibility, but comes into the actual world where it alters concrete circumstances. That which is every place and therefore no place comes to a place, wherever Christians are. That which is at all times and therefore timeless, comes also to have time, whenever Christians live. On the other hand, this world is idealized. Heaven is given to it. Heaven is not far off: "The kingdom of heaven is (come) unto you," (not "within you" in the sense of internality vs. outward events). The clue to conduct is to act as citizens of heaven, not worldlings. That which is confined to a place is given all places and therefore rises above the hampering restrictions of place. That which is at a time is given all times and therefore freed of the restrictions of time.

The duality also suggests difficulties. Heaven is the place, as the Lord's Prayer suggests, where God's will is done. Earth is the fallen place where God's will is not done. The two cannot be simply merged, as in mysticism and utopianism. The sinful otherness of earth is the measure of its reality. The holy otherness of heaven is a measure of its inaccessibility. Their coming together hampers heaven's spontaneous obedience, as evidence the allowances of Justification, the limited achievements of Sanctification. Their coming together destroys earth's sinful autonomy, as witness the universal cleansing of Justification, the renovating process of Sanctification.

IV. THE CHURCH IS TOTAL

We have now almost concluded our description of the Church. Several things, however, remain to be said. The first is that the Church, as we have conceived it, includes all men. Men do not come into it, because they are in it. The possession of humanity is possession of redeemed humanity, in an age of redemption, in a redeemed world. It is clear that the great acts that we have been describing cannot be restricted to professing Christians in Christian lands and to the Christian parts of the globe.

Here we must make a distinction between *what is believed* and *by whom it is believed*. It is clear that the 'what' of belief is not yet revealed, is not true, until someone believes it. So the 'by whom' it is believed is important. But if even only one person believes that all men are embraced in a new creative act which constitutes them a new mankind, then for him it is true. In his eyes, other men are in this new mankind as much as he is. If he speaks to others of this new humanity, it is not to invite them into it, but to bear 'witness' to the truth that they are already in it. Nothing they can do—not even believing—will bring them into it, seeing that they were included in the new mankind when it was constituted.

Belief does not create that which it believes; it responds to it. When St. Paul bade men to "reckon yourselves indeed to be dead unto sin," he bade them 'reckon' themselves so because they *were* so. This he explains when he says, "If one died for all, then were all dead."

The "by whom believed" is important, no doubt. It bears witness to the wonderful internality and unbreachable freedom of man. Man is bound to believe something. If he does not believe what we have been describing, he believes something else. Since what we have been describing is true, these alternatives are less than the full truth. They are belated. After the Second World War, a number of Japanese soldiers were flushed out of remote Pacific islands. In one instance they admitted that the war was over, demobilized and went home. In another case, they refused to believe that the war was over, regarding the claim as false propaganda. But the war *was* over and had been for some time, and any other idea with its ensuing conduct was out of date. For two thousand years now it has been recognized that the whole world has been redeemed. Any other idea with its ensuing conduct is out of date.

Sometimes men are belated about the Christian faith. In other phases of their lives they are premature. Take Justification, for example. According to Justification, man regards existence with its empirical flaws as cleansed, as identical with essential goodness. This he does *by living on*. The other alternatives are to live on because man has cleansed life or to die because he has not cleansed life. But these, as we saw above, are both impossible. The Christian knows that his ongoing life points to Justification. The Pagan lives on, but he does

not acknowledge the empirical flaws *or* if he does, he does not admit
responsibility for them. He feels only the tragic character of life. The
tragic "catharsis" is a kind of Justification, but partial, incomplete,
blind finally. The Jew acknowledges the Law and tries to live by it.
The prophetic Jew understands the impossibility of this and lives "in
hope." Justification is in the future for him, but his living on shows
that he is living in the present on what he believes to be only in the
future. While all men are in the new age, "not all have this knowledge"
and for this reason their thought and conduct is both belated and
premature. The difference made by the presence of faith is an important one. Baptism marks the presence of faith, the recognition
inwardly that all things have been transformed.

The terms *that which is believed* and *by whom it is believed* are
in some sense correlative. Yet belief does not create its object and
consequently *that which is believed* is independently and antecedently
true. In this case, it is first true that all men are incorporated into the
Church, the holy folk. From this point of view, all men are equally in
the Church, God's new creation of all mankind; "Church members"
are not in any more than non-Church members. No one can take
anyone in nor put anyone out.

It is important just now to emphasize this great truth about mankind rather than emphasizing the fact that some recognize it and some
do not. This latter throws an air of subjectivity over the truth, as if it
were dependent for its truth on the number who believed it. Autonomous man-centredness is the sickness of our age. The first sign of
health is to shift the emphasis to what man is dependent on rather
than what is dependent on him. When emphasis is put upon "that
which is believed," the quality of faith is changed. It becomes as spontaneous as a gasp of surprise or an exclamation of delight, as satisfying
as the unexpected sight of an old friend. Such faith is literally
wrenched out of man. Not to respond would be inhuman. Now that
the works of our hands are falling to pieces before our eyes and despair
is beginning to replace the ebullient hopes of yesterday, it is important
to have something to respond to, something which is unmistakably
independent, something which will not be denied.

There is another reason just now for emphasizing the object rather
than the subject of faith. It has to do with the character of the Chris-

tian enterprise, the manner in which the Gospel is preached. Many people say nowadays that they prefer the liturgy, the celebration of sacraments to preaching. The reason is that the liturgy is 'objective.' It is 'out there.' Something is done beyond the worshipper. On the contrary, in preaching one is asked to do something. One does not have the power to do what is asked and even if he did it would not be a very important act. If this is what preaching is, then liturgy is better, because preaching has forgotten to be itself.

Preaching is proclamation. The preacher is an herald, an emissary and to preach is to herald. It is also to bear witness, the witness describing himself as a participant in a fact which involves him. In any case preaching is declaratory. It points out what God has done, part of which deed is the report of His deed (*i.e.,* preaching). Preaching is in the present indicative. It does not first of all ask man to do anything, not even to believe! It declares what has been done in such a way as *to create* belief. Preaching is sacred work, too. It points out the kind of conduct arising from such belief and consonant with it. It says in one way what the liturgy says in another. Incidentally a liturgy which is only 'seen' and 'heard,' which is the same whether men are present or not, is a remarkable kind of "witness" of *verbum visibile,* as St. Augustine put it. If preaching can become too subjective,' liturgy can become too 'objective.'

So then everything is transformed. This is the "thing preached" and this creates our belief. The transformation is a new creation of the whole world as well as of man. The whole creation groaneth even as "we ourselves groan within ourselves" because of the mixed character of the fulfillment, previously discussed. But the fulfillment is theirs too, both as reality and as hope. The world which was one in fall is one in redemption. The wonder of a redeemed world is almost insupportable, a world in which the latest sub-atomic particle proclaims that all things have been made new, every hurtful thing overcome and hope made total.

Our present concern is with man rather than the whole world because our immediate interest is the Church. There is a Church because all mankind is newly created. This new folk is the Church. "Christians" are merely those who recognize the new mankind. Jews and Pagans belong to it, but their subjective participation is defective.

They are belated and premature. But their significance is more than merely negative. The Pagan reminds us of the liveliness of God's new humanity, the Jew of its sinfulness and subjection to radical judgment. God is king and all things serve His will.

There is one last feature to be added to our description of the Church. The Church includes the whole of man's life, his business, truly as his prayers. "State" and "Church" are alike included in it. Just as all men are in it, so all of man is under "the high and hospitable roof of God." There is no dualism here of sacred and secular, no invidious less or more. As man himself is one, so all of his life is equally in the mystery that embraces him, his "mind" and "body" as well as his "soul."

To be sure, there is a distinction between worship and life, between religion and economics, let us say. This distinction must be honored. The problem is to honor the distinction and yet let it not become a duality. This problem can be met in several ways.

First we can say that worship mirrors life. Worship is a celebration of the existence of the Church, the Church, that is, as the new creation of mankind. St. Augustine says something not unlike this. "That which is on the altar (i.e., the body of Christ) is the mystery of yourselves. Receive the mystery of yourselves." In worship, the Church recognizes itself as the people of God, recognizes and rejoices in this wonderful status. In the hour of worship the Church *looks* at the life which in other hours it *lives*.

Here we must guard against several misunderstandings. Worship is not self-worship. It is worship of that which grasps man, or of man as grasped by it. It is worship of the grace that enfolds man, of man enfolded by grace. It is worship of the love of God, of man as loved by Him. It is a worship of God, to whom alone worship belongs, but of the concrete God of the Church, of the God in the Church and the Church in Him. The creed uses the same word "believe" of God and the Church. "I believe in God . . . and in . . . the Church." The earliest form of the Apostles Creed added the word *"sanctam"* to *"ecclesiam"*—"I believe . . . in the holy ecclesia" or people of God.

Nor is worship a second-hand contact with God. The idea that worship mirrors life might lead to this misunderstanding, as if we *met*

God in life but only *remembered* Him in worship. No, we meet Him in worship. But the God we worship is the God whose revelation point is the Church. Here He has shown Himself and spoken. If we look away from the Church and its life, we do not see this God any more. We see only an abstract God, a mere possibility of a God. "God is not ashamed to be called their God." So when we look for Him and at Him, we look in the only place where He has shown Himself, that is, in connection with the actuality of the Church. Without Him the Church would not be there. But without the Church our God would not be available for our worship. He would still be the "unknown God," ignorantly worshipped.

The Church and its life cannot be counted out, not even out of its worship—especially not out of its worship. To do so is to separate the two. This means that there are two Gods, the God of worship and the God of life. This is to divide the one God, which is impossible. Or it means that worship knows God whereas He is denied to life. In this case, life has the second-hand contact, and in daily life we do not *meet* Him but only *remember* the God of the hour of worship. This is to make life meaningless and worship abstract. Both of these alternatives are monstrous and they are intolerable.

The interrelationship of worship and life is seen in Moses' alternating between Mt. Sinai, the symbol of worship, and the camp of the Hebrews, the symbol of life. On the mountain top Moses was told, "see that thou make all things according to the pattern showed to thee in the mount." This shows how closely worship is preoccupied with life. On the other hand, it was the exigencies of life that sent Moses up the mountain. In the story of Christ, the same pattern is repeated. It has been pointed out how closely his all-night vigils of prayer are related to "the crises of the Christ." The prayer in Gethsemane is at once the perfect paradigm of worship and absolutely concrete in intent.

There is another way to express the distinction between worship and life and yet keep it from becoming a duality. This is to consider that at one time the Christian principle is regarded *explicitly*. At another time it is *implicit* in the Christian life. In one case it is distilled, concentrated; in the other case it is diffused. In a relative and limited sense the two activities are beside each other. As soon, however, as they go entirely separate ways or one arrogates to itself a position above the other, the relative allowance has been transgressed.

It is permissible, then, to set aside holy days, holy men, holy acts, holy things, if it is ever recalled that the difference between these and other days, men, acts and things is only relative and provisional. Once these things become so holy that they are no longer things, and once their holiness deprives other things of all holiness, they become a threat to other things and must be opposed. Even though this exclusive development is a perennial danger, the impulse to set aside such special holy objects seems to be perennial too. This latter suggests that these special holy objects, the whole worship side of life serves a necessary purpose.

The ordinary activities of life are marked by a temper, a climate of mind which we might describe as "technical." For the moment, we set aside the independence of all things and control them. We ignore their individuality and combine them with others. Not their essential good-ness but their utility is our concern. For the time being we act as if the necessities of existence are all that matter. In the forefront of our mind are not the trailing clouds of glory with which all things come but the indispensable arrangements of a real world. "The butcher, the baker, the candlestick maker." Mankind cannot "live on love" any more than young lovers can.

This is necessary and great—it is our life!—but it is dangerous. The controllability of things makes us forget their independence of being. To the extent that this is so, we come to despise them and the value of being itself declines absolutely. Preoccupation with the limited calls for a reassertion of the whole. The difficulty and necessity of technical activity require a fresh grasp on the wonder of all things, including the wonder of technical activity!

For this reason, a special activity is necessary to recall and restate the wonder of things. But it is the wonder of all things that is being recalled and restated by the special activity. The holy activity is repre-sentative. By transacting it we recall and restate the holiness of all activity. The holy activity is an end in itself, but only when it repre-sents a life that is an end in itself. It is only when our daily bread is the bread of life that the Lord's Supper is an earnest of the Messianic

Feast. On any other, showing worship is irrelevant and life is meaningless.

With these words our description of the Church is complete. The Church is an entity whose existence is expressed by a series of analogies—body, bride, family, and nation. Its reality is constituted by Justification and Sanctification. It lives in time by the power of eternity. It is in but not of the world. It includes all men, though in a limited sense it is confined to believers. It includes all of life's activities, though it also expresses itself in special acts of worship.

V. THE CHURCH AND THE PRESENT CRISIS

The Church, so conceived, has much significance for the actual problems of our day. In the strictest sense of the word it is unnecessary to make special applications of our Church-idea to special problems, seeing that the rest of this book is filled with just that. If these concrete analyses are not demanded by the present concept of the Church, they are in accord with it. But even if special applications of our idea to the current situation are not demanded, they are not superfluous.

One of the difficulties of the present crisis is the so-called "godlessness" of the communists. There is undoubtedly a problem here, but it is a great gain to define it exactly. We cannot, to begin with, admit that this is godlessness in the strict and literal sense of the word. No man can live without faith and faith is ever the correlate of the divine. In every human situation, including that of the communists, God is known genuinely, though He may be known distortedly and partially. Though the "materialistic dialectic," "the economic process," or "the laws of economics" may be poor substitutes for "God," the religious quality in them is unmistakable. The "atheism" of the Russians is, like all atheism, a protest against a particular religion. In this case it is a protest at least partially justified by the social callousness and indifference of the Russian Church.

The problem with the communists is not that of a religious vacuum but that of a false religion. It is really the problem of self-worship. Self-worship does not mean the worship of the self as God or instead of God. No one has ever done just that. The essence of self-worship is the worship of a God who includes the existence of the self, so that the being of the God involves the existence of the self in its present and actual form. This is to eliminate any standard of judgment, to sanctify and crystallize present wrongs, to miss the significance of breakdown and death.

The Church, following the analysis of prophetic Israel, understands that man's existence is corrupted and self-defeating. Far from being involved in the being of God, it is judged by Him, "unto death." It lives not by its own virtue, which is insufficient, but by Justification. Due to Justification, everything as it stands is good and acceptable. Due to Sanctification a process is in being which will right wrongs, not by "justifying" them, but in the empirical sense.

This procedure does not equate the future with the present, as self-worship does, but lives in the present by the power of the future. It does not obliterate the absolute qualitative distinction of heaven and earth, as self-worship does, but lives on earth as citizens of heaven. It is the final overcoming of self-worship; or it is the worship of a creative-redemptive God whose being does indeed involve the existence of the church in its present and actual form, through Justification and Sanctification. This kind of "self-worship" is itself a sign of salvation: "I believe in God . . . and in the . . . Church."

A second acute problem of our period is group pretentiousness. There is the vertical type of the Nazis who inserted a barrier between the Teutonic master-race and the slave peoples doomed by nature to second-class humanity. There is the horizontal type of Communism which is concerned with men of all nations but only to the extent that they are or can become communists and proletarians. To be sure, there is the Stalinist revision of the basic Marxist "theology," a revision which contemplates the co-existence of communist and capitalist worlds. The problem here is the status of this revision. Is it only a tactical operation, like the "toleration" urged by certain religious groups when they are in the minority? To the extent that it is genuine, it represents an unresolved contradiction in their basic thought, since much of Communist theory and action reflects an exclusive claim to truth.

Both Nazism and Communism are post-Christian phenomena. Communism corrupts the universalism of the prophetic-Christian tradition, while Nazism turns its back on it, preferring an exclusive Teutonic racism. But in both cases we have a radical splitting of humanity which is possible only in a Christian era. The Church is the one unity with sufficient tenacity and profundity to overcome such a disruption of mankind. Even the difference between Christian and non-Christian is secondary in comparison with the unitary mankind created by the redemptive act in Christ.

It is not enough that mankind be created "of one blood," that men be one "in essence." War presupposes and employs this oneness as much as community. Indeed, there is an interior relation between war and community, since all communities are as limited and unjust as the men who realize them. No community, therefore, is really abiding, undercutting every conceivable disruption, unless it is a community which at once by-passes and redeems the efforts of community-realizing man. In a word, it must be a oneness which involves man's "existence" as well as his "essence." This is exactly what Justification and Sanctification do. In Justification it is existence itself which is declared to be one with man's essential state, including its unbroken unity. In Sanctification it is man's essential state which invades the disruption, beyond even the cleavage between Christian and non-Christian.

It is the very virtue of this unity that it is of God and not a moralistic production of man's will, that it is believed and never fully seen, with belief alone giving the clue to what is seen ("Spiritual things are spiritually discerned"). It is its virtue that it cannot be broken. This gives us the courage to face a time such as the present. For man has gained a power and profundity of disruption in this Christian era such as he has not had before. We can bear disunity when we know that unity is the deepest word about man, not only "essentially" but also "existentially." Thus we are saved from the necessity of producing a simple, visible unity—itself the perennial basis of disunity. This brings us to a third and final application of our idea of the Church, its value for man's "hope."

Much of the power of Communism, and also its evil, is connected with its Utopianism. It brings the future into the present, or rather only so much of the future as the present can contain. This present is then proclaimed to be the future, the summary fulfillment of mankind's hope for itself. This drastic performance is at least in part a reaction to a religion of pure futurity, of "pie in the sky, when you die."

The justice of this charge has never been fully met by Christianity. It must be admitted that the dynamic historical hopefulness of Communism derives from Christianity by way of Joachim of Floris and the Renaissance. But the prevailing Christian thought has been that of St. Augustine. For Augustine, history was a week of "days" of varying lengths. We are now in the sixth day, which is the millennium, in which Christ rules with his saints. There is complete fulfillment in the domestic life of the Church only, its worship and monastic perfection. For the empirical and communal factors we must wait till the end of history. In this transfer of hope to the pure futurity of eternity, the majority of Christianity has followed Augustine, leaving the Joachimite type of historical hopefulness for the secular world.

But the true Christian position we found to be "in this age by the power of the age to come." It *means* the future; the future has come into the present. We do not wait unfulfilled; "hope deferred maketh the heart sick." But it is the future only *as it can come into this present age,* therefore not simple, not simply visible. Partly it has to be believed in spite of the facts; partly it transforms a limited number of facts. On the other hand, this age remains. The present has not swallowed the future. But then it is not left alone, either. It is the present as truly indwelt by the future. We have passed out of death into life. It is neither simply present nor simply future but a life "between the ages."

Utopianism does not realize how characteristic of man is disruptive wrong-doing. It regards it as adventitious rather than reflecting what man regularly is. Or, in the case of Christian Utopianism, it considers that a simple transformation has occurred, making perfection possible. On the other hand, it is an un-Christian pessimism which does not recognize the profundity of the transformation wrought by Christianity. "Among them that are born of women there hath not risen a greater than John the Baptist: notwithstanding he that is least in the kingdom of heaven is greater than he." "We know that we have passed out of death into life—because we love the brethren." A limited, a modified Utopianism is open to us in the Christian era.

A fulfillment such as this is a half-loaf and if this is Christianity's last word we are only partly fulfilled. There is a "whole-loaf" by comparison with which this one is seen to be a "half-loaf." This, too, is in our hearts, but not only as a problem-raiser. We are not excluded from

it, or else we are not saved. We are reunited with it. Our partial fulfillment is related to this complete fulfillment as "earnest" as down-
payment and as promise of full payment. Thus we are guarded from
the Utopianism which is patient when it ought to "groan" and the
pessimism which groans when it ought to be patient.

The Church is no less than mankind in redemption, the human
enterprise regarded as created anew. It is a conception that is powerful
for every time and therefore also for our time. The Church is "there,"
and all that remains is to point to it and to acknowledge the sight.
Inspiring greatness and gentle tenderness meet and balance in this
noble reality—the Church.

The Church Between East and West

JOHN C. BENNETT

------------------------------ ✳ ------------------------------

JOHN C. BENNETT *is Professor of Christian Theology and Ethics at Union Theological Seminary. Educated at Williams College, Union Theological Seminary, and Oxford University, he has taught at Auburn Seminary and the Pacific School of Religion. He is well known for his participation in the ecumenical movement, and is the author of many books, including* CHRISTIANITY AND OUR WORLD, SOCIAL SALVATION, CHRISTIAN REALISM, CHRISTIAN ETHICS AND SOCIAL POLICY, *and* CHRISTIANITY AND COMMUNISM.

THE Christian Church lives amidst the conflict between East and West.[1] This conflict is the most difficult problem that it has had to face in our time. Not only are there Churches on both sides of the iron curtain but contrasting attitudes toward this conflict are the source of perplexing spiritual divisions in both East and West.

Karl Barth in his pamphlet,[2] which has the same title as this chapter, distinguishes between two conflicts: the conflict between nations, especially between Russia and America, and the ideological conflict over the issues raised by Communism as a system of ideas and a social system. He separates these two conflicts completely and advises the Church to have nothing to do with the first. About the second he is quite indecisive. I wish that these two conflicts could be separated as completely as Barth separates them, but most of the contemporary perplexity arises from the fact that in some measure the second conflict is embodied in the first.

----

[1] The use of the words east and west to describe this conflict is an inaccurate convention, for its reference is only partly geographical. It refers to the communist and non-communist worlds and India and Japan belong to the geographic east while Czecho-Slovakia and Hungary on the world map belong to the geographic west.
[2] Published in *Cross Currents* (Winter, 1951).

I believe that it is helpful to distinguish between four conflicts rather than two and to recognize that they cannot be separated, and that both the Church and the Christian citizen must be guided by the close interrelationship of at least three of them as well as by the necessity of making these distinctions between them. The four conflicts that I shall discuss are as follows: the international conflict which Barth emphasizes but which cannot be identified so simply with Russia and America; the conflict between Communism and Capitalism as economic systems; the conflict between Communism as totalitarian and a society that is open and pluralistic—whatever name one may give to it; the conflict between Communism as a faith and Christianity. I shall deal with the first of them last because its significance depends upon the others.

I. COMMUNISM VERSUS CAPITALISM

The conflict between Communism and Capitalism is the only one that can be in some measure separated from the others. The non-communist world includes nations that have rejected Capitalism. But Capitalism as a symbol has a very important part in the propaganda war and in the feelings of people on both sides of the iron curtain. There is a vast amount of confusion because the United States, the great center of Capitalism, has had its own economic revolution in the past few decades and its institutions are very different from the stereotype of Capitalism that still stirs emotions in Europe and Asia. The confusion is increased by the fact that many Americans use the slogans of nineteenth-century Capitalism and a considerable body of opinion, especially in the American business community, does not accept this American economic revolution but calls for a return to the practices of an earlier period. One of the chief representatives of this type of thinking said in my hearing that it was Lloyd George with his social legislation in 1909 who really caused the Anglo-Saxon world to go astray. There is a great deal of agitation in America for a purer economic individualism and this is often related to the more hysterical forms of American "anti-Communism." So, on the American side, Capitalism as a symbol creates much of the heat in the present conflict. In the communist world it creates even more heat, especially in the context of the assumption that imperialism is the product of Capitalism alone. Capitalism is a hated word in Asia because of its connection with imperialism. Also, in the western European countries there is a feeling that their necessary dependence upon American military power and economic resources may result in their being controlled by American Capitalism for purposes that are vaguely imagined but which are believed to be dark. Much of Karl Barth's own tendency to say "a plague on both your houses" arises from his own bitter feelings against Capitalism.

The Churches can say of this aspect of the conflict that they must not allow opposition to Communism to cause them to identify themselves with any economic system. The World Council of Churches at Amsterdam (1948), in the report of the third section of the Assembly, spoke for the Church as a whole when it criticized both Communism and Capitalism. This action offended many Americans but it expressed an almost world-wide feeling about Capitalism as a symbol and it did help to give the World Council of Churches a degree of detachment from the east-west conflict. At least the World Council could say that it had criticized not only Communism but also one of the west's emotionally charged symbols. This gained no favor either with the authorities in Moscow or with conservative Americans but it did help to give the World Council moral authority in western Europe and in Asia.

It is unfortunate that we have no word or symbol which suggests the very flexible combination of economic institutions which Americans call "Capitalism." These institutions have been astonishingly productive and they are favorable to political democracy and cultural freedom. The Amsterdam report criticized various tendencies which are characteristic of Capitalism and it criticized the principle of absolute economic individualism, but it did not intend to put this pluralistic type of economy which can be so readily changed by democratic processes on the same level with totalitarian Communism. Our need now is to avoid thinking in terms of slogans and doctrinaire stereotypes in the economic sphere. We should resist the propaganda in favor of absolute economic individualism, recognize the positive values in our mixed economic system, and respect the freedom of other nations to develop their own economic institutions. My chief interest in this discussion is to emphasize the conviction that the conflict between economic systems is a subordinate aspect of the present world struggle.

II. TOTALITARIANISM VERSUS FREEDOM

The second conflict is between totalitarian imperialism and a society that is open and pluralistic.[3] This is an essential aspect of the deeper spiritual and ideological conflict and of the international conflict but it needs to be emphasized because it is the one factor in the situation which, above all others, makes the east-west crisis so fateful. Communism with its base in the Soviet Union creates a vast totalitarian empire and threatens the political and the spiritual and cultural freedom of other nations. It is this fact that makes *political* resistance to Communism urgent. Communist totalitarianism is so thorough that, when once it gains control over a nation, it is extremely difficult for even a large majority of the people to change or overthrow it. The combination of political terror and the persuasion of many minds, and the combination of indigenous communist revolutionary movements and the power of the red army that is not far away from any country in Europe or Asia, constitute a real threat to the freedom of all the nations in both continents and eventually to the whole world. The red army does not have to march to do most of its work. When conditions are ripe for revolution its mere existence undermines the will to resist a well-organized communist minority within a nation. If Communism were not so unified by the power of the Soviet Union there would be less to fear from it even if in many nations it had at the moment the same totalitarian character. Many independent national communist experiments would not threaten other nations to the same degree and they would be more likely to be open to outside influences. The most hopeful fact about Yugoslavia is that it is now open to influences from the west.

It is well to keep in mind the distinction, emphasized by Professor Brunner, between dictatorship and totalitarianism. There may be occasions when a temporary dictatorship can be justified to prevent an-

---

[3] I am using these rather vague words, "open and pluralistic," because of the difficulty of finding any political label that is universally applicable. I shall refer later to aspects of "democracy" that are involved in any viable alternative to totalitarianism.

archy. And whether justified or not, the dictatorships which rise and fall in Latin American countries do not create a comparable danger to the world. A totalitarian state is a dictatorship that seeks to mould the whole culture of a nation on the basis of an official orthodoxy. The power of the state to intimidate and to indoctrinate is used to the utmost in this process. In the communist state the absolute teachers are also absolute rulers—a combination that leaves almost no space in which the human spirit can breathe.

What should be the attitude of the Church to this conflict between totalitarianism and an open and pluralistic society? The Amsterdam Assembly (the third section) surely spoke very generally for the Christian conscience when it said: "The Church should seek to resist the extension of any system that not only includes oppressive elements but fails to provide for any means by which the victims of oppression may criticize or act to correct it. It is a part of the mission of the Church to raise its voice of protest wherever men are the victims of terror, wherever they are denied such fundamental human rights as the right to be secure against arbitrary arrest, and wherever governments use torture and cruel punishments to intimidate the consciences of men." That is a clear enough witness against totalitarianism.

When we ask what the Churches can put over against totalitarianism the answer is less clear. They must be careful to avoid the identification of Christianity with Anglo-Saxon democracy. The temptation for Americans to do this is very great because of the contribution that Christianity has made to the development of our democratic institutions.

There are at least two elements in democracy as we know it which must be found in any alternative to totalitarianism that will be adequate in the long run. I refer to the participation of all groups of the people in government and to the safeguarding of the freedom of minorities to organize to become majorities. Such political freedom depends upon broad constitutional protections of freedom of discussion. How soon nations which have had a quite different cultural background will be ready to develop these two aspects of democracy in their own way, no one can say. Also, it must be admitted that these aspects of democracy are precarious developments which are never secure. We may not be able to use the word *democracy* to designate a universal alternative to totalitarianism but part of the substance of what we mean by democracy must surely belong to the goal of any society that seeks to achieve or to preserve spiritual and cultural freedom.

The confrontation of totalitarianism with democracy in the world struggle is greatly complicated by the fact that Communism often seems to speak to the immediate needs of the people of Asia better than those who represent democracy. Illiterate people naturally can hardly be aware of what they would lose or fail to gain under a totalitarian regime and the intellectuals are often so much under the spell of communist propaganda that they easily convince themselves that the oppressive elements in Communism are temporary accompaniments of the revolution. First-hand contact with communist terror seems to be the only cure for the illusions of these intellectuals. The fact that the bitter fruits of Communism are so little known and so readily discounted in Asia makes its promises extraordinarily appealing. In contrast to Communism, democracy seems to have no relevant program for Asia.

There is a common tendency to discount the extent to which poverty prepares the way for Communism and to stress chiefly the appeal of Communism as a faith to the souls of men who hunger for such a faith. This view is often a good corrective because it calls attention to the deepest dimension of the problem of Communism but it can be misleading for the following reasons: (1) Even the core of deeply committed communists to whom this idea applies most fully find the communist faith convincing because it seems to them to be immediately relevant to the social problems of their countries. It satisfies their souls because it is for them a way of combining thought and action which, according to their belief, fits the historical situation. (2) While the spiritual explanation of the power of Communism to win adherents is applicable to the fully convinced insiders, Communism gains political support outside that circle because of its capacity to exploit all the national grievances and to convince people that it has a program that will overcome poverty and other social ills of which they are the victims.

Our American emphasis upon freedom and upon democratic political institutions seems remote to people who need rice and security in land tenure, for whom the most important form of freedom may be freedom from debt or from the local landlord. The case against communist totalitarianism, however strong it is on Christian grounds in the light of its ultimate spiritual consequences, will not be convincing even to Christians if the only alternative is a shadowy promise of democratic freedom which offers no program of immediate deliverance from poverty and hunger. This consideration does not make the struggle against totalitarianism less urgent but it does indicate the dilemma of Christians, especially in Asia, who see on the horizon no relevant alternative to Communism either as a symbol or a program. When the world conflict is polarized as a conflict between Communism and democracy, the issue is all the more confusing to them when western powers support reactionary regimes in the east.[4]

The Churches are related in a very practical and bitter fashion to totalitarianism. Sooner or later in a communist society the Churches themselves become victims. It is a communist practice in the early stages of their power to play one Church off against another. Protestants may be favored for a time against Catholics, or Orthodox against Protestants, or one Protestant denomination against another. Always there is the official claim that the state grants religious liberty but this is so narrowly defined that it does not mean liberty for public teaching or for organized religious education. It does not mean liberty of prophecy. What internal liberty a Church has is bought at a price, the price of subservience to the state on political and social issues, especially, in these days, issues of foreign policy. It is difficult for an outsider to understand exactly how much health is left in Churches that have had to pay that price. There is evidence from some countries, notably Hungary, that the Churches have actually experienced a religious revival. In China many Protestant leaders entertained high hopes when the communist regime began but now these same leaders find themselves forced to make propaganda for the government, even to

---

[4] The World Council of Churches has come to use the phrase "the responsible society" for the constructive alternative to totalitarianism. This phrase covers the elements of democracy that I have stressed but it is an attempt to avoid the ambiguous word, democracy, as a slogan. One of the six sections of the next Assembly of the World Council of Churches is to be devoted to the subject "The Responsible Society in a World Perspective." See the pamphlet published by the World Council entitled "The Responsible Society."

denounce close colleagues as agents of American imperialism. Behind these public acts that are known to us there may be forms of resistance and of courageous witness to Christian truth of which we do not know.

It would be a great mistake to assume that a Christian Church cannot have vitality under a totalitarian regime for Christians learn quiet methods of resisting, and on an entirely non-political level they learn how to live with depth and power. But it is certainly true that the Church is greatly restricted in its functions. Moreover, a communist regime is implacably anti-religious and deals its heaviest blow to the Church by weaning the young away from it. It does not seek to destroy the Church by direct methods now, but it does count on being able to poison the mind of the next generation against all religion. The Church's opposition to totalitarianism must not wait until it becomes the victim. It must begin whenever the freedom of persons to be open to the truth, to be loyal to conscience is threatened by the power of the state.

III. CHRISTIANITY VERSUS COMMUNISM

The third conflict is the conflict of faith between Christianity and Communism. This obviously belongs on a different level from the others. If the communist faith did not generate a totalitarian political system this conflict would take an entirely different form. In that case the Christian as a citizen would not be involved in political or military methods to prevent the spread of Communism. Moreover, the spread of Communism would not threaten the Church's freedom of public witness and teaching. The Church should inspire its members to resist the extension of Communism politically, not because Communism is a different faith but because it is a totalitarian political system. The fact that it is a different faith does make the totalitarianism the more difficult for the Church and it does constitute the ultimate reason for the Christian's rejection of Communism, but it is important to keep these aspects of the conflict from turning it into a religious war.

How can the Church keep the religious conflict and the political conflict from being fused in such a way as to become a religious war? Quite obviously Christians from religious motives will engage in the conflict. The answer to that question is that the Christian should find in his own faith antidotes to the kind of self-righteous fury that we associate with a religious war. There are at least two such antidotes. First, there is the repentant recognition that the development of Communism is a judgment upon the Churches and upon the Christian world. It was patently the failure of the Churches to deal with the problem of social injustice under the conditions of early Capitalism that, more than anything else, caused the communist revolt to become a religious revolt. Churches that see this judgment upon themselves in the communist movement will resist Communism in a spirit free from self-righteousness and hatred. A second antidote is the recognition that Communism as a *faith* cannot be overcome by political or military methods. It can only be overcome by a positive witness to Christ in word and deed, and the deed must take the form of the effort to discover constructive alternatives to Communism. Understanding of Communism as the spiritual force that wins people because it promises deliverance from injustice and because it is a faith that gives meaning to their lives should cause the Churches to look upon communists as people with charity in the full Christian sense.

We must admit that the second antidote has a more limited application than the first. It is true that political or military action cannot overcome Communism as a faith among its contemporary adherents. But a communist regime can create a situation in which most people will not even be exposed to Christian truth, in which children are under such strong pressure from school and official youth movements that the influence of home and church is largely undercut. This external situation is a *political* creation and it can finally be prevented or overcome only by *political* means.

The difference between the spiritual and the political aspects of the conflict between Christianity and Communism may be seen in the fact that where political resistance to Communism is impossible, spiritual resistance remains a Christian responsibility. When Christians live under a communist regime it may be impossible for them to take any direct political action against it. Their only significant political act will be to draw the line at some point when they are asked to cooperate with the regime, especially in making propaganda for it or in acting as agents in its terror. But they can always find ways of presenting Christian truth as different from communist ideology. Resistance to the claims of Communism as a philosophy of life can always continue within the Church if there is clear teaching of the biblical faith. To keep clear the essential points of difference between Christianity and Communism among Christians themselves is most urgent. Christian idealism without religious depth and without theological understanding may sometimes lead to a synthesis of Christianity and Communism which distorts both or to the false assumption that Communism is the fulfillment of ethical Christianity in modern industrial society.

I shall state briefly the deepest issue between Communism and Christianity as faiths. On the surface the anti-religious teaching of Communism and its dogmatic atheism would seem to be basic but I believe that they are symptoms. The deepest issue is the absolute claim of Communism to have the only solution to the problem of human life. This absolute claim is possible because of the communist assumption that the only source of evil is to be found in the system of property. The failure to understand the perennial sources of self-centeredness and pride and the will to power in man makes it possible for the communist to believe that an external change in the system of property is the key to man's redemption. The inevitable loss and tragedy that are inherent in man's finiteness, even the fact of death itself, the communist is able to ignore. This absolute claim of Communism makes it natural for the communist scheme itself to become a substitute for God. Religion is crowded out as a superstition that accompanies suffering from evils from which Communism is expected to deliver man.

Communism has no place for God because it is an idolatrous substitute for God. The theoretical atheism of communist teaching is to be expected. The fact that this atheism is an organic part of a philosophy which is believed to be the true science is an important factor in closing the mind to anything that transcends the communist scheme. The teaching of Atheism may often be the way in which this communist absolutism is transmitted to the younger generation. Moreover, the communist society, because it is atheistic, knows no judgment upon it from beyond itself. It is this that makes the totalitarianism so intolerable.

The difference between the communist and the Christian attitude toward the individual person can be seen best in this context. For the Christian, every person—whether he is on the right political side or not, whether he is the enemy of everything that we may consider good or not—has standing before God. No society can cancel that standing. But for the communist, those who are opposed to his political scheme have no standing at all, no value and no rights that need to be respected. The result of this religious situation is that there is no mercy from heaven or earth in communist dealing with opponents.

One other facet of the communist scheme that develops from this absolutism and that most clearly indicates the conflict between Communism and Christianity is the illusion about the future which inspires communist action. This is implied in what has been said about the source of evil. The communist sincerely believes that if only he can drive through to a complete victory over all opponents of the revolution, the new society will be just and free. The dictatorship, it is believed, will disappear automatically if only it is successful in wiping out its enemies. This optimism about the future of the communist dictatorship is the most fateful miscalculation the communists make and it is a miscalculation that is basically theological. This expectation about the future makes it easy psychologically to justify any methods in the present. It also eliminates the need to prepare directly for freedom. It is not necessary to argue here about exactly how far Communism goes in the direction of utopianism. It is enough to call attention to its failure to understand the deeper roots of injustice and oppression that threaten every society. In this respect it is in conflict with the realism of Christian teaching about man.

The ultimate overcoming of Communism will depend in large measure on the outcome of a world-wide struggle for souls. Communism at the moment does occupy the place of religion in the lives of many people, especially young people. They will not be satisfied with either bread or power. They need a faith that will give direction to their lives. There will come a point at which many of them will begin to be disillusioned by the terrible contrast between the communist dream and the realities of the communist state or the shabby and cruel practices of communist parties. The Church has an opportunity to win them and many others who have not yet given themselves to Communism but who are attracted by it.

The Church will have to meet this opportunity in a fresh way. It must not present Christianity in a Marxist dress to make it look as much like Communism as possible; and it must not offer the Gospel as a conservative anti-communist weapon or as a means of escape from social and political dilemmas. The Church must show that it understands the need of social revolution in many countries. Indeed, it often needs to give evidence that it has learned from Marxist thought about the one-sidedness of its own understanding of the gospel. The Church can learn from Marxism about the importance of the material factors in history and about the self-deceptions of the dominant economic groups. What it learns it must keep under the judgment of the Christian revelation instead of accepting Marxism as an independent authority: and it must not exchange the self-deceptions of the middle classes for those of the new rulers of the "proletarian" society. Above all it is essential for the Church to proclaim those dimensions of the Gospel which make it relevant to human needs about which Communism knows nothing.

IV. THE INTERNATIONAL CONFLICT

The fourth conflict is the international conflict which is forever in our minds and which carries the threat of general war. I have referred to Karl Barth's attitude toward this conflict. He says of it:[5] "As Christians it is not our conflict at all. It is not a genuine, not a necessary, not an interesting conflict. It is a mere power conflict. We can only warn against the still greater crime of wanting to decide the issue in a third world war." That last sentence is true enough as against all who consciously or unconsciously *want* "to decide the issue in a third world war." But the statement as a whole is a reflection of Barth's olympian attitude toward political issues and it is based in part on the very mundane foundation of Swiss neutrality.

Here it is necessary to make clear two propositions which do not go easily together. The first is that the extension of the power of Russia and her allies and satellites means the extension of the area of totalitarianism which the Churches must oppose. The second is that the Churches of the West, including the American Churches, should be extremely uneasy about the dependence of the freedom of the west on American power.

As we discuss these two propositions it will be well to keep in mind

[5] *Op. cit.,* p. 67.

the fact that the shades of feeling and opinion about both of them will inevitably vary a great deal from country to country. There is no disembodied Christian mind that can be entirely objective about either of them. American Christians can only partly share the feelings of Christians in western Europe who know how vulnerable they will be in case of war and who, while they fear Russian aggression, also fear that war may be brought on by American recklessness. It is even more difficult for Americans to understand the feeling that is not uncommon in both Europe and Asia that America represents a culture that is not much less materialistic than Russian culture and in subtle ways almost as great a threat to the independence of other nations and to personal freedom. Here the symbol of Capitalism plays a great part. Americans can only read with amazement these words of a prominent French Protestant layman: "The Communist society rests upon the same essential postulates as capitalist society, and man is no more free on the one side than on the other. Everywhere in the world man is the slave of production, everywhere he is absorbed by the masses, everywhere justice is mocked, everywhere the same financial technique prevails and work is as inhuman in rationalized American factories as in Stakhanovism."[6] There are many other Christians in western Europe who would reject such a statement as nonsense and who are glad that American power is a protection against communist aggression. But they do not like to be so dependent on American power and they do fear aspects of American policy. The world is divided between east and west but the west is divided by these different attitudes toward America and we find these divisions very articulate in the Church.

The first proposition about the extension of communist power was in essence endorsed at the meeting of the Central Committee of the World Council of Churches in Toronto in the summer of 1950. The committee with only two dissenting pacifist votes gave support to the action of the United Nations in Korea. The support was given to the United Nations and it certainly would not have been given to America acting on her own. Also, this support was given before the first crossing of the 38th parallel which undoubtedly weakened confidence in the Korean action in both Europe and Asia. The Toronto resolution was bitterly attacked by Professor Hromadka and other spokesmen of

[6] Quoted in *Christianity and Society* (Winter 1950-51), p. 13.

the Churches on the other side of the iron curtain and also by many voices in the west, especially in France. It does, however, indicate that there is a considerable body of opinion in the Churches outside America which rejects Barth's judgment about the irrelevance of the international conflict. It also reveals the extraordinarily difficult dilemma of the World Council of Churches if it is to speak at all about political issues. It is sure to appear to range itself on the side of one group of nations against another group, and member Churches are present in both groups. Whether or not the Toronto action was strategically wise from the point of view of the World Council may be debated, but the conviction on which it was based that the Churches have a stake in the international conflict is surely sound. The freedom of persons from totalitarian rule depends upon the outcome of that conflict. The very existence of the ecumenical community depends upon it, but the Churches should not put that consideration ahead of the freedom of men and women from oppression.

Karl Barth is unfair in regarding the opposition to Russian power as a purely American interest. Much as the other western nations may resent their dependence on America, they have their own reasons for wanting to defend themselves against Russia. Given their fear of Russia they are dependent at present on America but their dependence on America does not create their opposition to Communism or their fear of Russian aggression.

The second proposition concerning uneasiness about the dependence of the freedom of the west on American power would be generally accepted outside America for some of the reasons that I have mentioned. It should be accepted by the Churches in America, though undoubtedly the feelings about it will be quite different because Americans do not share at first hand the anxieties of people on other continents. It is helpful for American Christians to see their country as others see it. The very fact of the concentration of power in America is a moral danger to America and to the world. It is essential that America accept the discipline that comes from loyalty to the United Nations rather than throw her weight around in a unilateral fashion.

The American Churches, in touch as they are with the worldwide ecumenical community, should emphasize points at which American public opinion and American policy need continuous correction. I suggest three such points for emphasis.

The first is illustrated by a remarkable statement that appeared recently in an article by a Canadian Roman Catholic in the Roman Catholic journal, *The Commonweal*: "I wonder if you have any idea of what it means to the rest of us to see a great nation become bewitched by a sterile anti-Communism."[7] It seems to be true generally that when people take their bearings chiefly from "anti-Communism" they do all of the wrong things. It causes them to join forces with the most reactionary movements so long as they are anti-communist, and in doing so they keep alive the very conditions that drive nations to Communism. It results in neglect of the constructive programs which are essential if alternatives to Communism are to be developed. Such anti-Communism is a threat to the free institutions and to the freedom of the mind in America when it creates fear of all dissent from the most conventional opinions. The most dangerous aspect of this anti-Communism is that it makes many people take lightly the risk of general war so long as it is war against Communism.

A second point of emphasis is to warn against the temptation to use American power to impose upon other nations American institutions and culture. There is no doubt that most of the non-communist world has real fear of America on this score. The conscious policy of the American government has been very scrupulous in this matter. But the impact of America on the world is not primarily a matter of conscious policy. It is therefore of great importance for the American Churches to keep their members and the American public generally aware of the danger of these less obvious forms of imperialism. The most needed corrective is a body of opinion that is sensitive to the feelings of other peoples and to values in other cultures and which is sufficiently self-critical to avoid the pretension that the American way of life is for all peoples.[8]

---

[7] March 16, 1951, p. 561.

[8] There is much needed balance between appreciation of American achievements and self-criticism. There is a type of American who has so specialized in self-criticism that he is blind to much that is precious in American life. He can have little influence on American opinion and he increases confusion and unfairness in the attitudes of other nations to America.

The third and most important point of correction is the subordination of the military approach to the world conflict to the role of ideas and constructive programs. The military power of America is a necessary counterweight to the military power of Russia and to preserve this power is a service to the freedom of the west. We may regret that this is the case both because we dislike military power in itself and because we regard the present polarization of the world with only two nations of comparable strength as a bad state of affairs, but it is the case. And yet, it is a mistake to overrate the importance of military power in this conflict and to underrate its danger.

If Communism spreads to western Europe it will be chiefly because of the power of the red army, for western Europe has enough social health and enough sophistication about Communism to ward it off except as a military threat. There may be exceptions to that— Italy perhaps—but in general it is true. In Asia the opposite is the case. If Communism continues to spread in Asia—and it is more likely to spread in Asia than in Europe—it will be because of the poverty and the internal weakness of governments rather than because of the strength of the Russian and the Chinese armies. The curious fact is that there are many Americans who are almost willing to write Europe off but they are eager to use military force in Asia where its use is less relevant to the main sources of communist strength.

If the international conflict should lead to general atomic war it is doubtful if victory for the west would destroy Communism. It is even more doubtful if it would prevent the spread of totalitarianism. We are in the difficult plight of having to risk war to deter the Soviet Union from using military force to extend its power. But if general war should come it would probably leave the world so poor and broken that it would be ripe for any movement that would promise bread and security at the expense of freedom. The Churches should use their influence to prevent war without playing into the hands of those who with slogans of peace attempt to undermine resistance to communist power. World war and world tyranny are the two threats to humanity. There is no clearly marked road to the prevention of both. But it is both world war and world tyranny that the Churches must strive to prevent.

V. CONCLUSION

As one looks back over these four conflicts, it should now be clear how closely they are related. The Church is most deeply involved in the conflict of faith. Against Communism as a faith only Christian witness and deeds which embody it can have any power. But Communism as a faith does lead to a totalitarian society which must be resisted by political action. This totalitarian society has behind it the enormous power of the Soviet Union and at times may be extended from country to country by military force. The Church, where it is free to do so, should support the effort to preserve as large an area of the world as possible from communist domination. In doing so, the Church should keep before the nations the deeper causes of Communism in injustice and poverty. It must constantly remind the nations of the west of the temptations that accompany their power and their confidence in their righteousness.

The Foundation and Pattern of Christian Behavior

PAUL L. LEHMANN

———————————————— ✳ ————————————————

PAUL L. LEHMANN *is Professor of Applied Christianity at Princeton Theological Seminary. Educated at Ohio State University, Union Theological Seminary, and the Universities of Zurich and Bonn, he has taught at Elmhurst College, Eden Theological Seminary, and Wellesley College. He is the author of* FORGIVENESS, DECISIVE ISSUE IN PROTESTANT THOUGHT *and is a frequent contributor to theological journals.*

SINCE its inception, the Frontier Fellowship has been chiefly concerned with the bearing of the Christian faith upon Christian action. Our debt to Reinhold Niebuhr is immeasurable and unrequitable. He has formatively shaped our understanding of the ethical situation and the ethical task which confronts us. He has uncovered and restored to us the ethical vitality and substance of biblical and Christian thought as "the rock from which [we] were hewn," "the quarry from which we were digged."[1] And he has encouraged and emboldened us—each in his own way, and where he is set down—to take up the difficult and diverse responsibility of ethical reflection and conduct.

No member of the Fellowship could undertake this responsibility in terms of simple obedience to unambiguous ethical demands. Niebuhr has permanently shattered the illusion that such a course is possible, and chiefly for the reasons set out in *Moral Man and Immoral Society* (1932) and in *An Interpretation of Christian Ethics* (1935). The former volume analyzed the psychological and socio-political complexity of the ethical situation. The latter volume undertook to explore the foundations and the terms of an independent Christian

———

[1] Cf. Is. 51:1, Revised Standard Version.

93

ethic and reached the conclusion that such an ethic, derived from the pure love commandment of Jesus, could only be dialectically related to the actualities of human behavior. The unqualified and unmixed selflessness required by Jesus' own demand and exemplification of love is both expressed and denied in every ethical act. The pure fulfillment of the love commandment is a trans-historical possibility and hope.

I. THE SIGNIFICANCE OF THE FRONTIER FELLOWSHIP FOR CHRISTIAN ETHICS

The ongoing life of the Fellowship has confirmed this analysis. We have, in a word, been trying by theological and political analysis, to chart a course of Christian behavior in the world. In this undertaking, most of us discovered that the orthodox doctrines in terms of which the Christian faith had come down to us, contained insights into the depth and range of human experience which had been obscured by traditional creedalism and ignored by the stress upon life rather than doctrine in theological liberalism. We came to see that the real business of theology is the disciplined reflection upon the biblical and historic Christian view of God and man and the world whereby Christianity emerges as a specific and meaningful faith for living. What has often been described as a "shift to the right, theologically," was really a shift in the direction of a more explicit grasp of the intrinsic content of Christianity and of its significance for what is going on in a changing world.

From the first, the Fellowship understood that what is going on in a changing world is pre-eminently a matter of politics. For politics, in the broad sense, have to do with the foundations, structures, and ends of human community. What happens in the world has human relevance insofar as it makes human community possible or problematical. The dynamics of change in the world are compounded of natural processes and social forms and, sooner or later, make political analysis and political responsibility imperative if human life is to be worth living. What has often been described as a "shift to the left, politically," on the part of the Fellowship, was really a shift in the direction of a more explicit grasp of the concrete character of our political situation. For this reason, we were Marxists, and still are; not in the doctrinaire, but in the historical sense of the word. Marx was the first to grasp and to explore the fundamental and far-reaching significance of an industrial economy for the human community. He is and remains one of the architects of the modern world in the sense that one cannot understand the contemporary situation unless one has an understanding of the central elements of Marxian thought.

The structural and programmatic operation of Marxism, however, has been quite another matter. On this point, the Fellowship has, so to say, had "the rug pulled out from under it." We thought, when we began, that socialism—with its promise of an effective correlation of the political structures and traditions of liberal democracy with the structures and processes of an industrial economy—provided the concrete context of Christian behavior. But between the two world wars, this prospect lost rather than gained in actuality. And alternatives have been increasingly denied us by the accelerating tempo of technological industrial organization and achievement, on the one hand, and the feverish political struggles for the mastery of technological power, on the other.

It would have been possible, of course, to move in the direction of the Leninist-Stalinist intensification and absolutization of Marxism. But, especially after the collapse of Nazism, this road clearly ended in the fruitless fluctuation between political anarchy and political tyranny. Here was the perversion of politics from its authentic, community-creating function to a device for aggravating the anarchic potencies of social life in order to establish totalitarian political control. Another possibility would have been the abandonment of the political concern of the Fellowship and the pursuit of the pure trans-historical aims of the Christian faith. But this road would have led us either into a flight from history into eschatology or into a too rigid adherence to the possibility of implementing a trans-historical ideal. In the first instance, theological considerations of a rather formal and doctrinal sort would be required to explain the bearing of Christian faith upon Christian action. In the second instance, the already unstable alliance between Christian faith and idealism (philosophical or moral), characteristic of theological liberalism, would be re-established. In either case, the basic conviction of the Fellowship that there can be no simple obedience to unambiguous ethical demands would have been surrendered.

Unable to accept either a Stalinist analysis of the political situation or an a-political theological analysis of the human situation, the Fellowship has been increasingly committed to a pragmatic approach to personal and historical choices. Our theological analysis found it difficult to offer ethical direction beyond the choice of the lesser of two evils and to explain this predicament in terms less general than the divine activity in history and the sinful pretensions which corrupted and imperiled all personal and social creativity. This is not said to detract in the least from the serious theological concern and the genuine theological insights which inspired our understanding of the basis and the direction of Christian behavior. On the contrary, the Fellowship fostered a theological and political realism which made possible a sensitive concern for the concrete doing of God's will without the illusory prospect and encouragement that God's will could or had to be done in accordance with our aspirations and efforts. We knew that theology and politics belonged inseparably together in authentic Christian behavior. In the midst of an immoral society we were drawn on, not undermined, by the impossible-possibility of the Christian ethical demand of love.

Nevertheless, the specifically *Christian* nature of our ethical concern has been less explicity related to our behavior than it ought to have been. The Fellowship recognized that behavior could be said to be "Christian" in at least two senses: a) in the sense that an individual or group undertook to deal with the ethical ambiguities of every concrete human situation in terms of the insights into the total situation of man in the world supplied by biblical and Christian thought; and b) in the sense that a given action or course of action moved in the *direction* of changing existing patterns of thought and social structures in conformity with the insights of the Christian faith. For us, the direction of Christian behavior has been indicated by the struggle for justice in our common life. But how the concern for justice followed from our faith was never satisfactorily stated or explained. We were clearer about the context of the ethical situation than we were about the context in which we proposed to work out a "Christian" line of behavior. The Fellowship tended rather to juxtapose what was most often called "the insights of biblical and Christian faith" and "the ethically ambiguous situation," instead of exploring the ethical signifi-

cance of the fact that we were a "Fellowship" concerned to pursue
a certain course in an ethically ambiguous situation.

These insights and oversights of the Frontier Fellowship set the
problem and the task of this chapter. The problem is whether the
foundation and the pattern of Christian behavior can be clearly defined
and convincingly related to the conditions and decisions of life in
this world. The task is to try by systematic ethical analysis to set out the
terms in which this problem may be stated and resolved. *The nature
of Christian ethics* is not a speculative question about which various
interesting or uninteresting things could be said, but an actual and
urgent question affecting what, in fact, Christians are doing in the
world.

II. CHRISTIAN ETHICS AS A PART OF THEOLOGY

Christian ethics, as a theological discipline, has to do with the
"ethos" of Christians. The word "ethos" is derived from a Greek verb
εἴωθα meaning "to be accustomed to." The idea is that what one is
accustomed to gives stability to the human situation and thus makes
conduct possible and meaningful. By some such correspondence between language and reality, "ethos," as a noun, meant "dwelling"
or "stall." What was originally referred to animals as giving stability
and security to their existence came also to be applied to human relations. So, the ethos of a society denotes that which gives stability and
security to human behavior. Ethos is, so to say, "the cement of human
society"; that without which it cannot hold up, cannot be a society
at all. On this etymological substratum the distinction came gradually
to be drawn in ethical thinking between *morality* and *ethics*—morality
being broadly reserved for behavior according to custom, ethics for
behavior according to reason, that is, according to the presuppositions
and criteria of conduct ascertainable by reflective analysis. Insofar as
the presuppositions and criteria of conduct can be ascertained by
theological analysis, Christian ethics can be distinguished from other
types of ethical thinking, for instance, non-Christian (*i.e.*, religious
ethics other than Christian) and non-theological (*i.e.*, philosophical)
ethics.

Christian ethics, then, is that part of theology which undertakes to
state and explain the presuppositions and the criteria of Christian be-

havior. This is a *methodological* definition, arrived at by asking about the "field" of inquiry and the method of getting at what is going on in the "field." But this definition does not yet express the heart of the matter. It does not say what Christian ethics is in terms of its *content*. At this point the ways divide; and Christian ethics has been and may be variously defined.

Is Christian ethics, for instance, identical with New Testament ethics? Such an identity has commended itself from time to time in Christian history and to certain groups of Christians. If one can say that Christian ethics is New Testament ethics, the way seems to open to pure and simple presuppositions and criteria of Christian behavior. Such a way cuts through the ambiguity and complexity of the ethical situation and tells a Christian man in absolute terms what he ought to do. The focal point of this identity is obviously the teaching of Jesus which is regarded as universally applicable. What man requires is the single-minded will to carry them into practice. Christian ethics as a theological discipline cannot achieve the simple purity of such a conception of Christian behavior. But Christian ethics as a theological discipline tries at least to face the formidable facts that the teachings of Jesus are not so simply and purely accessible to knowledge and that the Church has not in the main taken this course.

Indeed, the early Church itself was heavily burdened by the difficulty of moving from the New Testament presuppositions and criteria of Christian behavior into an ethical situation dominated by oriental asceticism and the Hellenic vision of the excellence of the soul uncorrupted by sensory involvement. The earliest ethical literature outside the New Testament consists of tracts covering various phases of Christian behavior. There is no systematic ethical reflection. Instead, the love ethic of the New Testament retains its purity by a kind of imperceptible transformation into the ascetic virtues of charity (alms) and the restraint of passion. It is perhaps not accidental that what may be the earliest systematic Christian ethics, the *De Officiis* of Ambrose (c. 391 A.D.) deals with the morals of the clergy. Those under Holy Orders must, of course, set an ethical example. But the main thrust of Ambrose's work confirms the monastic conviction that the real way to live the Christian life is to forsake the world.

We cannot follow here the course of Christian ethical reflection between Ambrose and the Reformation.[2] The Protestant Reformation tried to get at the content of Christian ethics in still another way. Luther and Calvin recognized that the complexity and ambiguity of ethical action acutely raised the question of salvation. The force of the tension between the righteousness of God and the unrighteousness of men carried the Reformers through to a rediscovery of the basis of ethics in the saving activity of God. The point of departure for specifically Christian ethics became what God has done in Jesus Christ. But until the publication of Emil Brunner's *The Divine Imperative*,[3] this point was never thoroughly elaborated in a systematic Christian Ethics. Instead, the successors of the Reformers, insofar as they did not attempt to identify Christian ethics with the ethics of the New Testament, either fell into an unhappy tangle over the relations between Law and Gospel or fell back upon philosophical presuppositions (idealism) in terms of which to interpret the ethical insights of the Reformation.

Brunner's ethics breaks new ground in the history of Christian ethics as a part of theology. It does so chiefly because Brunner sets out frankly to write an "evangelical ethics." He tries to work out a theory of Christian behavior on the presuppositions of the sixteenth-century Reformers, chiefly Luther and Calvin. After showing how justification through grace alone is the foundation for the Christian understanding of what is good, Brunner defines Christian ethics as "the science of human conduct as it is determined by divine conduct."[4] With this definition, the present discussion has no quarrel. The matter can be put this way; and certainly Brunner's analysis has carried us a great way forward in understanding Christian ethics as a discrete and concrete way of thinking about Christian behavior.

Nevertheless, I venture to suggest that Brunner's analysis turns a wrong corner soon after it is under way, a mistake which permanently obscures his evangelical point of departure. "In the Christian view," writes Brunner, "that alone is 'good' which is free from all

---

[2] The classical foundation of medieval ethics may be found in the Secunda Secundae of the *Summa Theologica* of St. Thomas Aquinas.

[3] Translated from the German by Olive Wyon. The German edition appeared in 1932 under the title, *Das Gebot und die Ordnungen*, Tübingen: Mohr. The English translation was published in 1936 under the title, *The Divine Imperative* (Philadelphia: Westminster Press, 1936).

[4] *Ibid.*, p. 86.

caprice, which takes place in unconditional obedience. . . . But this obedience is rendered not to a law or a principle which can be known beforehand, but only to the free, sovereign will of God. . . . Man only knows what the love of God is when he sees the way in which God acts, and he only knows how he himself ought to love by allowing himself to be drawn by faith into this activity of God."[5] So far so good; this is the unique understanding of human behavior of an evangelical or Protestant ethics. But then Brunner goes on to declare that "the will of God, as it is made known to faith through revelation, is both a gift and a task; . . . as the Will which demands, as the Command of God it can only be known by us through the law in its three-fold sense."[6] This is not so good, for this means that Brunner has slipped with the successors of the Reformers, even with the Reformers themselves, into that fateful retreat from the sovereign priority of grace into the traditional and deadly ordering of the ethical life *from* the law *to* the gospel. This is not good; for this means that Brunner's ethics is primarily an ethics of obligation rather than of free response (despite all that he says about responsibility as freedom-in-response). When the will of God regarded as demand overshadows the will of God regarded as gift; when obligation overshadows freedom in "unconditional obedience," then the will of God tends to be detached from its concrete context in the redemptive activity of God, and to be welded instead to the sterile and abstract uniformity of the divine law. In a word, the content of Christian ethics is, as the translator of Brunner's book rightly puts it, "the Divine Imperative." But an ethic, based upon the self-revelation of God in Jesus Christ, is more concerned about "The Divine Indicative" than it is about the "Divine Imperative." The primary question is not, "What does God command?" The primary question is "What does God do?"[7]

---

[5] *Ibid.*, pp. 83-4.

[6] *Ibid.*, p. 92.

[7] The ethics of Karl Barth, though not yet complete, appears to be involved in the same difficulty. The priority of grace is more strictly adhered to than in the argument of Brunner. Whereas Brunner's thought moves from the revelation of God's gracious forgiveness of the sinner to creation and then to redemption, Barth discusses the ethics of creation *after* he has laid the foundation for what he calls "general ethics" in the gracious will of God which man knows through God's self-revelation in Christ. What man knows in this way is that God through Christ has "elected" man into fellowship with Himself and into obedience in the world for God's sake. Election and ethics are the two parts of an accurate Christian interpretation of God's

The experience of the Frontier Fellowship shows that we were try-ing to explore the nature of Christian ethics as *indicative* rather than *imperative*. We were trying, in other words, to understand the will of God in terms of God's concrete activity in the affairs of men. Rein-hold Niebuhr's ethical thinking had made us almost instinctively aware of the sharp juxtaposition of the will of God *and* the pragmatic realities of every ethical situation. But what we did not see was that our own existence as a fellowship provided a clue to the nature of Christian ethics which could help us to understand more accurately the foundation and the pattern of Christian behavior. Niebuhr's ethics had, so to say, correctly pin-pointed the ethical target, but it had not satisfactorily explained how to live constructively in the gap between the will of God, theologically understood, and the concrete human situation, pragmatically understood. We were all in some way or other, believers in Jesus Christ; and we were engaged in trying to express the ethical insights of this faith. But we were all also, actually and unavoidably, members of a society of believers; and the ethical signifi-cance of this fact we did not see. We tended instead to be divided over theological formulations with the result that our real consensus was political. Had we understood the theological significance of our exist-ence as a *fellowship*, we might have achieved a more explicit and persuasive consensus about the *Christian* presuppositions of our be-havior, and thus a more adequate foundation for our political concerns.

The problem, then, is whether the nature of Christian ethics can

gracious covenant with men. Election and ethics are the two parts of the answer to the question: what does God will for man? So far so good; but then, exactly as with Brunner, the imperative overshadows the indicative, what God *commands* over-shadows what God *does* in relating Himself to man and the world. The point is not that the command, the law, has no place in ethics. The point is that in Christian ethics command and law do not have the definitive place. With Barth and Brunner, as with the Reformers, the same theological presuppositions require a different start-ing point for ethics than "the Command." *Ethically speaking*, the will of God is not first of all command; it is first of all a definite divine action. (*Cf.* Karl Barth, *Kirchliche Dogmatik*, II/2 par. 36; especially, pp. 564-67, 595-600; III/4, par. 62.) The fragmentary and posthumously published ethics of Dietrich Bonhoeffer wrestles with this same problem and tries to break away both from the formal and the con-crete rigidities of the conception of command. "The command of God," Bonhoeffer writes, "is the permission God gives to man to live in His presence. . . . It is to be differentiated from all human laws in this basic respect, namely, that the command of God commands freedom." (*Cf.* D. Bonhoeffer, *Ethik*, Munich, 1949, p. 218.) To put the matter this way has the two-fold advantage of emphasizing in Christian ethics, the personal relations between God and man established by God's action and the *will*, rather than the *command* of God.

be stated in terms of its *content,* and in such a way that the presuppositions and the actualities of Christian behavior correspond. I think this can be done by exploring the following definition of Christian ethics: *Christian ethics is the disciplined reflection upon the question, and its answer: what am I as a believer in Jesus Christ, and as a member of his Church, to do?*

III. CHRISTIAN ETHICS AS "KOINONIA" ETHICS

The basic answer to the definitive question of Christian ethics is *the will of God.* But how we arrive at this answer is not self-evident. And when we have arrived at this answer, it is not self-evident what the will of God is. The definitive question of Christian ethics, therefore, immediately raises two subsidiary questions: how do I know that I am to do the will of God? and, what is the will of God which I am to do? The remainder of this chapter must concern itself with a brief suggestion as to how these questions might be answered.

Everything depends, in thinking about Christian ethics, upon the point of departure. This is really what makes one interpretation of Christian ethics different from another. The point of departure in the present instance is the concrete fact of the existing Christian fellowship. For reasons, which our analysis ought to bear out, this existing Christian fellowship may be designated by its New Testament term: *Koinonia* (κοινωνία). Koinonia, in the New Testament, is the characteristic word for describing the concrete results of God's specifically purposed activity in the world. Accordingly, we may say, that Christian ethics is *"koinonia" ethics.* And this means that it is from and in the *koinonia* that the will of God becomes the norm of Christian behavior. It means also that it is from and in the *koinonia* that we get the clue to what the will of God is, and what, in consequence, a Christian is to do. This was exactly the point made by the Apostle Paul in some of his most influential correspondence. "God," he once wrote to the existing Christian fellowship in Corinth, "is utterly dependable, and it is He who has called you into fellowship (*koinonia*) with His Son Jesus Christ, our Lord."[8] And towards the end of his

---

[8] I Cor. 1:9. Unless otherwise listed, the New Testament passages are quoted from the translation by J. B. Phillips, *Letters to Young Churches* (New York: Macmillan, 1950).

life, Paul wrote to the existing Christian fellowship at Philippi, "my constant prayers for you are a real joy, for they bring back to my mind how we have worked together (literally, "the fellowship [koinonia] of you") for the Gospel from the first."[9]

Perhaps, the most impressive passage in which Paul connects the Christian *koinonia* with Christian ethics is in the letter to the existing Christian fellowship in Ephesus (Chapters 4-6). Although the term *koinonia* does not occur, its nature and ethical significance are more explicitly put forward in terms of the relation between Christ and the Church. "We are not meant," he declares, "to remain as children at the mercy of every chance wind of teaching and the jockeying of men who are expert in the crafty presentation of lies. But we are meant to hold firmly to the truth in love, and to grow up in every way into Christ the Head. For it is from the Head that the whole Body, as a harmonious structure knit together by the joints with which it is provided, grows by the proper functioning of individual parts to its full maturity in love. . . . Live life, then, with a due sense of responsibility, not as men who do not know the meaning and purpose of life but as those who do. Make the best use of your time, despite all the difficulties of these days. Don't be vague but firmly grasp what you know to be the will of God . . . And 'fit in with' each other, just because you all recognize that God is the Supreme Power over all."[10] There follows a discussion of the relations between wives and husbands, children and parents, employees and employers, which defines their behavior after the manner of Christ's relation to the Church.[11]

It appears from these Pauline writings that the Christian *koinonia* is a fellowship called into being by God, a fellowship with His Son Jesus Christ our Lord. The *koinonia* is a fellowship of working together for the gospel. And the *koinonia* is a fellowship of organic integration and growth of its several parts, whose vitality and integrity are derived

---

[9] Phil. 1:5.

[10] Eph. 4:14-16; 5:5-17, 20.

[11] It is instructive to note in this connection that the celebrated Pauline discussion of Christian Love in I Corinthians 13, is preceded by the almost as celebrated discussion of the body and the members (chap. 12). For an illuminating treatment of the biblical foundations of this organic conception of the Church, and of its social importance, see F. W. Dillistone, *The Structure of the Divine Society* (Philadelphia: Westminster, 1951).

from the Head, and in which men learn the meaning and purpose of life, learn, too, what their responsibilities in life are.

A *koinonia* ethic starts from the concrete reality of the Church.[12] To start to think about ethics from this point gives to Christian ethics a clarity and relevance otherwise unattainable.

1) A *koinonia* ethic is, in the first place, an ethic which is always concrete and contextual. This means that Christian ethics start with certain facts which are simply "there," and which make up what may be called, "the ethical situation." These "facts" moreover, are significant ethically—not as isolated fragments of what is "there"—but as part of a pattern and a framework of relationships. Some grasp of the far-reaching importance of this point for ethical understanding may be provided by contrasting a "contextual" with an "absolutist" appraisal of ethical problems. Is it, for instance, wrong to tell a lie? Is a Christian required always to tell the truth, the whole truth, and nothing but the truth? Christian ethics, along with philosophical ethics, has tended to give an affirmative answer to both these questions. But the answer has been based upon some conception or standard of "the truth" which was held to be ethical in itself, and indeed, precisely to the extent that such a "norm of truth" was not involved in the facts and the relationships of the ethical situation. This is the hallmark of "absolutist ethics" which declares that the proper answer to the question What ought I to do? is supplied by an absolute, that is a standard of conduct which can and must be applied to all people, in all situations, in exactly the same way. The standard may be an idea or an ideal, a value or a law; its ethical reality and significance lies in its absolute character. The price of absolutist ethics is abstraction from the stubborn diversity and complexity of the actual situation out of which the ethical problem arises. The consequence is that the gap between the ethical demand and the ethical act is wide and unbridgeable.

---

[12] The Pauline passages just cited suggest that in the New Testament the elemental meaning of "church" is *koinonia*. The two terms are interchangeable; and for reasons that lie deep in the Old Testament background of New Testament thought. One could, therefore, speak of a "church ethics," as well as of a *"koinonia* ethics." This usage would underline the theological point that the doctrine of the Church is the foundation of Christian ethics. The word, "church," however, is burdened by the ecclesiastical associations of a long institutional history, so that to speak of a *"koinonia* ethics" is better designed to keep the fundamental point in view. The concrete reality of the *koinonia* is inseparable from the visible institutional structures of the Church; but the visible institutional structure of the Church is not identical with the *koinonia*.

A contextual ethic, in contrast, regards the concrete complex of the actual situation out of which the ethical problem arises as itself ethically significant. There are basic ethical facts, there is a concrete ethos of human behavior without which it is impossible to regard that behavior as human. "Men make ethical judgments all the time. They decide that this kind of act would be wrong, that kind right to do, often without hesitation and with satisfaction to all . . . He who does not know such facts, who does not know that peace is good, that the world is not the best possible and should be improved, that love is better than hate, is insincere or mad . . . No one has ever taken every supposed ethical fact as genuine . . . But if we are to make an open investigation, if we are to make a genuine attempt to clarify and certify, we cannot rightly begin except by accepting what we have available."[13] And when we do begin "by accepting what we have available," it appears that every concrete ethical question involves determining what is actually to be done with reference to a certain pattern or context of relations.

If a man is selling his car to a prospective buyer, what does it mean to tell the truth? Obviously, it is not telling the truth to remark that the sun is shining, even if it is. Such a remark, having nothing concretely to do with the buyer and the car, could make the buyer suspect that he was not going to be told the truth. But as regards the buyer and the car, what should the owner of the car do? There are at least three possibilities. The owner can refuse to tell the buyer anything; he buys as is, and at his own risk. Or, the owner can tell the buyer everything the owner knows about the car; at the risk of losing the sale. Or, the owner can answer only those questions which the buyer asks; and risk only the buyer's praise or blame, according to the actual performance of the car.[14] An absolutist ethics, it would be argued, would take the second of these three courses of action. But

---

[13] Paul Weiss, *Man's Freedom* (New Haven: Yale University Press, 1950), pp. 179-81. Professor Weiss' work is important in this connection, partly because he makes a thorough-going attempt to move from the relativity of ethical concreteness to an ontological ethical principle without falling either into absolutism or into relativism. His work is also worth citing because Professor Weiss does not know—how could he?—that Christian ethics, as *koinonia* ethics, starts exactly where he does. Contrary to Professor Weiss, *koinonia* ethics includes as basic ethical fact, the concrete existence of the *koinonia*, which he chooses to ignore.

[14] I am indebted for this vividly concrete illustration to Mr. Charles P. Taft. Mr. Taft is, of course, not responsible for the use to which his account of an actual situation is here put.

there is no guarantee in an absolutist ethics either that the owner had told everything he knew about the car (he might have forgotten something), or that what the owner knew about the car was the truth. Nor could the owner's *intention* to tell the truth cover the fact that he had actually not told the truth.

A contextual ethics, on the other hand, recognizes that telling the truth is, as Dietrich Bonhoeffer has put it, "a matter of accurate and serious consideration of the actual circumstances. The more complex the circumstances of a man's life are, the more responsible he is and the more difficult it is for him 'to tell the truth.' . . . Therefore, telling the truth must be learned. . . . Since it is simply a fact, that the ethical cannot be detached from the real situation, the increasingly accurate knowledge of this situation is a necessary element of ethical action."[15] Telling the truth about the car, on these terms, would not be identical with optimum verbal veracity. It would be different for a high school adolescent than for a man in middle life; for a man who had two cars than for a man who had to dispose of the only car he had in order to pay for his wife's burial; for a humanist than for a Christian. But in each case, telling the truth would be a matter of saying the "right word," or better, "the living word." "The living word is as alive as life itself."[16] The living word is the verbal expression of the full complexity and totality of the existing concrete situation, the ethos of which is always the dependable openness of all the human beings concerned to one another. Insofar as the "right word" is instrumental to such openness, telling the truth is ethically real. If the buyer and the seller of the aforementioned car come, through that transaction, to be linked together and open to each other as human beings, and each in his own concrete situation, then, whether much is told, or little is told about the car, whatever is said is the truth. If such human relatedness, if the ethos is missing from the transaction, then, whether much or little has been said, the truth has not been told.

A *koinonia* ethic claims that such human relatedness, such an ethos, is possible and actual, only in the context of the concrete reality of the Church. If we are to begin by accepting what we have available, it is not enough to know that men made ethical judgments all the time,

---

[15] *Op. cit.*, p. 284.
[16] *Ibid.*, p. 285.

that love is better than hate, that the ethical situation is contextual rather than uniform. It is also necessary to take seriously the empirical reality of a fellowship which is by foundation and by destiny designed to express in the world the ethos of man's interrelatedness and openness for man. The empirical reality of the Church violates in many ways the ethos which is the true occasion of its existence and without which it cannot be the Church. Nevertheless, the empirical reality of the Church is a basic ethical fact as the laboratory of the living word. Here, in an ongoing experiment in the concrete reality and possibility of man's interrelatedness and openness for man, the human ethos acquires a framework of meaning and a pattern of action which undergird the diversity and complexity of the concrete ethical situation with vitality and purpose.

2) A *koinonia* ethic is, in the second place, an indicative rather than an imperative ethics. This does not mean that there are no ethical demands. What it means is that the ethical demands acquire meaning and authority from the specific ethical relationships which precede and shape these demands. What am I, as a believer in Jesus Christ, and a member of his Church to do? The answer is, "I am to do what I am." "He who does what is true comes to the light, that it may be clearly seen that his deeds have been wrought in God."[17] "For me to live is Christ. . . ."[18] Dante has strikingly and movingly made the same point, in the concluding lines of his pilgrimage into Paradise. "Already my desire and will were rolled—even as a wheel that moveth equally—by the Love that moves the sun and the other stars."[19] But whereas Dante derives his grasp of the ethical indicative from his vision of the Church Triumphant, a *koinonia* ethic derives this indicative from the reality of the Church militant. The Church militant is the existing *koinonia*, the body of which Jesus Christ is the Head, the purposeful work of God in the world. To be in the *koinonia* is to be in the sphere and on the line of God's activity in the world. It is this activity of God which establishes and defines the relationships and the pattern of what is ethically real. The existence of the *koinonia* is itself the evidence that certain relationships between God and man,

---

[17] John 3:21, Revised Standard Version.
[18] Phil. 1:21.
[19] *The Paradiso* (London: J. M. Dent and Sons, 1926), canto xxxiii, 11.143-45.

and man and man are facts. It is also a fact that these relationships give to Christian behavior a certain pattern. One may not like the facts, or one may try to ignore the fact that they are "there." But this does not alter the evidence of the divine activity. Christian ethics deals with this evidence. It regards what God has done and what God is doing as determinative of the ethical situation. *Koinonia* ethics is indicative because it gives primary attention to what is.

What *is* the relationship between God and man, and man and man which takes concrete form in the existing *koinonia?* The answer can only be given in terms of the story of God's ways with men in the world recounted in the Bible. This again is simply a fact—that the *koinonia* and the Bible are inseparable. The mind of the Church has been notoriously divided on *how* the *koinonia* and the Bible belong together. But there can be no denying that they do go together without denying what is there. A decent respect for the facts ought to make it clear that the existence of the *koinonia*—and consequently a *koinonia* ethic—presupposes the basic conceptions with which Christian theology has wrestled in its effort to understand and to communicate God's activity in the world set out in the Bible. That God acts characteristically in an historical way is plain from His convenant with Israel. This covenant is, according to the Bible, anchored in the structure of creation; and is, indeed, the point of it. The destiny of God's covenant people is to bring to all people God's ways with men in accordance with God's way of making Himself known. God's covenant with men expresses God's will to include men in fellowship with Himself and to establish the conditions under which men really could be themselves in being related to each other. God's covenant will is God's love offered to men in faithfulness and trust to be faithfully and trustfully received. "It is plain," however, "to anyone with eyes to see that at the present time all created life groans in a sort of universal travail. And it is plain, too, that we who have a foretaste of the Spirit are in a state of painful tension, while we wait for that redemption of our bodies which will mean that at last we have realized our full sonship with Him."[20] For reasons best known to Himself, God's covenanted will to fellowship did not exclude the risk and the pain of disavowal and deliverance. With the same historical actuality, God

---

[20] Romans 8:22-23.

displaced the "old covenant" by a "new covenant," sealing it this time, not by the law and the prophets, but by the incarnate life of His only Son. "It is true that God chose Him to fulfill this part before the world was founded, but it was for your benefit that He was revealed in these last days—for you who found your faith in God through Christ. And God raised Him from the dead and gave Him unimaginable splendor, so that all your faith and hope might be centered in God. . . . It is for you now to demonstrate the goodness of Him who has called you out of darkness into His amazing Light. In the past you were not 'a people' at all: now you are the People of God. In the past you had no experience of His mercy, but now it is intimately yours."[21]

If we in the Frontier Fellowship had been clearer about the presuppositions of a *koinonia* ethic and the bearing of this ethic upon our existence as a Fellowship, we would have been less likely to imagine that we could pick and choose from the storehouse of Christian knowledge and experience to explain what we ought to do and why. The *koinonia* is the always contemporary reality of God's will to fellowship with men and for men with one another. It is in the *koinonia* that this will of God defines what men in fact are, and are meant to become. It is in the *koinonia* that the will of God, in Bonhoeffer's phrase, "commands freedom," for we are simply bidden in word and in act, to be what we are.

3) A *koinonia* ethic is, in the third place, a social rather than an individualistic ethic. This follows from the nature of the *koinonia* as the expression of the will of God. A *koinonia* ethic obviously does not exclude individual behavior. It is to the *koinonia* and its relationships that the individual is committed. It is as individuals that we are to heed the Pauline admonition "firmly (to) grasp what you know to be the will of God. . . . And 'fit in with' each other." Nevertheless, the understanding of what the will of God is, is not derived from what individuals are doing but from what God has done and is doing in the world. And in the *koinonia,* following as it does the Scriptural line, it is plain that what God is doing in the world is bringing His kingdom in. The drive and the direction of God's activity are social. They erupt on the boundary line between the "old age" and the "new age." The Christian breathes the air and the power of the *Magnificat.* His "soul

---

[21] I Peter 1:20-21; 2:9-10.

magnifies the Lord, and . . . rejoices in God (its) Savior. . . . He has shown strength with his arm, he has scattered the proud in the imagination of their hearts, he has put down the mighty from their thrones, and exalted them of low degree; he has filled the hungry with good things, and the rich he has sent empty away."[22] "For look at your own calling as Christians, my brothers. You don't see among you many of the wise (according to this world's judgment) nor many of the ruling class, nor many from the noblest families. But God has chosen what the world calls foolish to shame the strong. He has chosen things of little strength and small repute, yes, and even things which have no real existence to explode the pretensions of the things that are—that no man may boast in the presence of God. Yet from this same God you have received your standing in Jesus Christ, and He has become for us the true Wisdom, a matter in practice of being made righteous and holy, in fact, of being redeemed."[23] The *koinonia* is the outpost of God's judgment upon every social pattern and structure which seeks to preserve and to justify itself by the idolatry of the *status quo*. And the *koinonia* is the outpost of God's renewal, establishing new patterns and structures, commensurate with God's new possibilities of living on the other side of those which are played out. The ethical reality of the Christian life is being, in fact and in anticipation, ready for God's next move.

A *koinonia* ethic thus provides the basis for the inseparable connection between theology and politics; and indeed, between a theology of the "right" and a politics of the "left." In this, the Frontier Fellowship was instinctively on the correct path. For a theology of the "right" acknowledges and explores the sovereign freedom and initiative of the divine will at work to conserve the divine purposes. And a politics of the "left" recognizes and explores the nature and the direction of social change in the making and re-making of the human community according to the patterns of the kingdom of God.

IV. LIVING IN THE KOINONIA

We have been suggesting that it is in the *koinonia* that the answer to the central question of Christian ethics can be made. As a believer

---

[22] Luke 1:47ff.
[23] I Cor. 1:26-30.

in Jesus Christ, and as a member of his Church, I am to do the will of God. It remains now to suggest an answer to the question; what is the will of God which I am to do?

Perhaps the most frequent and familiar answer to this question is that the will of God is love. So Jesus unforgettably put it; "You shall love the Lord your God with all your heart, and with all your soul, and with all your mind. . . . You shall love your neighbor as yourself. On these two commandments depend all the law and the prophets."[24] And certainly, as ethical formulations go, the New Testament is completely at one with Jesus. "Love hurts nobody: therefore, love is the answer to the Law's commands."[25]

But it takes almost no reflection at all to realize that these formulations do not settle the problem of what the will of God is; they raise it. What does the love of God and neighbor mean? And how shall one go about it? In dealing with these perplexing questions, Christian ethics has tended to fall between two stools. Every concrete situation which calls for love reduces the understanding of love in relation to behavior to one of two possibilities. Love is either a statement, precept, law; or, an attitude of benevolence, sympathy, mutuality. But in both cases, the precise meaning and relation of love to the concrete action is obscure. Behavior meantime goes on; and decisions are arrived at either purely pragmatically or with the aid of some value system in which Christian love has a difficult time eking out a discrete existence.[26]

It is precisely this difficulty which a *koinonia* ethic resolves. And it does so by spelling out the meaning of love in terms of what God is doing and has done in the world. The concrete behavior situation is, so to say, invaded by the *indicative* nature of God's activity. The whole complex of man's pragmatic choices is drawn into the orbit of

---

[24] Mt. 22:37, 39-40, Revised Standard Version.

[25] Romans 13:10.

[26] This problem has been particularly well set out in Professor Paul Ramsey's *Basic Christian Ethics* (New York: Charles Scribner's Sons, 1950). Christian ethics is, according to Ramsey, an ethics of obedient love. In distinction from philosophical ethics, Christian ethics asks, not "what is the good?", but "whose good?" This is effectively stated. But when Ramsey goes beyond this formulation, the difficulties begin. He rightly refuses to limit Christian ethics to statements and attitudes. A Christian can and must act with "enlightened" not "unenlightened" unselfishness. But the criteria of "enlightenment" are to be sought, according to Ramsey, in philosophical idealism rather than in the *koinonia*.

what God has set up and is setting up in the world. It has not, I think, been sufficiently noticed, that this is the characteristic New Testament way of spelling out what love means. "Already we have some experience of the love of God flooding through our hearts by the Holy Spirit given to us. . . . The proof of God's amazing love is this: that it was while we were sinners that Christ died for us. . . . If while we were His enemies, Christ reconciled us to God by *dying for us,* surely now that we are reconciled we may be perfectly certain of our salvation through His *living in us.* Nor, I am sure, is this a matter of bare salvation—we may hold our heads high in the light of God's love because of the reconciliation which Christ has made."[27] "To us, the greatest demonstration of God's love for us has been His sending His only Son into the world to give us life through Him. We see real love, not in the fact that we loved God, but that He loved us and sent His Son to make personal atonement for our sins. If God loved us as much as that, surely, we in our turn, should love each other!"[28]

This is the way the love of God looks from within the *koinonia.* And this is what it means. Love is God's concrete action in Christ, establishing a bridgehead of forgiveness in the world. And life in the *koinonia* is first of all, simply being oneself on this bridgehead; and then doing whatever one does with all the pragmatic resourcefulness required by God's unyielding maneuvering, on the one hand, and the actualities of enemy resistance on the other. The aim is to extend the bridgehead until the enemy and all the territory under enemy occupation are brought into the orbit of God's reconciling action in Jesus Christ.

In the *koinonia* one learns to understand and to talk about the will of God as one sees it in action. A *koinonia* ethic, therefore, defines the will of God as forgiveness and justice and reconciliation, rather than as love. This does not mean that the will of God is something else than love. It means, on the contrary, that the concrete reality of love in the *koinonia* in the world, is forgiveness and justice and reconciliation.

The mention of "justice" brings us to the central concern of the

---

[27] Romans 5:5, 8, 10-11.
[28] I John 4:9-11, Revised Standard Version.

Frontier Fellowship and to the end of this chapter. The foregoing pages have been devoted to the theological understanding of the foundation and the context of justice because justice is the crucial problem of Christian behavior. If the significance of justice in Christian ethics is to be rightly set out, the clearest possible grasp of the exact place of justice in the thinking and the behavior of Christians must be presupposed. Since it is at this very point, as we have seen, that the thinking of the Fellowship also required clarification, it is appropriate to conclude with a suggestion about where and how the responsibility for justice arises in a *koinonia* ethic.

The suggestion is that justice belongs with forgiveness and reconciliation in defining the pattern of Christian behavior. Christian behavior moves along a line, which may be plotted graphically by three points. The first point is forgiveness, which is the gift, free and undeserved, of a new possibility of life, dead in the middle of a dead-end street, when every existing possibility has become "old;" is, in fact, played out. At the other end of the graph is reconciliation. Reconciliation is the actual condition which emerges whenever the alienation of enmity has been transmuted into fellowship. And in between—not in the middle, but somewhere along the line—on the concrete way from forgiveness to reconciliation—is what the Bible calls "justice." Justice is God's setting right what is not right in the doing of His will in the world. This happens—as it looks from within the *koinonia*—whenever existing cultural and social patterns, existing structures of power and pretension, whether corporate or private, are broken down and overthrown, while others are built and planted.[29] God's justice (righteousness) is being concretely applied in the world in which God's will is being done, whenever and wherever the exalted are brought low, and those of low degree are exalted. Here is the line of battle for the bridgehead. And here, forgiveness and reconciliation are deprived of abstractness and inwardness and become real in the concrete struggle for justice, when the actual enmities of men are transformed into the love of the brethren. Living in the *koinonia* is living in terms of the pattern and the direction of the forgiveness, justice, and reconciliation, "for God so loved the world that he gave his

---

[29] The allusion is to Jeremiah 1:10, Revised Standard Version.

only begotten Son, that whoever believes in him should not perish but have eternal life."[30]

When he came, the people that sat in darkness saw a great light. Simple ones and great ones met each other there, where he was born; and bowing there, they became members one of another, in the *koinonia* of his body in the world. By a remarkable, yet scarcely accidental correspondence, Martin Luther, who re-discovered the heart of the gospel for the reformation of the Church, and W. H. Auden, who re-discovered the heart of the gospel for the reformation of contemporary culture, have come upon a common metaphor. Borrowing upon it, we could say, that *koinonia* ethics is the "ethics of the Manger."

The Wise Men say:

> Led by the light of an unusual star,
> We hunted high and low. Have travelled far,
> For many days, a little group alone
> With doubts, reproaches, boredom, the unknown.
> Through stifling gorges. Over level lakes,
> Tundras intense and irresponsive seas.
> In vacant crowds and humming silences,
> By ruined arches and past modern shops,
> Counting the miles, And the absurd mistakes.
> O here and now our endless journey stops.

And the Shepherds say:

> We never left the place where we were born,
> Have only lived one day, but every day,
> Have walked a thousand miles yet only worn
> The grass between our work and home away.
> Lonely we were though never left alone.
> The solitude familiar to the poor
> Is feeling that the family next door,
> The way it talks, eats, dresses, loves, and hates,
> Is indistinguishable from one's own.
> Tonight for the first time the prison gates
> Have opened. Music and sudden light
> Have interrupted our routine tonight,
> And swept the filth of habit from our hearts.
> O here and now our endless journey starts.

And then, in intermingled conversation, the Wise Men and the Shep-

---

[30] John 3:16, Revised Standard Version.

herds, and the echoing chorus of the by-standing world, already being drawn into the orbit of God's indicative action in the world, say:

> Our arrogant longing to attain the tomb,
> Our sullen wish to go back to the womb,
> To have no past, no future, is refused.
> And yet, without our knowledge, Love has used
> Our weakness as a guard and guide. We bless
> Our lives' impatience. Our lives' laziness,
> And bless each other's sin, exchanging here
> Exceptional conceit with average fear.
>
> Released by Love from isolating wrong,
> Let us for Love unite our various song,
> Each with his gift according to his kind
> Bringing this child his body and his mind.
> . . . .
> Love is more serious than Philosophy
> Who sees no humor in her observation
> That Truth is knowing that we know we lie.
> . . . .
> Love does not will enraptured apathy;
> Fate plays the passive role of dumb temptation
> To wills where Love can doubt, affirm, deny.
> . . . .
> Love knows of no somatic tyranny;
> For homes are built for Love's accommodation
> By bodies from the void they occupy.
> . . . .
> Love does not fear substantial anarchy,
> But vividly expresses obligation
> With movement and in spontaneity.
> . . . .
> The singular is not Love's enemy;
> Love's possibilities of realization
> Require an Otherness that can say *I*
> . . . .
> Not In but With our time Love's energy
> Exhibits Love's immediate operation;
> The choice to love is open till we die.
> . . . .
> O living Love, by your birth we are able
> Not only, like the ox and ass of the stable,
>   To love with our live wills, but love,
>   Knowing we love.

O living Love replacing phantasy,
O Joy of life revealed in Love's creation;
Our mood of longing turns to indication:
Space is the Whom our loves are needed by,
Time is our choice of How to love and Why.[31]

---

[31] "For the Time Being," from *The Collected Poetry of W. H. Auden* (New York: Random House, 1945), pp. 442-47.

Towards a Contemporary
Doctrine of Vocation

ALEXANDER MILLER

———————————————— ✳ ————————————————

ALEXANDER MILLER *is Lecturer in Religion at Stanford University. Born in Scotland, and educated in New Zealand and Great Britain and at Union Theological Seminary, he is the author of* THE CHRISTIAN SIGNIFI-CANCE OF KARL MARX, CHRISTIAN FAITH AND MY JOB, *and* BIBLICAL POLI-TICS, *as well as a frequent contributor to religious periodicals.*

THE Frontier Fellowship could be identified historically by reference on the one hand to the recovery of biblical and Reformation social theology which appropriated, re-interpreted and deepened the concerns of the Social Gospel; and on the other by reference to the insights of classical Marxism, which corrected the illusions of a non-dialectic political liberalism.

This creative debate between biblical Protestant thought and the insights of classical Marxism can be usefully illustrated by a discussion of the doctrine of vocation, which was a pre-occupation of the Reformation and of Puritanism, and which in a refracted form was close to the prime concerns of the Marxists. It has become again an anxious concern of Protestantism, as witness the plethora of commissions working in and for the World Council of Churches and the National Council, and the frequency with which this theme is slated for discussion in church groups of every kind. And not only is the theory of the matter up for discussion, but certain of the most influential experiments in Protestantism, the Iona Community for example, have focussed their activity right at this point.

I. PRELIMINARY THESIS

It is tempting to see a dialectic scheme in the historic fate of the Reformation doctrine. The form of it was relatively constant from Luther through Calvin and Puritanism, with some degeneration as the Puritan pattern of life felt the corroding touch of industrialism. The Industrial Revolution negated it entirely, or almost entirely, and insofar as it survived in the Church at all the forms in which it was expounded in the late eighteenth and nineteenth centuries were anachronistic and often fatuous. The twentieth-century Church is the heir of this debacle. Hence the contemporary demand for a relevant modern statement of the doctrine.

Meanwhile, however, the problem persisted, and it was dealt with in the nineteenth century; not by Christian theology, for the social insights of the Reformation were at a discount, but first by Hegel (who abandoned Protestant theology for philosophy), and in succession to him by Marx and Engels. The analytic sections of their social theory are in a true sense a refraction of the Reformation doctrine of the calling. The discussion of *Entfremdung* (estrangement: alienation) which played so large a part in the thinking both of Hegel and of Marx is the most relevant nineteenth-century treatment of the relation between man and his work. If industrialism—to continue a risky figure of speech—negated the received doctrine of vocation, Marxism is the ideological account of this negation. At the level of theory, then, the Reformation doctrine is the thesis, Marxism the antithesis, and the problem for the contemporary Church is to find a synthesis which reappropriates the insights of the Reformation, enriched by the Marxist critique of industrialism. Into the synthesis, however, additional elements will have to go, for the one hundred years since the *Communist Manifesto* have brought radical and momentous changes within capitalist industrialism itself, shifting the pattern of work—and property—relations associated with it. Obviously the most significant change is the growth of the power of workers' organizations, their corresponding political strength, and the new relationship between workers' power and industrial responsibility.

There is a growing volume of empirical material touching the effect of recent industrial development upon the relation between a man and his work, and it is this empirical material which must be brought together with the theological restatement of the doctrine to give us the ingredients of a relevant and contemporary formulation. It would seem that along these lines we might make a non-casuistic approach to a problem which the Puritans as late as Baxter treated in a casuistic fashion. In any event, the point of view on theological ethics which is implied in these essays makes the attempt inevitable.

II. A SKETCH OF THE HISTORY

a. *Luther*

For our purposes we can ignore the refinements of the debate between Max Weber and his critics. Albert Hyma and others appear to have shown that Luther's use of the word *Beruf* (calling) to refer to secular occupations is less original than Weber maintained.[1] But nonetheless we shall have to take account, as a starting-point for our study, of the "Copernican revolution," as Anders Nygren calls it, which Luther wrought in the whole universe of religion.

By analogy with Karl Marx' self-confessed relationship to traditional philosophy, what Luther propounded—it may be without full comprehension of what he was up to—was a "religion to end all religion." Leaving aside the terms in which he made his point, what he did was to extricate Christianity from its post-Pauline entanglement with the "religious" concern about salvation, and to substitute for it a sole concern about *agape*-obedience.

For Luther—as for Paul—the religious quest, in every conceivable form of it, is over, because the issue of our salvation has been taken care of by One who not only loves us more than we love ourselves and can do more about our salvation than we could do for ourselves, but in fact has done, in Christ, in fact and in history, all that is needful. As he said in controversy with Erasmus,[2]

> God has taken care of my salvation . . .

and in *Christian Liberty*:

> . . . no one can do God greater dishonor than not to trust him.

---

[1] A. Hyma, *Christianity, Capitalism and Communism*, p. 4 ff.
[2] In 1525. Quoted A. Hyma *op. cit.*, p. 43.

The Christian, then, relying simply and solely on the assurance the Gospel brings that the root of all anxiety has been cut, forthwith renounces all anxiety and will henceforth treat "religious" concern as a type of unfaith. The quest for the *summum bonum* gives way to a simple compulsion to give back love for His love who has given us "all good things, and also salvation," and has espoused us to himself by the wedding-ring of faith.

> Quite voluntarily and without recompense, the Christian does all that he does without thereby seeking his own advantage *or salvation . . .* What is done is done just to please God thereby.[8]

By this loving subjection to the saving and commanding will of God the Christian man gets back the primal dignity which he lost by his rebellion. He is a son of the most high God, his rights immeasurable. He has a status "higher than that of a bishop."[4] "The common status of a Christian is the holiest on earth."[5] Specifically, his loving service of God will be expressed first in his life as a loyal churchman, a member of the community of the justified; this is the heart of it, and the emphasis of Luther and the Reformation at this point amounts to a high doctrine of the Church which is a world removed from the extremes of "Protestant individualism." But the service of God relates also to the orders of creation, to the perennial forms of social life; to the family, the political order, and the economic order of property and labor.[6]

Our particular business is with the third of these, but in Luther's thought the calling to a special work of hand or mind in one's particular vocation is held in close relation to the work of citizenship, inasmuch as both express the love of the neighbor, and the service of the

---

[8] This section quoted and paraphrased from *Christian Liberty*. English Translation of Bertram Lee Woolf. (London: The Lutterworth Press, 1937.) (Italics ours.) We discern how pervasive and persistent was this *motif* in Protestantism and through Puritanism, when we find Oliver Cromwell describing the motivation for his political and military endeavors in words reminiscent of Luther's. "Truly no creature hath more cause to put himself forth in the cause of his God than have I. I have had plentiful wages beforehand, and I am sure I shall never earn the least mite." Cromwell's *Lectures and Speeches*. Thomas Carlyle. Vol. 1, p. 81. Everyman edition.

[4] *Works*. Erlangen Edition, 21:281.

[5] *Works*. 50:248.

[6] The most comprehensive and influential contemporary exposition of this pattern of obligation is in Emil Brunner's *The Divine Imperative* (Philadelphia: Westminster Press, 1936).

commonwealth. Luther was peculiarly tough-minded and discon-
certingly logical about this.

> Should you see that there is a lack of hangmen, beadles, judges,
> lords, or princes, and find that you are qualified, you should offer
> your service and seek the place, that necessary government may by
> no means be despised and become inefficient or perish.[7]

One must concede that there is no record of Luther's volunteering
for hangman's duty, and one must concede further that there were not
likely to be jobs going vacant in the "lords and princes" bracket: but
this reference at least seals the connection in Luther between social
necessity and the Christian's citizenship obligation and vocational
responsibility. Whatever is necessary to social health is wholesome
work for the Christian.

This is, of course, the end of monasticism and the cloister. "Conscientious fulfilment of the duties of one's earthly calling takes the
place of all self-chosen ascetic practices."[8] It denies any priority to
the narrowly "religious" occupation, and makes the whole area of
the common life the arena of holiness. It has not sufficiently been
noticed, and it particularly needs to be noticed in our day, that a high
estimate of the office of Christ is here implied. How often it is suggested that the "Catholic" doctrine of the person of Christ takes him
out of reach of the common man, and makes his example of no use
to us. What Luther in fact suggests is that if the earthly example of
Christ is made the prime significance of His Person then the logic
of the matter is the cloister, or at least celibacy and the teaching ministry. But if it be recognized that the work which Jesus as the Christ
did was a unique work, a work which only He could do and for which
He chose the conditions, then it becomes possible to believe that the
common man's best service of Christ is not the mechanical following
of his earthly example in celibacy and the renunciation of the normal
work of citizenship, but the acceptance and faithful performance of the
work Christ lays on *us* in home and state and particular vocation.

> You ask, Why did not Christ and the apostles bear the sword?
> Why did He not also take a wife, or become a cobbler or a tailor?

---

[7] *Secular Authority*. Works. Philadelphia Edition, III, p. 241.
[8] Edgar M. Carlson. *The Reinterpretation of Luther* (Presbyterian Board, 1948),
p. 96.

If an occupation or office is not good because Christ Himself did not occupy it, what would become of all occupations and offices, with the exception of the ministry which alone He exercised? Christ fulfilled His own office and vocation, but thereby did not reject any other. It was not meet that He should bear the sword, for He was to bear only that office by which His kingdom is governed and which properly serves His kingdom. Now it does not concern His kingdom that He should be a married man, a cobbler, a tailor, a farmer, a prince, a hangman or a beadle, neither is the sword or secular law of any concern, but only God's Word and Spirit, by which His people are inwardly governed.[9]

It is not for the Christian man to open the kingdom of heaven to all believers, or in any sense to perform that work which alone Christ could perform, and which he once and for all has performed. "It is meet that they should have some other . . . by which God may also be served."

This is the root of the doctrine of vocation by which the Churches of the Reformation are still governed, insofar as they are true to themselves.

It is necessary to see in briefest outline what was the fate of this doctrine, through the succeeding centuries.

b. *Calvin*

In contradistinction to much of what passes for Protestantism in our day, Luther and Calvin were essentially of the same mind. The difference over which Luther appears to have hesitated was the appearance in Calvinism of a restlessness which could not be at peace in the love of Christ and could not find the meaning of vocation in the simple joy of serving Him and the neighbor for His sake. In Calvin the rigorous logic of God's sovereignty and its corollary in predestination made it necessary to devise some way, in the context of the doctrine of the Reformation, of finding religious assurance. It could not be, as in the old Church, by reliance on the word of the priest; nor, as in Luther, by the simple consciousness of the presence of Christ with His gift of forgiveness. For alongside the promise of forgiveness was the inscrutable mystery of God's election. How do we know that we are among those whom He does forgive and receive?

---

[9] *Secular Authority. Works.* Philadelphia Edition, III, p. 246.

Only one possibility remains. If in his achievements he can discover so great progress that he must admit a power greater than his own, then he knows that God is in him and that he is of the elect.[10]

If the word of the priest is without complete authority, and if our "experience" of forgiveness is as vulnerable to deception as all human experience, then we can "make our calling and election sure" only by working to demonstrate the fruits of it to ourselves and to others. Hence the mysterious combination of what looks like religious fatalism with a relentless activity.

But in spite of this emergence in Calvin of an *ethos* distinct from that of Luther, there are still wide areas of agreement between them; and at the point which concerns us particularly the coincidence is very close. For Calvin as for Luther the kind of activity peculiarly acceptable to God, and therefore most congenial to a full and Christian vocation, is that which serves the neighbor. In Calvin, in point of fact, this criterion is more explicit than in Luther, and his conception of a truly Christian calling is correspondingly more critical.

He is not content, as Luther on the whole was, to accept each task which the existing society sets a particular man, and construe it as a Christian vocation. He is interested directly in the social consequences of the work. He waxes sarcastic about the uses to which the doctrine of vocation can be put:

> If a lawyer wants to get fine fees, if he helps one party to oppress the other, if he crushes the good cause to favor the wrong, he is not to blame! For each must follow his vocation. If merchants destroy the world with monopolies, if they counterfeit and disguise their goods, if they perjure themselves every hour to defraud and circumvent, if they plunder and consume all they can snatch, let nobody speak! For that would blaspheme the vocation of the Lord.[11]

Luther had been concerned to make Christian men perform without restlessness the work that lay to their hand; Calvin will have them seek out a true Christian vocation.

> For Luther, as for most medieval theologians, (the calling) normally meant the state of life in which the individual had been set by Heaven, and against which it was impious to rebel. To the Calvinist, Weber argues, the calling is not a condition in which the individual is born, but a strenuous and exacting enterprise to

[10] Einar Billing. *Var Kallalse* (Our Calling). Privately translated and printed.
[11] "Contre la Secte des Libertins," *Opera*, vii, p. 211.

be chosen by himself, and to be pursued with a sense of religious responsibility.[12]

On this basis Calvin is explicit about a man's right to change his occupation, a right about which Luther had been at best half-hearted.

Yet neither Luther nor Calvin is to be bound in a formula. In Luther as we have seen there is some flexibility in terms of particular social necessities: "Should you see that there is a lack of hangmen . . . etc." And in Calvin, while the emphasis falls otherwise than in Luther, there is still a strong regard for the existing and accepted pattern of social life as determining the form of the calling for the majority of men.

> (God) gave one authority over the other, or enriched one with more talents than the other, in order that the man with more talents should serve the man with less, and in him serve his God.[13]

Conversely, of course, the man with few talents has his responsibility toward the man with more. This becomes important for our understanding of the relationship of masters and servants, in Calvinism and later in Puritanism. The servant should serve his master and "in him serve his God." Both master and servant stood under the moral law, and their responsibilities were mutual; but the relationship itself was unquestioned because the Scripture endorsed it.

> Calvin really is not interested in justifying this arrangement to his own moral sense. He is interested, in a fashion quite unintelligible to us, *in what the Scripture says.*[14]

That is all very well, but the same Calvin is prepared on another issue, the issue of usury, to subject the Scriptural word to radical criticism in terms of his own moral sense and the needs of the age. The fact is that in Calvin the interests of the employer, who is also the entrepreneur, who needs to hire servants and who also needs to rent money, curiously determine the rigidity or adaptability of the biblical word. Yet what adaptation was made was made generally under the governance of the Gospel and under a concern for justice and the general good. The use and abuse of usury was judged by this norm,

---

[12] R. H. Tawney in "Foreword to Max Weber," *Protestant Ethic and the Spirit of Capitalism* (New York: Scribners, 1930), p. 2.

[13] A. Kuyper, *Calvinism* (Grand Rapids: Eerdmans, n.d.), p. 27.

[14] Georgia Harkness, *Calvin: The Man and His Ethics* (New York: Henry Holt and Company, 1931), pp. 213-214.

and there is no sign in Calvin of any general sanction on unregulated money-getting. There is in fact very little emphasis upon diligence in secular work such as Weber found in the seventeenth and eighteenth centuries. The work which makes the calling and election sure is work directed to the glory of God; but this is by no means identified with the kind of work which brings prosperity. There is still the traditional suspicion of wealth, if anything quickened and pointed against the very opportunities for wealth-getting which the new economic situation opened up.

> We may not think that God acted without reason (against Tyre), for the inhabitants of Tyre were proud, ambitious, lewd and licentious. These abuses follow in the train of wealth and prosperity, and commonly abound in mercantile cities.[15]

c. *Puritanism*

The earlier Puritans—Sibbes, for example, Perkins and Ames—continued the characteristic Reformation witness, and Richard Baxter (1615-1691) gave it its most influential statement. We can leave the critics of Weber[16] to hew away at him, and to argue whether the manifest corruption of the doctrine in the interests of money-getting which took place from the middle of the seventeenth century is a degeneration which results from elements in the Puritan doctrine itself, or whether men like Richard Steele are no longer within the authentic Puritan tradition.[17] It is clear, in any event, that from the latter part of the seventeenth century the enhanced opportunities for wealth created by nascent industrialism corroded the old restraints upon money-getting, and forced the adaptation of the "calling" doctrine in the interests of industrial and commercial acquisitiveness.

> The rules of Christian morality elaborated by Baxter were subtle and sincere. But they were like seeds carried by birds from a distant and fertile plain, and dropped upon a glacier. They were at once embalmed and sterilized in a river of ice.[18]

---

[15] *Opera*, xxxvi, p. 391.

[16] The article *Puritanism and the Spirit of Capitalism*, by Winthrop S. Hudson in *Church History* (March 1949), represents the type of criticism to which Weber at this point is vulnerable.

[17] Winthrop Hudson, *op. cit.*

[18] R. H. Tawney, *Religion and the Rise of Capitalism* (New York: Pelican Books, 1947), p. 188.

No doubt part of the trouble was plain human sin and selfishness: but the fact was that industrialism was creating new forms of property and, necessarily, also, new forms of work-relations in which the older formulations of the doctrine had very little meaning. The older Puritan formulations were shaped by a proprietor class and by a clergy whose class-affiliation was with the proprietors. An ethic of responsibility was meaningful to those who held responsibility, and the employer who ruled in patriarchal fashion both his family and his workshop (or his counting-house) accepted it as a high calling that he should rule his little kingdom well. As for his employees—their work was obedience. They were to serve God by serving their employer. Let them thank God if the latter were benevolent, and if he were malevolent, let them examine themselves to see for what sin they were chastised. On both employer and employee the code of the calling laid the uniform obligation of hard work. The significant difference was that the harder the employer worked the richer he became, while the harder the employee worked the richer the employer became. In theological theory—and no doubt largely also in the consciousness of the age—the difference was insignificant since the hope of heaven and the fire of hell burned equally for both, but communities of men do not live entirely or for long solely by the hope of heaven or the fear of hell, and this Puritan stability could not maintain itself in the face of the growth of the acquisitive society on the one hand, and the impulse of simple justice on the other.

d. The Industrial Revoltion

By the end of the eighteenth century the strong Puritan discipline had been emasculated in the interests of unregulated money-getting and adapted to become the ideology of a predatory industrialism, while the workers whom it had tutored to obedience were taken out of the patriarchal household and put to work at the machines, machines whose authority was to become as absolute as that of the old Puritan proprietors, and a good deal less considerate. It was the beginning of an enslavement which an observer later described this way:

> While the engine runs, the people must work—men, women and children are yoked together with iron and steam. The animal ma-

chine—breakable in the best cases, subject to a thousand sources of suffering—is chained fast to the iron machine which knows no suffering and no weariness.[19]

The earlier part of the eighteenth century had been a transition period with British production still largely based on agriculture and home industry, but the beginning of the nineteenth century the moderated autocracy of the old proprietor had given way to the unregulated tyranny of the industrial boss, whose survival as mill- or mine-owner depended on the ruthless exploitation of wage-labor in the interest of mounting profit on a limitless market.[20]

The Church's tragedy was a double one. In the first place, it paid the price of utter docility for the sake of the patronage of the industrial *nouveaux riches;* in the second place, it had nothing wherewith to tutor the workers except the anachronistic *ethic* of docility. As Tawney puts it, the Church by now had ceased to matter, for the Church itself had ceased to think. It was worse than that in the measure in which the failure of the Church was more than an intellectual failure.

The contemporary Church inherits this debacle. We have never been able to grip the situation with decisiveness either in theory or practice. Evangelicalism redeemed the position in part by importing a measure of meaning and community into working-class life; but the Methodist leaders were at odds with the Chartists, and while the "chapel" produced religious and political forces which mitigated the worst effects of industrialism (notice the connection between the chapel and the industrial organizations of labor), yet in another aspect of it both the evangelical and the modern missionary movements represent a diversion—a "spiritualization" if you like—of the Reformation drive for the provisional santification of secular life. By 1792, when William Carey kindled the spark of missionary enthusiasm, the pattern of British industrial life had become intransigeant to any Christian or humane discipline, and it is symbolic that Carey himself was put to cobbling because his father feared the dire effects of work in the cotton-mill.

---

[19] Quoted in J. L. and Barbara Hammond, *The Rise of Modern Industry* (New York: Harcourt, Brace and Company, 1926), p. 208.

[20] For the full horror of what followed read the books of the Hammonds, or Friedrich Engels, *The Condition of the Working-Class in England.*

While the foreign missionary movement went forward during the nineteenth century the Church at home[21] had virtually nothing but outworn and increasingly fatuous formulae for the guidance of an industrial society. The worker who kept a semblance of humanity could react to the implacable tyranny of the machine either by debauchery or by revolution: the Church forbade him both, but had little else to contribute to an interpretation of his situation. Here again there were mitigations. Christian Socialism made its voice heard in the Establishment, and elements of non-conformity, as we have seen, had a hand in the early labor movement; but the general picture is one of "the more industry, the less Church," until by the beginning of the present century main-line Protestantism was largely isolated from the urban masses on both sides of the Atlantic, and as Max Weber puts it, "The idea of duty in one's calling prowls about in our lives like the ghost of dead religious beliefs." It survives for the middle-classes in the idea of stewardship which is the fruit of evangelicalism, but for the manual worker it scarcely survives at all.

III. HEGEL AND MARX

It is worth noticing that Hegel's *Early Theological Writings* coincide almost exactly as to date with Carey's initiation of the modern missionary enterprise. It would not do to attach much more than symbolic importance to this, since industrial development in Germany was tardy compared with England; but the fact is that during the period when the Protestant Churches virtually resigned their responsibility of interpreting the situation of industrial man, this undertaking was taken up first by Hegel (a Lutheran turned philosopher, as we have noticed) and by Marx. What we have in the Hegel-Marx analysis of man-in-industrial-society is a refraction of the Reformation, lacking, however, the final dimension of forgiveness.

Hegel turns on Luther for the "senseless sophistic reasoning" which leads him to say in *Christian Liberty* that "the soul will not be touched or affected if the body is maltreated, and the person subjected to another's power." On the contrary, according to Hegel, the subjection of the individual worker to the tyranny of industrialism and the

---

[21] . . . and in America, *Cf.*, Henry F. May's *Protestant Churches and Industrial America* (New York: Harpers, 1949).

expropriation of his labor-power by the mechanical processes of the market represent a deep offence against the very center of man's personality. It is, in very truth, "soul-destroying"; it robs life of meaning and purpose; it destroys the possibility of a true "vocation."

On this point there is strict continuity between Hegel and Marx.

> The worker alienated from his product is at the same time alienated from himself. His labor becomes no longer his own, and the fact that it becomes the property of another bespeaks an expropriation which touches the very essence of man.[22]

From this point of view, as Paul Tillich says:

> Socialism is the fight of man for his creative freedom against the forces of industrial society that transform him into a thing.[23]

This alienation of the worker from his work and therefore from himself is a situation which Reformation theology ought to have been able to understand and to interpret in its own more profound terms. It ought to have been able to relate the dimension of nature and society (which was the pre-occupation of Marxism) to the more ultimate dimension of forgiveness and justification by faith, but the implications at the secular and political level would have been revolutionary, and for this the Church was not ready. Nineteenth-century German theology, which was confronted directly by Marxism, was not sufficiently governed by the doctrine of justification to spell out an intelligible relation of justification to justice. And it is clear that the later development of the Social Gospel in America was mis-directed by nineteenth-century German theology into the shallows of a "Kingdom of God" progressivism which could not deal with the problem of the alienation of industrial man because it was informed neither by the full insights of the Reformation nor by the radical Marxist analysis of capitalist industrialism. In any event, in spite of the Copec movement in England, Rauschenbusch in America and Ragaz in Europe, by the present generation the Church was without an adequate doctrine of vocation and had resigned itself to mitigating the worst excesses of industrialism by the doctrine of stewardship.

---

[22] H. Marcuse. *Reason and Revolution* (New York: Oxford University Press, 1941), p. 279. Marcuse deals exhaustively with the continuity between Hegel and Marx. The sentence quoted is a paraphrase of an extended discussion by Marx of the theme of "alienation."

[23] *Christianity and Society* (Winter, 1949-50), p. 9.

IV. THEOLOGICAL REVIVAL AND CONSEQUENT UNEASE

In our generation the Church is in a real dilemma. On the one hand, it has a quickened sense of responsibility about its own evangelical task, and finds that the urban groups in every industrialized country have passed largely beyond its influence. On the other hand, it has learned that its evangelical responsibility must be interpreted much more profoundly and much more socially than was understood by nineteenth-century individualism. It has a concern about the patterns of social life as well as about the hearts of men. It knows how truly and how deeply the hearts of men are shaped by social pressures (for this it is indebted very greatly to Marx), but more significantly, it knows that the claim of Christ is total, and that a disorderly industry is as sinful as a divided mind.

In the sphere of industry it discerns that certain patterns of industrial life may frustrate the Christian intention for the lives of men, and that men for whom the meaning of life is obscured by the conditions of their work can neither—as they sense it—apprehend the claim of Christ nor obey it. So from the contemporary Church comes a true *cri du coeur,* spoken both by the theologians and by the Church gathered in Council:

> Within this soulless economic order, which destroys personal relations and reverses the order of nature, is it possible to do any "work" that rises above the level of things, work which is offered as a service to the community and is done to the glory of God? Is it possible to realize the personal meaning of labor in such an anti-personal economic system? Can, indeed, the proletarian or the capitalist understand at all what we theologians on the mere fringe of this terrible soulless world are saying about the idea of vocation, about the idea of service, and about the meaning of labor?[24]
>
> The part of the ordinary worker in much of modern industry has been trivialized to the point of boredom, and preclusion of self-respect. Snipping endlessly the paper and split-leather soles for bargain shoes; feeding endlessly the rods, wire and cheap metal that become ten cent hardware; . . . Who is fool enough to look for God, even if one were sure there is a God, in this dreary modern warehouse?[25]
>
> The only forms of occupation open to many men and women,

---

[24] Emil Brunner, *The Divine Imperative* (Philadelphia: Westminster Press, 1936), pp. 422-423.

[25] Robert L. Calhoun, *God and the Common Life* (New York: Scribners, 1935), p. 30.

or the fact that none is open at all, prevent them from finding a sense of Christian vocation in their daily life.[26]

Statements of this sort could be multiplied endlessly. Many of them reflect a clerical tendency to over-dramatize the situation of the worker, which has a residual richness and provides certain satisfactions even where, to the more academic observer, it looks like sheer and visionless drudgery. But the problem is real enough and the concern is deep enough to have brought some of the best minds of the Church to bear on the issue, so that both in Europe and America we now have commissions working on behalf of the ecumenical movement and a growing body of theoretical material which is good as far as it goes. But the theoretical work is vitiated constantly by the fact that the thinking of the contemporary Church is not fertilized by the actual experience of working men.

The most hopeful points of penetration are the groups which do their theorizing from within the actual structure of industry, but these are few.[27]

V. PREFACE TO A SOLUTION

In the Preface to a volume of selections from Richard Baxter's *Christian Directory*, Bishop Charles Gore wrote:

> Confessedly there has been in recent times no adequate attempt to produce a systematic casuistry for ordinary Christians who want to know and do their duty. Indeed, great districts of human life have been allowed to escape altogether from the jurisdiction of the divine law, which nevertheless was intended to control and sanctify the whole of human life.[28]

We have been exploring one of these "great districts of human life," and the need which Bishop Gore describes is patent. But from the point of view on Christian social ethics which is here presupposed it cannot be met by any kind of casuistry, not even of the qualified type

---

[26] The Report of the Oxford Conference (Chicago: Willett and Clark, 1937).

[27] One of the most fruitful of these is the French Roman Catholic Movement represented by the Mission de Paris, whose work is described in the books *France Pagan, Priest-Workman* and *The Priest and the Proletariat*.

The Iona Community in Scotland and the Laymen's Academies in Germany represent a more Protestant attempt at the problem, and they have made some real advance. In this country and beyond it one of the most fruitful approaches is through the Student-in-Industry camps and other short-term projects. But progress so far is minimal.

[28] *Chapters from a Christian Directory*. Selected by Jeanette Tawney (London: G. Bell and Sons, 1925), p. vii.

of a *Christian Directory*. The modern movement in theological ethics which is generally represented in this volume has moved so far from natural law, in the sense of rational standards rationally perceived, that it calls in question the possibility of such a "systematic casuistry for ordinary Christians" as Bishop Gore apparently desired.

What kind of approach to the contemporary problem of vocation does our point of view require? It involves bringing together the Gospel and the situation, the Faith and the facts, the Christian's absolute loyalty and his pragmatic choice. It requires the conjunction of theological and empirical material; the exposition of the Gospel on the one hand, which is the business of the theologian, and on the other hand, the close and scientific analysis of the dynamics of modern industry, the kind of material which is the preoccupation of the economist, the sociologist and the industrial psychologist. Both the theologian and the empirical scientist will do their work well in proportion as they live close enough to the actual stuff of industrial life to feel the pulse of it and apprehend in living fashion how its pressures bear upon the lives of ordinary men.

A fruitful approach to the present problem will require the following ingredients at least:

1.) The theologian must provide a critical restatement of the classical doctrine of vocation as it comes from Luther through Calvin and Puritanism. A "critical" restatement it must be, because, as Paul Tillich says, it is the essence of Protestantism that "it has no classical period"; but nonetheless if we are to understand ourselves and our dilemma we need to realize afresh what it was that for two centuries fruitfully shaped our Protestant mind, if only to discover how it was that we were diverted into the present *cul-de-sac*.

We shall have to recognize that, on the whole, the received doctrine was directed too exclusively to the relation between the particular man and his particular work. The social matrix in which the work was done was taken for granted and assumed to be both wholesome and self-regulating. If each man did his work well, the commonwealth would profit. Where warnings were given, they were pointed to individual motivation and not to the pattern of social life; warnings against greed, ostentation, etc., directed to the proprietors; against sloth, refractoriness and envy directed to the workers. It was not made explicit:

a. That each type of work must be seen in its relation to the developing social pattern, and measured by justice.

b. That, as Paul Tillich puts it, "there are social structures which unavoidably frustrate any spiritual appeal to the people subjected to them."[29]

A further difficulty is that what does duty nowadays for a doctrine of vocation is governed by the accidents of traditional Protestantism but has little to do with its theological substance. The high ethic of responsibility which was given its last influential formulation by the Puritan divines is congenial and intelligible to the bourgeoisie, though even by the professional person and the entrepreneur it is interpreted much too narrowly. But it is unintelligible to the industrial worker, and it has the further effect that the terms into which it is translated for contemporary use put a false premium on professional and middle-class standards and occupations.

This becomes clear at once if one has any considerable dealings with young people in the Protestant Churches; especially with students, who are relatively articulate about such matters. The assumptions which underlie the thinking of such groups are somewhat as follows:

i. The meaning of a vocation is to participate in "the building of the Kingdom of God." This dynamic enterprise of reconstructing society after a Christian pattern is the expression and fulfilment of personality.

ii. It follows that the point of a vocational choice is to find a position of public influence, in which Christian intention may have scope to operate, and Christian personality may have space to express itself fully and influentially.

iii. In these terms the first choice, for those who are whole-hearted enough to surrender the financial rewards offered by business or the secular professions, is the ministry or other "church professions," teaching or Christian social service or the like.[30]

iv. A second-best choice, which can be accepted without surren-

---

[29] *The Protestant Era* (Chicago: University of Chicago Press, 1948), p. xviii.

[30] A full discussion would include particular reference to the home as the focus of a vocation for women. It clearly stands outside the generalizations which are here being made.

dering a Christian intention or fatally cramping "Christian personality," is represented by professional and business life, or by intellectual occupations like administration or the work of a publicist. Here there is a measure of responsibility and public influence and an *entree* into the relatively spacious life of the middle-classes. I recall that back in 1940 an American correspondent of an English paper, weighing Mr. Wendell Willkie's Presidential chances, reported as follows:

> Mr. Willkie has admitted that this is the class to which he will direct his appeal, on whom he will turn his vote-getting smile: the farmer who owns his piece of land or hopes to do so one day, the man with a telephone and a motor-car and a few thousand dollars in life insurance, the small shopkeeper, the doctor, the lawyer, the *man who goes to church on Sunday.*

This is, without intention, a description of the general social group within which the received doctrine of vocation is intelligible, and it represents the group within which Christian young people expect to find their place and their calling, if they don't mean to "go all out" in the full-time service of the Church.

Now I am not certain that it is a job for the systematic theologian purely as such; but it is clear that the Church as a whole, with a powerful "assist" from the systematic theologian, must find ways in which to speak of Christian vocation so that it becomes intelligible not only to the doctor and the lawyer and the small proprietor, but also to the automobile worker, the steel worker, the longshoreman and the New York hackie.

For myself I would incline to make it a test of every allegedly popular exposition of Protestant and Christian doctrine that it be tried on a New York hackie; and I have a hopeful conviction that the authentic Protestant categories of forgiveness, justification by faith, and a calling determined by personal skills related to downright social usefulness, would bear the test of such a translation better than the more "modern" categories of personality and "Kingdom of God" progressivism.

2.) But if this kind of re-appropriation and translation of the received doctrine is to go forward, the importance of our second ingredient becomes apparent. For as we have seen, the classical Marxist analysis is at least symbolic of the fact that the full Christian dimension of forgiveness and obedience, while it describes life's ultimate meaning, is related to secondary dimensions of meaning which are determined by social patterns, and by moral coherence between a man and his work and the purpose to which that work is put. It is not enough to declare salvation by grace in a purely perpendicular and individualistic fashion. There has to be a search for what Paul Tillich calls "a *Gestalt* of grace" within the actual structured relationship between the man and the work; the worker and the employer; the worker, the employer and the total life of society.

Marx was bound, within the terms of his presuppositions and the dimensions of nature and society, to identify *Entfremdung* with damnation and its healing with redemption. He was wrong. Even if it were true that socialism would get rid of alienation at this level, yet socialism is not the kingdom of God, which is "righteousness (justification), and peace, and joy in the Holy Ghost" (Rom. 14:17). Yet while Marx is wrong to identify the overcoming of social alienation with the achievement of salvation, he is not wrong to relate them. For when life is distorted at the level of man's work and therefore in the sphere of his social relations, it cannot be seen clearly or seen whole, and the dimension of salvation is obscured. Man's final alienation—from God who is his home—will not be healed by socialization, but it may be that without socialization of life and labor it cannot even be understood.[31]

Marx in his fashion posed the problem of what patterns of property and work-relations would sustain responsible work. His thesis was that Capitalism undercut it and that socialism would restore it. We are probably agreed that this is too simple, but the problem remains. Here the work of the theologian shades off into the work the economist, sociologist and psychologist; or rather, it has to be brought into relation to their conclusions. The connection between the theology of vocation and the empirical science of industrial life probably cannot be made at the level of theory. The synthesis of these elements can be made only in the sphere of decision; not simply the decision of the

---

[31] I use "socialization" here in the very broadest sense to mean the importation of a greater degree of social significance into the world of work. I assume this can be done only by modifying the "private" character of large scale industry, but I should be prepared for every kind of pragmatic experiment and for variant solutions of the problem here.

man who has a particular job to do or a particular job choice to make, but the decision of all Christian men and men of goodwill about the type of social and economic order they want to live in.

The faithful handling of these two ingredients may give us a doctrine rooted in the fundamental faith of the Reformation, but more critical and therefore more political than the formulations which were developed in the sixteenth and seventeenth centuries.

VI. INCENTIVE STUDIES AND THE LIKE

We noted early that if you have in some sense a thesis in the Reformation doctrine, the negation of which by industrialism was interpreted by Marxism antithesis, the synthesis must not only take account of the Marxist analysis but must include also an analysis of the developments in industry and society which have taken place since 1883. The salient fact is the vast growth of workers' power and their powerful participation in industry, either directly as in Britain or indirectly by bargaining from strength as in this country.

The material that has to be dealt with here ranges from detailed incentive-studies such as were pioneered by the Harvard Business School and have now proliferated in every business school of any account in the country, to broader analyses of the significance of workers' power like those of Tannenbaum, Lindblom, and C. Wright Mills.[32]

In this area the necessary questions touch the character of ownership, in a society where "the tools of a free man's trade are (frequently) bolted down to the floor of another man's factory"; and the problem of relating the power of the workers' organizations to real responsibility.

Raise the problem of vocation and stay with it long enough and it points directly to a double injury; the hurt of the people of God represented by the alienation of the manual workers, and the hurt of the manual workers represented by their alienation from their work. The first will not be healed without the second, and neither will be lightly healed.

---

[32] Frank Tannenbaum, *A Philosophy of Labor* (New York: Knopf, 1951).
Lindblom, *Unions and Capitalism* (New Haven: Yale University Press, 1949).
C. Wright Mills and Helen Schneider, *New Men of Power* (New York: Harcourt, Brace, 1948).

The Person in a Technical Society

PAUL TILLICH

————————————— ✳ —————————————

PAUL TILLICH *is Professor of Philosophical Theology at Union Theological Seminary. Born in Starzeddel, Prussia, and educated at Berlin, Tübingen, and Halle, he taught at various German universities before becoming professor of philosophy at Frankfort-am-Main in 1929. When Hitler took power in Germany, Tillich came to America and since that time has taught at Union Theological Seminary. He is the author of many books and articles, among them,* SYSTEMATIC THEOLOGY, THE PROTESTANT ERA, THE SHAKING OF THE FOUNDATIONS, *and* THE COURAGE TO BE.

IT IS my understanding of the movement which is called Existentialism and which is at least one hundred years old that it rebels in the name of personality against the depersonalizing forces of technical society. For the sake of my special subject as well as in the spirit of this volume, I want to begin with some references to the earlier history of Existentialism. This history, going on since the middle of the nineteenth century, has determined the fate of the twentieth century in all spheres of human existence. The immense tragedy of our political as well as the creative chaos of our spiritual situation are foreshadowed and deeply influenced by the Existentialist rebels of the nineteenth century. Moreover, the tradition, out of which this book is written and out of which he to whom it is dedicated has worked, is rooted in the protest of the lonely prophets of the nineteenth century against the threatening destruction of humanity and personality by technical society. Finally, it is my conviction that the new beginning, of which this volume is supposed to be a symbol, should be and, I hope, will be a continuation of this tradition under new conditions and with new means. But the aim should be what it was in the preceding movements of protest: a fight for humanity, which includes both community and personality, against the dehumanizing power of modern society.

I. KIERKEGAARD AND EXISTENTIALISM

It is usual to refer to Kierkegaard as the instigator of Existentialism. For the theologians especially this is the natural start. Historically, however, this is incorrect, since people like Pascal, Schelling and others had raised the Existentialist protest before Kierkegaard. They had done it for the same reason and with the same purpose as Kierkegaard: to resist a world in which everything was transformed into a thing, a means, an object of scientific calculation, psychological and political management. Kierkegaard saw that, in spite of many romantic elements in Hegel and in spite of his doctrine of freedom as the purpose of history, *this* was the meaning of his attempt to subject all reality to a system of logical forms: The existing individual was swallowed, the deciding personality was eliminated. The world-process, playing with the individual, gave him the feeling that he was deciding for himself, while the process, governed by dialectical necessity, had already decided about him. Kierkegaard's metaphor of the "leap" embodying his protest against Hegel's logically determined world process is the idealistic mirror of the realities of the modern world. This was its greatness and this was the reason why the revolt against our world found its most successful expression in the protest against this mirror. Kierkegaard made his protest on the basis of classical Protestantism. But classical Protestantism had ceased to be an immediate reality. It had been lost and had to be regained. How? By being put in its place in the whole of the dialectical process, answered Hegel. By being reached through the leap of faith, answered Kierkegaard. Hegel's answer makes classical Protestantism a useful element within the frame of technical society; Kierkegaard's answer asks the individual to break away from this society in order to save his existence as a person. Therefore Kierkegaard's loneliness, therefore the pathological traits in his dealing with marriage, vocation and Church, therefore the lack of any effect in his own time. All this is understandable if the existing person can only be saved by a leap. Our own period, in which Kierkegaard has shaped philosophy as well as theology in the Existentialist direction, has shown this clearly. Philosophical

Existentialism demands the leap of the individual out of all traditions and social obligations into the freedom of normless decisions. Theological Existentialism demands the leap of the individual out of his given cultural and intellectual situation into the acceptance of a sacred tradition formulated hundreds of years ago. The leap liberates, but does it not enslave again? The personalities of Sartre's novels have absolute freedom, but it is actually the freedom of falling under the compulsion of the internal or external situation of the moment. And the Neo-Orthodox Christian subjects himself through the leap of faith to traditional ecclesiastical dogmas. He is free in the moment of his leap. But his leap into freedom involves the sacrifice of his freedom. The power of technical society is manifest in this conflict between rational necessity and the leap of freedom. The person is lost if rational necessity prevails. He tried to save himself by the leap which, however, leads to new forms of servitude, natural or supranatural ones. Only if we face realistically this situation, which even more than Hegel's and Kierkegaard's is our own situation, can we realize the seriousness of the problem: "The person in a technical society."

II. MARX AS EXISTENTIALIST

While Hegel provided the idealistic mirror of technical society, Marx gave its realistic description. This accounts for his ambiguous relation to Hegel, his opposition to him, insofar as the idealistic side is concerned, his dependence on him, with respect to the dialectical analysis of present day society. Marx saw much more clearly than Kierkegaard that it is not a system of thought, but the reality of modern society which is responsible for the reduction of the person to a commodity. His famous descriptions of the dehumanizing effects of economy in the industrial age center around the proletariat, but they are meant for all groups of society. Everyone, insofar as he is drawn into the all-embracing mechanism of production and consumption, is enslaved to it, loses his character as person and becomes a thing. Marx did not think that it is the technical method of production as such which destroys personal freedom, but that the social structure of the class society is responsible for it. He believed in possibilities of humanizing the technical process, but he did not believe that this could happen within the frame of the class society. Therefore he became a political rebel against the social and economic structure of bourgeois society and a tremendous historical force, not only in the countries which became "Marxist"—at least in pretense—but also in those which avoided a radical transformation by fulfilling demands of the Marxist movements within the framework of bourgeois society. This latter fact should not be forgotten by those who are still interested in an unprejudiced, scientific criticism of Marx. The way in which Marx envisages the salvation of the person in technical society unites in an highly ambiguous way dialectical necessity with political decision. Marx, the sociologist, follows Hegel's method of structural analysis and derives from it not what Hegel did, a systematic glorification of the present, but a necessary, calculable development into a glorious future. At the same time he appeals to the action of the proletariat, especially the vanguard which consists of proletarians and people from other groups who have joined them. Appeal is senseless without the presupposition that it can be accepted or rejected. He did not believe that the "person" in the proletarian was extinguished to such a degree that political appeals would be meaningless. This view is supported by the two concepts which characterize Marx's view of man, the concept of "dehumanization" and the concept of "real humanism." Both presuppose that man can be distorted by social conditions in such a way that his humanity is lost, and both presuppose that there will be a state of things in which his community is reestablished. Both show that Marx is concerned with the loss and the salvation of the "person" in the technical society as he experienced it.

But again, as in the case of Kierkegaard, the power of this society became manifest as soon as the question was: how can one break away from it? The answer seems to be easy: through the dialectical process and the revolution it will bring about. But social dialectics and revolution occur through human beings, and this introduces alternatives which are as difficult as those we found in Kierkegaard's doctrine of the leap. If those in a state of complete depersonalization are carried by the dialectical process into the "realm of freedom," how can they use it without radical transformation from thing to person? But if they are still persons they introduce an incalculable element into the situation. The proletarians may not see their real interest or their enemies may be unexpectedly strong or groups may become active who do not fit the simple class scheme, or the proletarians may carry through their demands to such a degree that they cease to be proletarians in the genuine sense of the word. All this has actually happened and has produced two contradictory reactions. The one is the reaction by what is called today "the free world," namely, the attempt to save the person within the frame of the bourgeois-capitalistic society by methods of reforms (whatever they may be called). The other is the reaction by what is called today Communism, namely, the attempt to save the person in a future state of history by removing in the present those personal elements which might endanger the future. This has led to the establishment of the communist system in which all technical refinements are used to eliminate the risks involved in personal resistance against the system. A type of technical society has been created in which the person of the present is completely sacrificed for the sake of the expected person of the future. A movement which started with a passionate fight against depersonalization has turned into one of the greatest powers of depersonalization in all history.

III. NIETZSCHE'S PROTEST

The fight of Existentialism against the dangers of the technical society was done, at the same time, on a third front, on that front which determines more than the two others the present fight against depersonalization. It was in the name of life that Nietzsche fought against the "nihilism" of the technical culture. Many followed him in all spheres of spiritual creativity. He and the movement of which he is the most conspicuous symbol saw more sharply than Kierkegaard and Marx the deepest roots of the dehumanizing and depersonalizing implications of modern society. Technical society—this is the message of all adherents of the "philosophy of life" (whether philosophers or poets or writers or artists)—destroys the creative power of life. Man becomes, according to Nietzsche, a cog in the all-embracing machine of production and consumption. This self whose center is the will to realize itself has nothing to will any more, and, therefore, it wills the "nothing." Only a new beginning of the will which wills itself can save life from a complete disintegration. This will (misleadingly called by Nietzsche the "will to power") is the self-affirmation of life as life against everything which transforms it into an object, a thing, a tool. Only a small group of people are the bearers of this new beginning, persons acting in the sense of heroic self-affirmation. They are the saviors of personal existence, through whom the power of life will reappear. On this basis the philosophers of life denounce the technical mass civilization, the egalitarian ideals, the subjection to the system of values which are accepted in this civilization, including the Christian values insofar as they are amalgamated with the ideals of the modern society. Only a few romanticists amongst the philosophers of life attacked the technical development as such (just as a few ecstatics amongst the socialists, and a few pietists amongst the followers of Kierkegaard). Generally speaking the technical world was accepted as a meaningful creation of life. But the way in which this creation turns against its creator produces the wrath of all philosophers of life. They want to restitute the integrity of creative life by looking for something below the split into subject and object. On their way they meet the depth-psychology, the emphasis on the unconscious, or the instincts, or the demonic, or the unreflected and unbroken self-realization. From the beginning in the early nineteenth century to their full development at the end of the nineteenth and the first half of the twentieth century depth-psychology, philosophy of life and Existentialism were intimate allies. Their common enemy was and is the objectifying, depersonalizing power of technical society. They do not look for the religious liberation through the leap of faith as did Kierkegaard, nor to the political liberation through the social dialectics as did Marx, but they look at the liberation which comes out of the depth of the personal life itself, his unconscious ground, his drives and instincts, his unity with nature, his self-affirming will. Sometimes they look back into the past, not in order to return to it, but in order to discover in it examples of undistorted life, *e.g.*, in the Middle Ages, or in the archaic periods of the ancient cultures, or in the so-called primitives. Some go even beyond this and use the unreflected animal life to symbolize the ideal they put against the realities of technical society (note the use of animal symbols in Nietzsche's *Zarathustra*).

IV. CONTEMPORARY PROTESTS

Again the protest is profound and forceful. But is it able to pierce the walls of the society and its depersonalizing magic? Obviously not. It is driven to fateful self-contradiction. It has to fight the state of reflection with the tools of reflection. Politically the fight against the intelligentsia, and for the primitive and the genuine—in its extreme form for "blood and soil"—has produced the most sophisticated and technically elaborated tools for suppressing every genuine expression of life which did not fit the demands of the political system. Man in this society was pressed into a scheme of thought, action and daily behavior which reminds more of machine parts than of human beings. Even the faces of the storm troopers, for example, were as stereotyped as normal industrial tools. Any indication of personality and individuality was removed. The attempt, made in the name of life, to overcome the rule of depersonalized things, has produced the complete removal of humanity in the supporters of this attempt. And its victims (including many followers) were transformed by terror into slaves, not less obedient than the slave which is called machine. The only way in which the original emphasis on life was maintained was the unrestricted realization of formerly repressed drives toward power, pleasure and destruction. This was done in the name of vitality, against rationality. But the result was a mutilated, self-destroying vitality united with bestiality and absurdity. The power of the technical world proved again to be overwhelming.

Recent Existentialism (Sartre) tried to break its power by isolating the individual from the embracing structure of technical civilization. It tries to save the person by asking him to create himself without norms, laws and principles, without anybody else or anything else. True humanism is declared to be the message of the individual making himself. Since "man's essence is his existence" no criteria are given to him for his self-creating activity. The will willing itself, the decision deciding for the sake of deciding and not for the sake of a content, the freedom maintaining itself by the rejection of any obligation and devotion—all these descriptions of the existential situation express the protest of Existentialism against our technical world. They are in analogy to Kierkegaard's "leap"; and their freedom is as much a leap into the dark as Kierkegaard's leap would have been without his participation in the Christian Lutheran tradition. By surrendering all norms they deliver the person to the contingencies of the situation, they depersonalize him.

Much more successful in saving the person from the dehumanizing power of technical society seems to be the third ally in the fight for genuine life, the depth-psychology, especially in its latest development in which all emphasis is put on the analysis and synthesis of the personal life. "Personality" has become the central concept of the post-Freudian psychotherapeutic development. The analytic attempt to liberate the unconscious from the repressions, forced upon it by the society, to liberate the Ego from the authoritarian representatives of the "Superego," to liberate the person from the compulsive drives which subdue the personal center and eliminate its power of making personal decisions—all this seems to be the way to the salvation of the person in the technical society. Many people believe that it is, and feel that their own experiences support this belief. So we must ask: Is psychotherapy the way to break through the otherwise unconquerable fortress of technical society? Is it the way to save the person from becoming a thing amongst things? Or is there a similar problem as that in the other attempts to save personal existence, namely the problem of transition, "the leap," the breaking away from the tyranny of the technical civilization. For two reasons it seems to me that the situation is not essentially different: first, because the individual person is not isolated; second, because the method of liberating him may strengthen that from which it tries to liberate. The first reason points back to Marx, the second to Nietzsche. A philosophical analyst once said to me: "What is the use of my work with my patients even if most successful, when I have to send them back into *this* society?" More and more psychotherapists have discovered that the conflicts of their patients are partly and often largely conditioned by the social situation in which they live, the competitive, technical, post-puritan society with the repressions, the anxiety, and the compulsions it produces. This, however, means a limit to the healing power of analysis and the demand for a social transformation for the sake of the person and his salvation from the depersonalizing forces.

But psychoanalysis has not only its "Marxist" problem, it has also its "Nietzschean" problem. It is the question: can a method, a technically elaborated procedure, save the person from technical society? Two answers can be given to this question. The one would say that psychotherapy is indeed a technique and works like every technique through adequate means towards a definite end. The end is healing of pathological states of mind; the means are determined by their methodological adequacy to their end. If this answer is accepted, the psychoanalyst no more saves the person than does the internist in bodily medicine. The opposite answer would say that within the psychotherapeutic method elements are present which transcend the mere technical sphere, above all a person-to-person relationship which may be saving for the patient as person. If this answer is accepted it means that the analyst implicitly and indirectly exercises priestly functions. This is quite possible and certainly very often real. But then it is not a psychotherapy as psychotherapy which saves the person, but the spiritual substance in which both the analyst and the patient participate. And the question remains: What is this saving power?

V. TWO SHORTCUTS

The result of all this seems to be quite negative. It seems that the Existential revolts against technical society have been futile. From Kierkegaard to present-day psychotherapy, the problem of transition is decisive for the failure to save the person within the technical society. The "leap" in all its variations is more an expression of despair than an answer. Nevertheless, the Existentialist revolt is the decisive event, theoretical and practical, of the last one hundred years. It has shown the problem and it has given different solutions, each of which proved the superiority of the technical society over all those who attacked it. But the attack itself was and is most significant. Whether victorious or not, it kept alive the consciousness that technical society is the great threat against the person. This is the reason why almost all important creations of the last decades were creations by those who belong to the movement of rebellion against the technical society.

These attacks have led to attitudes and systems of life and thought which challenge the contemporary bourgeois society. What, then, about this society and the attitude toward it by groups who largely agree with the criticism made by the one hundred years of Existentialist protest and who, at the same time, are aware of the tragic self-contradictions into which the protesting ideas were driven when they succeeded politically or spiritually? It seems to me that such groups, *e.g.*, the contributors of this volume and the movement they represent, must avoid two shortcuts, the one to return, in a state of disappointment, to a full affirmation of present-day technical society, the other, to use the Christian message as a *deus ex machina*, which solves all problems, unsolved by the other movements!

The first shortcut is an understandable reaction to the chaos of disintegration and the horrors of attempted reintegration which we have experienced in our period. A conservative mood today pervades, not only the disappointed members of the older generation, but also the younger people who without a revolutionary impetus and without visions concerning the future adapt themselves, in a matter-of-fact way, to the concrete demands of the given reality. It is a practical positivism, but without the forward looking enthusiasm of the earlier positivism. It is a realism of resignation. One hardly can resist this mood in a world in which small groups under the protection of political and military secrecy rule mankind; and in which the dependence on production of a highly technical character subjects everybody more and more to a new kind of fate—as incalculable and threatening as that towards the end of the ancient world. Nevertheless, one can resist this mood, not by closing one's eyes to this actual situation, not by glorifying our own reality because it is not as bad as the reality elsewhere—certainly it is better, yet the threat is the same—not by pointing to the improvements of the social situation in the western world—certainly there are improvements, yet the conflict between person and industrial society is not removed—but by transcending the whole situation and seeing it from a point beyond it.

This point, however, is not the Christian Church and her traditional message. To say this would be another shortcut. One must ask, especially on Christian ground, why the Church and her message are so powerless in their fight against the depersonalizing forces of the present world. The reason cannot be that they are in themselves without power. The opposite is true, not only for the vision of faith, but also for sociological and psychological observation. The reason that the Church and her message are unable to resist the progressive annihilation of the person within industrial society is something else. It is the unintended participation of the Church in the essential structure of industrial society. Step by step, the Church, including the way she has shaped and communicated her message, has been determined by the categories of life and thought which characterizes the industrial society. The Church became a section of that against which she was supposed to defend the person. The process of depersonalization has caught up even with the churches and their members. One should not close his eyes in face of this situation, and one should not glorify the churches as more protected against depersonalization. Certainly, they are more protected in principle, namely, by their foundation, their message, their community—but this is not a necessary protection in the actual churches. They have means of resisting depersonalization in their traditions, their symbols, their rites—but these means can be transformed into powerful tools of dehumanization. They emphasize the infinite value of the individual person—but they are in danger of depersonalizing the person in order to preserve his infinite value. One must transcend not only society but also that section in the society which is taken by the churches, in order to see the situation in its threatening power. Only from "beyond," can industrial society and its dehumanizing forces be resisted and finally overcome.

VI. MAN AND THE NEW REALITY

Two shortcuts have been rejected: the conservative acceptance of the state of things within the so-called "free world," and the ecclesiastical acceptance of the churches as the means of saving the person in the industrial society. It is obvious that the widespread combination of the two shortcuts does not provide for the right way. What, then, is the direction in which we must look for the right way? It is the Christian message of the New Reality, seen in the light of the Existentialist criticism of the old reality, and of its special expression in the industrial society. This, it seems to me, must be the program of a group as that which is represented by this volume. It is now possible to point to some basic implications of this idea.

The first critical statement to be derived from it is directed against the reality of such a thing as "Industrial Society." Its meaning is a society whose character is determined by man's industrial activity. Man certainly is *homo faber*, industrial man. The being which invented the first tool *as* a tool for permanent use transcends by this act everything given and was potentially the creator of a world beyond the given world. The importance of this fact can hardly be exaggerated in a theological or philosophical doctrine of man. But this power of transcending the given is not an isolated element in man's nature. It is interdependent with many other elements within a total structure. The industrial man is at the same time the man who is able to speak because he has universals, and he is social man because he is able to have I-Thou relations, and he is theoretical man because he is able to ask and to receive answers, and he is moral man because he is able to make responsible decisions, and he is religious man because he is able to be aware of his finitude and of the infinite to which he belongs at the same time. Man is all this because of the basic structure of being which is complete in him; he has a centered self in correlation with a structured world. He looks at both of them, he is free from and for both of them, and he can transcend them both.

If one element in this structure is developed in isolation and put into control over the others, not only the whole structure is distorted, but the special element itself loses its power and its meaning. If, for instance, industrial society transforms the universities into places of research for industrial purposes, not only the universities lose their function of asking radically for the truth, but the technical development itself will be stopped in the long run—the danger of present-day America. On the other hand, if the universities isolate their function of asking for man's existential concern, *e.g.*, the social, they lose their significance and fall victims to unanalyzed ideologies—the danger of past Germany. Many similar examples about the self-destructive consequences of the isolation and imperialism of a special function of the human mind can easily be given. In all of them the result is depersonalization, for the person is a centered whole to which all his functions are subjected. As soon as one function is separated from the others and put into control over the whole, the person is subjected to this function and through it to something which is not itself. It *becomes* this function. This is even true of religion. The abominable word "religionist" implies that a man has dissolved his personality into the religious function, that he is, for example, not free to ask radically even for the truth of religion, that he cannot transcend his functional limits—an implication which is not in vocational names as artist, economist, statesman, bishop. If religion makes "religionists," it destroys the person as much as industry by producing an industrial age. Not industry but the isolation and imperialism of industry is the threat for the person in our age.

Homo faber, the industrial man, makes tools; this is the only thing he can "make." The "world above" the "world" he produces is the world of means, leaving open the question of the ends. One previous consideration has shown that the person is either the end for which everything else is means, or the person becomes a means and then not only the person but also the end is lost. There is no end in the chain of means and ends except the person. And if the person himself becomes a means, an endless chain of means-and-ends-and-means is established which crushes purpose, meaning and person. But one may ask the question: Is it not the person for whose comfort and well-being the whole technical world is produced; and even more, is not the creation and the use of tools, from the hammer to the artificial brain in itself an expression of man's power over nature and a confirmation of his personal superiority? To this one must answer that, certainly, only man as a person is able to produce this "second world," but that in doing so he can become himself a tool for the production of tools, spiritually as well as economically, centered in "gadgets" and considered as a part of the production and consumption power. And although the tool serves the comfort of the person, it cannot serve the person as person, that which makes him a person. It can make communication easier. But that which makes the person is the content of what is communicated, and it may well be that the ease and the content of the communication are inversely proportional. Another question could be raised, namely, whether the person is the end which cannot become means without being destroyed. Is not the glory of God or the Kingdom of God or, in more secular terms the realization of values, the ultimate end for which everything must become means, even the person? But such a question is self-contradictory. The meaning of, for instance, Kingdom of God is not the unity of things or functions, but it is the unity of persons including their relationship to the whole non-personal realm. Through persons, *i.e.*, through beings who can decide for or against them, values and the glory of God are actualized. To say that God is the ultimate end is saying that the person is the ultimate end.

VII. CONFORMITY VERSUS MAN

Western technical society has produced methods of adjusting persons to its demands in production and consumption which are less brutal, but in the long run, more effective than totalitarian suppression. They depersonalize not by commanding but by providing, providing, namely, what makes individual creativity superfluous. If one looks around at the methods which produce conformity one is astonished that still enough individual creativity is left even to produce these refined methods. One discovers that man's spiritual life has a tremendous power of resistance against a reduction to prescribed patterns of behavior. But one also sees that this resistance is in a great danger of being worn down by the ways in which adjustment is forced upon him in the industrial society. It starts with the education of "adjustment" which produces conformity just by allowing for more spontaneity of the child than any pre-industrial civilization. But the definite frame within which this spontaneity is quietly kept, leads to a spontaneous adjustment which is more dangerous for creative freedom than any openly deterministic influence. At the same time, and throughout his whole life, other powerful means of adjustment are working upon the person in the technical society; the newspapers which choose the facts worth reporting and suggest their interpretation, the radio programs which eliminate non-conformist contents and interpreters, television which replaces the visual imagination by selected pictorial presentations, the movie which for commercial and censorship reasons has to maintain in most of its productions a conscious mediocrity, adjusting itself to the adjusted taste of the masses, the patterns of advertisement which permeate all other means of public communication, and have an inescapable omnipresence. All this means that more people have more occasions to encounter the cultural contents of past and present than in any pre-industrial civilization. But it also means that these contents become cultural "goods," sold and bought after they have been deprived of the ultimate concern they represented when originally created. They cease to be a matter of *to be or not to be* for the person. They become matters of entertainment, sensation, sentimentality, learning, weapons of competition or social prestige, and lose in this way the power of mediating a spiritual center to the person. They lose their potential dangers for the conformity which is needed for the functioning of the technical society. And by losing their dangers they also lose their creative power, and the person without a spiritual center disintegrates.

VIII. THE STRUGGLE FOR PERSONS

To struggle for the right of the person under the conditions of technical society should not become a fight against the technical side of mass communications; it should not even become a fight against their adjusting power. The technical development is irreversible and adjustment is necessary in every society, especially in a mass society. The person as a person can preserve himself only by a *partial nonparticipation in* the objectifying structures of technical society. But he can withdraw even partially only if he has a place to which to withdraw. And this place is the New Reality to which the Christian message points, which transcends Christianity as well as non-Christianity, which is anticipated everywhere in history, and which has found its criterion in the picture of Jesus as the Christ. But the place of the withdrawal is at the same time, the starting point for the attack on the technical society and its power of depersonalization.

It is the task of the Church, especially of its theology, to describe the place of withdrawal, mainly the "religious reservation." It is the task of active groups within and on the boundary line of the Church to show the possibilities of attack, to participate in it wherever it is made and to be ready to lead it if necessary.

Looking back at the three great movements of protest against the dehumanization in the technical society, we can say that he who fights today for the person has to become an heir of all three of them. He must join in the rebellion of creative life against the degradation of person into an object. This is the first frontier of a Christian action today. Together with the philosophers of life, the Existentialists, the depth-psychologists, and whatever new allies appear, it must show how the "structure of objectivation" (transforming life and person partly into a thing, partly into a calculating machine), penetrates all realms of life and all spiritual functions. It must show especially how even the religious symbols have been misinterpreted as statements about facts and events within the whole of objectivity, thus losing their inborn power to transcend this realm of the subjective-objective, and to mediate visions of that level of reality in which life and personality are rooted. Christian action must be as daring as that of the Existentialists in their analysis of the human situation generally and the present cultural and religious situation especially. It must be as conscious of the infinite complexity of the human soul as that of the depth-psychologists, fully aware of the fact that religion is responsible as much for the complexities and conflicts of the mind as it can contribute to the solution of the conflicts. Christian action today must, like the philosophers of life, have the courage to join the rebellion of life against internal repression and external suppression—in spite of the risk of chaos. But in joining these allies, Christian action must show that it comes from a place of withdrawal where it has received a criterion and a power able to overcome the danger of losing the person while attempting to save him.

And Christian action today must be aware of the second front: together with all movements for social justice whether they are called socialist or not, it must show how the competitive society produces patterns of existence which destroy personality because they destroy community, and which increase that all pervading anxiety which characterizes our century. Christian action today must preserve, in spite of political and social odds against it, the tradition of social criticism which runs from the enthusiasts of the Reformation period through the bourgeois revolutionaries of the eighteenth century to the social critics of the nineteenth century of whom Marx was the most passionate, the most profound and the most dangerous. In alliance with all these movements Christian action must attack wherever social patterns become visible by which persons are treated as means or transferred into things or deprived of their freedom to decide and to create, or thrown into anxiety or bitterness or hate or tragic guilt. But in joining these allies, Christian action must show that it comes from a place of withdrawal where it has received a criterion and a power able to overcome the danger of sacrificing the person in order to save him.

And Christian action today must be aware of the third front:

Together with all the movements within and outside Christianity which have rediscovered, partly in dependence on Kierkegaard, man's existential situation and the ultimate conflict which underlies all other conflicts, his estrangement from the ground of his being and meaning, Christian action must point to the ultimate roots of personal being. It must show that man can maintain his nature and dignity as a person only by a personal encounter with the ground of everything personal. In this encounter, which is the living center of religion and which, against rational as well as mystical criticism, has been defended by Christianity, the person is established. In showing this, Christian action shows also the place to which it withdraws from the technical society in order to attack this society. This place is that which transcends every place, even the Christian Churches. It is the New Reality which is manifest in Christ and against which even technical society and its power of destroying the person as person cannot prevail. Only out of the ground of the personal can the personal be saved. Only those who withdraw from action can receive the power to act. Christian action today rests on two poles, the one which transcends the structure of technical society—the new reality of which Christianity is the witness; the other which is present within the structure of technical society—the movements which struggle, from different sides, against its depersonalizing power. In the correlation of these two poles Christian action must find a way to save the person in the industrial society.

Christian Liberty and Totalitarianism

EDUARD HEIMANN

---------------------------------- ✳ ----------------------------------

EDUARD HEIMANN *was born in Berlin and received his Ph.D. from the University of Heidelberg. He taught at the Universities of Cologne, Freiburg, and Hamburg before coming to the United States in 1933. Since that time he has been Professor in the Graduate Faculty of the New School for Social Research, more recently also lecturer at Union Theological Seminary. He has lectured widely in the United States and in Europe and is the author of* COMMUNISM, FASCISM, OR DEMOCRACY?, HISTORY OF ECONOMIC DOCTRINES, *and* FREEDOM AND ORDER *and of many articles. His books have appeared in four foreign languages.*

IN THIS volume and outside, totalitarianism has innumerable times been confronted with Christianity and found incompatible with it. The logic of a totalitarian system in subjecting all human activities to one supreme secular criterion precludes any compromise with the Christian principle of surrender to God's loving grace, if this is to be more than a subjective sentiment, if it is to be a dynamic force.

(Incompatibility in principle does not preclude compromises of a purely power-political nature, fencing off some reservation which the totalitarian state does not invade. But this invalidates not only the totalitarian claim but also the absoluteness of the Christian commandment, which knows no delimitation even though it is never lived up to by sinful Christian men. Compromise is the stuff of which political life is made; it is, by definition, the product not of redeemed virtue but of expediency in an unredeemed world. Hence, it is impossible to say from without whether compromise is or is not permissible in the individual situation. It seems that a case can be made, *e.g.,* for many of the diplomatic actions of the Vatican in the fascist period; the Concordats with Italy, Spain and Portugal did save the lives of uncounted

Jews on their way through these countries. Whether this was worth the price of giving support to the dictators may be arguable, but the fact should not be ignored. On the other hand, one does not see what Rome's Concordat with Hitler could have achieved; an outsider cannot decide whether this was miscalculation or something worse. Again, however, it cannot be argued that the bad intention is proved by the contrast between the Concordats with all Fascist powers and the absence of one with Soviet Russia; it is most likely that the Vatican was quite eager to come to terms with the Soviet too, but failed because the latter preferred a compromise with the docile Russian Orthodox Church, the age-old rival of Rome, to one with Rome. These few remarks are only designed to suggest the area which is not to be discussed here: that of practical policies.)

It is customary to say that the Christian way of life is superior to the totalitarian one because it includes the creative element of liberty which totalitarianism denies by definition. The Lord in Heaven, throwing us on our unique responsibility before Him, thereby prevents our unqualified submission to any lord on earth—we have, in the extreme case, to obey God rather than men—we are free.

The supreme truth, to be sure, is today abused in a most shameful manner, which ignores the divine discipline and claims that the highest value taught by the New Testament is simply the individual, the goal of human life his self-realization, the institutional framework of a Christian society, the system of unregulated free enterprise, etc. It is no less revolting, on the other hand, to give Christian freedom a purely sentimental interpretation without social and political significance or outlet—the perversion of which too many systems of social and political authoritarianism, using religion as opiate for the people, have been guilty. But abuse either way, of course, is not refutation. If Christian liberty means anything in the historical-political sphere, if it is to be more than a theory or a moral demand, if it is a reality, man and society in the Christian era must be different from what they are without it. What, then, is Christian liberty?

I. CHRISTIAN APOLOGETICS AND TOTALITARIANISM

The question in its entire breadth is hardly discussed even by the leaders of Christian thought in this age. Christianity has been reduced to a defensive position by modern culture, and the historical-political writings of Christians are, for the most part, of an apologetic nature, taking this word in its highest sense, which denotes something indispensable. That is, Christian thinkers, interpreting the Christian message in the light of contemporary events and teachings, warn non-Christians against the illusions to which the modern belief in progress, idealism, and science falls prey; this belief is more cruelly punished as it becomes more presuming. Science is not a substitute for or an alternative to the Christian religion, whose problems are on a plane beyond the reach of science; so the modern structure of life built on the foundation of science is dangerously cracking and may collapse because its foundation is inadequate—neither comprehensive nor profound enough. The dangers of sin in all its ever new forms can be somewhat adequately met only if they are understood instead of being argued away. Even then, of course, enough perplexing problems remain with us. But the insoluble paradoxes of the human situation become acceptable in the light of the Christian comfort, while without it they drive the secular mind to exasperation over their intractability and to more furious, more illusory, and more ruinous ventures. Such apologetic warning, in addition, includes suggestions for reforms, wisely concentrating on that which is necessary because it is possible and refraining from utopian promises.

Warning, safeguarding, and guidance are to validate the Christian message to the estranged. Reinhold Niebuhr's unique moral authority in national and international discussions rests on the penetrating insights into modern thought which his Christian understanding gives him (see his *Nature and Destiny of Man* and his *Faith and History*) as well as on the moral firmness and pragmatic flexibility with which he uses his absolute standard of judgment in the intricacies of present-day political problems (see his *Children of Light* and his *Irony of American History*).

The apologetic analysis of contemporary tendencies has much that is pertinent to say about totalitarianism. It is true that there are wide differences between the various totalitarian systems. On the one hand, there are the rationalist ones, that is, those claiming ultimate reason for their rulers, and on this basis either individualistic in the tradition of the French revolutionary slogan of "forcing people to be free" (Rousseau) or communist in the Marxian style, where the Communist Party guarantees the "correct understanding" of the workers' interest, which the workers themselves do not yet correctly understand. Christian writers have revealed the presumption and utopianism of rationalist totalitarianism, the absurdity of its claim to absolute rationality above the all-human temptation of power, and the ensuing atrocity of its practice in destroying critics and controlling the minds by fear. On the other hand, there are the irrationalist systems, as in the various branches of fascism, where man's spiritual life is despised and denounced altogether and his biological qualities are what matters. Of course, mixed systems are logically possible as, *e.g.*, individualism and fascist nationalism. In all these different systems the Christian apologetic literature has revealed the atheism explicitly or implicitly underlying them all as the source of their atrocious policies.

Such apologetic approach is indispensable, but it is not enough. This can be seen from the reaction of many Christian intellectuals, particularly in France and Italy, of whom only a few can be suspected of consciously or subconsciously accommodating themselves to the possible prospect of military occupation by Russia. If they say that the difference between secular democracy and totalitarian systems is only one of degree, their argument is inadmissible because it judges in terms of absolutes while everything human is relative and there never are differences except of degree. But then they go on to say that there are certain things to be commended in Soviet Russia, such as strict ethnic and racial equality or the systematic care of health, etc., and that Christians should judge, not on the basis of the ideology of governments as discussed by the apologetic literature, but pragmatically on the basis of practical achievements or failures. Now this piecemeal judgment, while correct on traditional political developments, misses the point in totalitarianism, which is its monolithic logic—the strict logical derivation of all measures and policies from the supreme goal which they are to serve. For while a pragmatic system takes man as the God of history has made him, a totalitarian system explicitly takes man as manipulatable, capable of, and in need of being made over in the image of its own representative figure—be it "Nordic man" or the "proletarian man" who "correctly understands" his class interests in the way the Marxist intelligentsia does in admitted contrast with the empirical aspirations of actual proletarians. It should be clear that the manipulation of the nature of man cannot be judged pragmatically and piecemeal.

II. CHRISTIAN MAN IN HISTORY

The man to be made over by them—the man whom the God of history has made and is daily remaking in and through us—is Christian and post-Christian man, whether believer or unbeliever. It is he to whom our apologetic literature is addressed, and whom it takes as its theme. If the manipulators have their way, he is not to continue, and obviously he has not always existed; he is a product of, as he is the maker of, Christian history. He is not, naturally, the "true Christian" who never exists, as we know from the Gospel stories themselves; as Tillich puts it, Jesus is the Christ because he alone achieved complete surrender to and identification with the will of the Father. Hence to speak of Christian man is a scandal to many orthodox theologians. What we mean is not a sinless man, but a man equipped by Christian history with distinct insights and qualities; after all, Christianity must mean something in history even though sin continues. But both theologians and political theorists—among them the present writer—have in general dealt with the present type of man and do not see man in a sufficiently wide historical perspective.

Jacques Maritain has, among contemporary Christian scholars, the most radiant trust in "the quiet work of the Evangelical inspiration in the profane conscience," which accounts for his confidence in a real growth of moral sensitivity among modern men and in the emergence of Christian democracy in the end, even though the forces of evil can never be eliminated. Maritain thus is a progressivist, but a Christian progressivist. What he gives, however, is a most eloquent plea rather than historical demonstration. The question of whether there is a distinctly Christian type of man in history and what he is can best be addressed to historians—historians of sufficient scholarship and profundity of mind.

Among the historians Toynbee has, in his rich conceptual structure, the characteristic Christian notions of pride and abuse of freedom on the one hand, and of creative response to the challenge of the emergency on the other hand. The supreme effort of the creative response is not always possible, according to Toynbee; it requires that the threat be very grave but still not totally discouraging. It is because of pride and abuse, he says, that civilizations perish, dying, as it were, at their own hands; and it is through the creative response that they can gain a new lease on life and thus break through the hopelessness of the cycle of life from birth to death which is proclaimed by the Greek philosophers and historians. Man and his society are nature and confined in this natural cycle of life; but they are also spirit and may rise above cyclical determinism by concrete action, by setting, through a supreme effort, a new fact which could not be predicted and whose addition to the complex of effective causes gives history a new direction on a new plane.

Christians understand history as meaningful because it is centered around a unique climax and directed towards a fulfillment beyond itself, to which all events in history are positively or negatively related, while the classical view subsumes history under the cyclical law of nature. This contrast is well known to students. But how strange that it is always treated as a difference in theory, as if man's understanding of history, that is, of himself, could possibly have remained without consequence in his making of history. It is true that in this approach the word "Christian man" must be understood with certain extensions forward and backward in history. It includes many persons and groups in societies of Christian tradition who, for themselves, cherish the moral and cultural inheritance but have lost the understanding of the dogmatic center from which everything flows, and may go so far as to criticize it in the name of their culture. Not that this could go on forever; but our secularized and weakened Christian civilization is tragically full of persons and groups who, for the time being, benefit by the fruits of the Christian tradition but deny it. On the other hand, whatever Christian men may have achieved in history cannot have been without occasional anticipation among pre-Christian men if Christianity, as the revelation of the supreme truth, could be received only by minds prepared for such revelation by a long process of divine education, as shown in Tillich's discussion of revelation (*Systematic Theology*, pp. 137ff). Examples of such pre-Christian achievements are precisely what Toynbee gives in his Christian categories without discussing the qualitative nature of Christian man as such.

But this is what Rosenstock-Huessy does in his majestic panorama of the last one thousand years of Occidental history.[1] He finds the classical theory of the rotation of forms of government—from monarchy through aristocracy, democracy, and tyranny back to monarchy—the adequate reflection of classical history, where man is under a strict deterministic law; the history of Christian man, however, is defined by periodic renewals, which break through the cycle and start history anew on the new level, even though evil, too, assumes new forms there. Christian history thus creates a unique and meaningful sequence of achievements, each of which is made imperative by the unsolved problems of the preceding phase and will likewise give rise to further dynamic urges. For one thousand years of incessant stress and strain—since the imperial and monastic revolution of the tenth century, the Gregorian revolution of the eleventh century and the Franciscan revolution of the thirteenth century—Europe has not been broken; it has always done that which could not have been predicted, in "creative response to the challenge" of the emergency. It has preserved its unity and tradition throughout all revolutions by limiting each of them to its own national section and integrating its spiritual, political and social results into reforms adopted in all other national sections so as to present the picture of an army "marching in echelons" from goal to goal. It has thus conquered new problems and created new forms of life at every step because Christianity has taught it the mystery of regeneration, the power to rise above one's past failures. All the weaknesses and vices of man, to be sure, harass him on the new level as they did on the old, and for each problem solved a new one emerges. There is thus no room for an utopian belief in redemption through history. But what matters is the experience that, after all, problems can be solved and new levels reached. Christianity, in other words, has taught man a new dimension of his life; it has invalidated the classical doctrine of the law of the natural cycle controlling and frustrating his aspirations; it has given him hope.

All this is another way of saying that Christianity has delivered man from the law. This is a most familiar proposition, however dif-

---

[1] *Out of Revolution* (New York: Morrow, 1938).

ficult to understand; it is certainly emasculated if it is given a purely subjective, sentimental, psychological, or moralistic interpretation. The New Testament promises to us the glorious freedom of the children of God; it promises that the truth, which is Jesus Christ, shall make us free. It has kept the promise if freedom means the power to do something unpredicted, the spontaneity which transcends necessity even though it does not eliminate necessity—the logic of the new situation asserts itself at once; but it is a new situation. In this sense, freedom and creativity are the same thing; freedom is the power to conceive and realize something not previously existent. Man, naturally, does not create as God does, he does not add to the stuff of which the world is made. His every creation is, in physical terms, only a transformation and rearrangement of things which existed before; it is, in this sense, dependent on and limited by the necessities of his material. But creation is spiritual: it gives life a concrete new meaning, a significance unknown before. Because creation creates the unknown, there cannot be a theory of creation; social theories are and always must be stated in terms of known necessities, of existing forces and tendencies even though rearranging them. The most ambitious of these theories expects the growth of large-scale industry from and over many smaller and less productive plants to lead to the final unification of all production and all producing mankind under one will. This development is supposed to be the consummation of science, and is supposed to be certain because it is logical. If Christian history is to continue, this prediction will be invalidated as the Christian era has invalidated the Platonic-Aristotelian-Stoic-Polybian theory of the mere rotation of forms of government throughout history.

But it is not certain that Christian history will continue; to do so will require Christians—again, not in the sense of their being morally pure but in the sense of their being aware of their power over and freedom from the law. That this awareness is weakening is the most frightening of the many frightening signs of the times. For Christian freedom has not eliminated necessity and can never do it; while the immense effort, which is freedom, can work only intermittently, the necessity and logic inherent in the structures of reality are always at work. Hence the law stands ready to take over if and as freedom fails. This is the issue of totalitarianism versus Christianity in these anxious days. (We do not deny that all future history, however inscrutable to us, will be God's and Christian in this sense, even if the world should go down and make room for something different. We use the words *Christian history* to denote the history of Christian man as a specific type whom we have come to know in the Christianized parts of the globe. There should be no objection to this factual, non-theological use of the word.)

III. COMMUNIST VERSUS DEMOCRATIC UNDERSTANDING OF LIBERTY

In Communism, according to its own presentation, necessity reigns supreme. Friedrich Engels defines communist freedom as the appreciation of necessity.[2] The test of this communist freedom is in the "withering away of the state," the agency of organized coercion. If and when nobody's understanding is corrupted by divisive interests vested in private property, necessity as proclaimed by the authorities in scientific terms will be understood and voluntarily submitted to by everybody. Then organized coercion can be dispensed with because people have no more use for pre-scientific, unscientific, or anti-scientific liberty. The "leap from the realm of necessity to the realm of freedom" means precisely this: the understood and approved necessity represented by the communist authorities is no longer felt as a pressing weight, it loses its despotic sting as people recognize it and identify themselves with it. All of which makes clear that freedom, in the communist utopia, is bound to and inferior to necessity—"appreciation of necessity"—and loses its identity as a separate mode of life, while to the Christian understanding, freedom ontologically transcends necessity although it may historically fail to do so. What a Christian civilization tries to defend is the possibility of freedom—not the existence of freedom because freedom is not a state of things. What communist society tries to do is stamp out that possibility in favor of a politically enforced scientific certitude; the coincidence of communist liberty with that strict order is brought about by the definition of liberty as nothing but the absence of coercion. On condition that people do

---

[2] "Hegel was the first to state correctly the relation between freedom and necessity. To him, freedom is the appreciation of necessity. Freedom of the will therefore means nothing but (Sic!) the capacity to make decisions with real knowledge of the subject." *Anti-Duehring.*

not use the absence of coercion to do anything spontaneous but comply with the all-inclusive scientific order laid down by the authorities, there will be no coercion—this is hardly more than a tautology.

In the materialistic philosophy which is the Soviet creed, necessity is not simply a philosophical but also an institutional concept; necessity is incorporated in the Soviet authorities. The necessity of their actions is strongly activistic, and one may quite well argue that theirs is a considerable margin of freedom. That would equally strongly bring out the necessity which Soviet rule and compliance with its demands impose upon the Soviet people. The "jump from the realm of necessity to the realm of freedom" is attributed to "mankind," that is, not individual persons acting spontaneously but the rationally organized collective represented by the science-guided authorities. Theirs is the science-guided freedom, the people's is the science-guided necessity of compliance—abuse of the dialectic permits to identify the two.

Christian liberty, if it is to remain a reality, must appear in institutional form, too. There were, in the medieval set-up, a number of specific liberties for different groups; best known among them are the liberties of the craftsmen's guilds, which built the huge cathedrals. Of equal importance, however, was academic liberty incorporated in the jealously guarded self-rule of the Christian universities; we shall briefly come back to this point. Christian liberty, for our present understanding, demands democratic liberty for a number of reasons which cannot systematically be discussed here. As Reinhold Niebuhr beautifully puts it: "Man's capacity for justice makes democracy possible; but man's inclination to injustice makes democracy necessary."[3] Nobody is good enough to be given full powers over others, and everybody is entitled to that life which his Maker intends him to live. This is his just claim, which love covets to give him; love and justice demand liberty. The liberty of the person in the community is thus oriented toward God and is limited by, as it is demanded by, justice. In the extreme case this liberty soars above any other consideration to its supreme pinnacle where obedience to God requires defiance of men— but it is obedience, not arbitrariness. And in the divine dispensation the thus defined liberty becomes the means to political regeneration.

---

[3] *The Children of Light and the Children of Darkness* (New York: Scribners, 1944), Foreword xi.

The democratic liberties, which include the right to non-conformity and criticism for the sake of obedience to God, "are a sign of democracy's humility before the absolute, before the Lord of Justice. . . . They are the opening through which an unexpected new truth, whenever it pleases, can invade and transform a given body politic. Democracy is to be defined as that system which does not claim to be just but only to strive for justice."[4]

Now this Christian liberty, which is the essence of democracy, is rejected by millions not of the worst people even in the free countries, in favor of communist liberty, which is submission to authority. This proves how much the Christian concept of liberty has become perverted and discredited. Perhaps we should say that it was unavoidable that Christian liberty should be corrupted by sin; the limitation of man's freedom is much emphasized by medieval and Reformation theology—more than this writer's fragmentary understanding seems to justify. But the very concept of sin suffices to prove that our freedom can never be understood to be completely absorbed into divine necessity. Prayer itself is an act of our freedom, even though the prayer is for a greater power to come to the aid of that frail freedom—these are the two sides of the Christian message. The corruption of our freedom would not be sin if it were not our freedom that is corrupted.

Anyway, the Christian freedom, which ultimately is the freedom to obey God rather than men, has become the freedom to use one's superior intelligence, cunning, financial strength, social connections, etc., to gain advantages over one's neighbors. The misunderstanding goes so far that the most ambitious of the social scientists, the economists, offer the study of the policies which the individual must adopt to maximize his income under varying conditions as their contribution to the teaching of democratic freedom. If individual liberty is thus emancipated from divine discipline and thereby lifted above justice and community, there is little wonder that many disgusted people should turn to a system which subordinates liberty to an order supposedly incorporating justice and community. This has often been said and need not be explained here.[5]

---

[4] Eduard Heimann, *Freedom and Order* (New York: Scribners, 1947), pp. 289ff.
[5] *Cf.* "A Christian Looks at Communism," in *The Christian Demand for Social Justice*, W. Scarlett ed., Signet Book No. 744, 1949.

But it refers only to the old countries, where secular liberty, derived from Christian liberty even though abusing it, has been supreme for a while. It does not refer to the young countries throughout the Eurasian continent where liberty has remained unknown to this day. Those who have tasted of the fruits of liberty prove, in general, to be immune to communist propaganda; they may be dissatisfied but realize that restoration of liberty rather than its abolition is the indicated remedy. But the argument as formulated so far has no force in the undeveloped countries, Russia and China and the former colonial countries of Asia. Russia, a signally Christian country but divorced from the West by the specific tradition of the Eastern Church, has not shared in the political and social growth of the West; it was left to the Soviets to bring it the medical and educational facilities developed in the West and thus aspire for leadership in the even more neglected countries of Asia. The present misery in Asia is precisely due to these countries being excluded from western material and political progress by the champions of that progress, who declared the "natives" to be too unintelligent for it and kept schools and facilities from them. Democratic liberty must thus appear to those "natives" as a privilege of the master race and may be repudiated with control by the master race. The absence of a Christian background—whatever the affinities with Christianity of the other high religions—removes from the picture the starting point for any true understanding of western liberty. We have not even begun to explore and appraise the gravity of this situation.

But the communists have. Communism never forgets its own historical (dialectical) derivation as heir and beneficiary of that western civilization which it opposes. It presupposes a phase of liberty on the way to its own goal, to emancipate people from traditional "irrationality" and teach them the elements of its own rationalism for use in industrial and political organization. In old countries it finds those requirements realized; it takes them as its own starting point and tries to proceed beyond them. But in underdeveloped countries, where liberalism either has had no chance yet or sacrificed its chance to racial prejudices of imperialists, Communism must bring the people, not liberty indeed but liberation from decaying feudal rule or exploitation by landlords or tax collectors and accompanying superstitions, in order to be then able to impose on them its own control, which it presents as the supreme achievement of science. Certainly for an Asian peasant the liberty which he does not have must appear, first of all, as liberty from oppression by his landlord and his tax collector—and in some countries from white exploiters—which is precisely what the West—in violation of its own principles—has failed to give him and what he now receives from Communism. For non-western countries it is plausible to present Communism as a movement of preliminary emancipation, thus turning the Western standards against the West.[6]

The obvious countermove of the western world, realized late and inadequately, is a program of land reform and other social, medical, and educational improvements to give the neglected what they need, lest they must ask it of Communism. But, speaking concretely, of whom shall they now ask it? The United States and the United Nations are committed to the political *status quo,* in consequence of their respect for sovereignty. They cannot directly interfere in China or Indo-China or the Arab countries; they must achieve whatever they can through the constituted governments, members of the United Nations. But these governments are not governments in the western sense of the word, where the term denotes an agency equipped not only with armed force and compulsory taxing power but also with an administrative organization manned by trained, competent, and honest personnel and capable of building or rebuilding the social and economic structure in a deliberate way. To appeal to governments for reforms makes sense where there are governments capable of carrying out these things. But it is becoming more and more clear that such is the case only on the soil of the west and in some countries just emerging from western rule. From the eleventh century on, the great Christian universities—first, Paris and Bologna, then, Oxford and Cambridge, later, Prague and Vienna, Heidelberg and Wittenberg, Basel, Leyden, Upsala and Cracow, and others—set up the standards of knowledge on things divine and human and of responsibility in this light, and taught ministers and counselors of secular and ecclesiastical princes and magistrates.[7] They thus created the sense of commonwealth and public service, which, however tainted by class

---

[6] *Cf.* "Marxism and Underdeveloped Countries," in *Social Research,* Sept. 1952; and "Schumpeter and the Problems of Imperialism," *ibidem,* June 1952.
[7] *Cf.* "On Academic Liberty," in *Christianity and Crisis,* July 7, 1952.

interests and limited to domestic affairs, lifted western governments above the merely confiscatory policies of their counterparts in most of the other sections of the globe, with the signal exception of Japan. Communist governments, of course, are in that western tradition of personal honesty and technical efficiency and could be counted upon to carry out their reforms in all countries through officials trained in Moscow. That is why we, on the other hand, are unlikely to get anywhere in those countries unless and until we can give them governments capable of receiving our technical and financial aid without embezzling it in more or less contractual form.

Speaking more generally, what the underdeveloped parts of the non-communist world need is modernization without disruption of the social fabric by an industrial revolution of the type imposed on the mother countries of modern life by the rise of industrial capitalism. There are two alternative ways to Communism: either through refusal of modernization, or through a modernization which disrupts the moral fibre and atomizes society. The path to success is steep and narrow. Only with governments honestly and competently dedicated to the cause can we hope for any success at all; and the question of whether and where such governments can be had without some form and degree of political revolution should be given top priority. This question should not be mixed up with secondary and contingent matters such as parliamentary elections or freedom of the press, which can be good only where there is some approximation to a sense of public service and commonwealth. And the problem should certainly not be encumbered by considerations of an international law which is the outgrowth of western thought and western governmental experience, and is not meant to protect highwaymen in the disguise of governments.

IV. SECULAR EDUCATION FOR TOTALITARIANISM

Such a program may fail not only for reasons in our partners but also because we may not, or no longer, be competent for the mission.

The totalitarian danger to the United States is dual. Externally, of course, it comes from the international tensions where our adversary is communist Russia. But no sane person can believe that Communism is our chief danger at home, however seriously the danger of communist espionage at home must be taken in view of the international situation. The chief danger at home has some distinctly fascist traits such as an idolatrous nationalism with a strong admixture of racialism. The institutional program to which those forces are committed is individualistic in the right-wing American tradition, with free enterprise including free monopoly, the free press, etc. Now this individualism is not simply the opposite, but the dialectical opposite of Communism, connected with it in fundamentals and easily changing into it. This is no academic speculation; Marxists have long studied the period of terror in the French Revolution as part of their own history; and it is this tradition of radical French individualism and of the positivism of Auguste Comte which to this day has been the way to Communism for many French politicians and groups. There is the distinct possibility of a collectivism in the institutional forms of individualism. For if personal independence and spontaneity are precluded by definition, totalitarianism may very well standardize the individual owner so as to make him pliable and responsive to the will of the authorities, as in the fascist countries of the thirties.

According to communist theory, the chief force in liberal society making for Communism is economic. The glaring injustices of economic stratification in a system where everybody is expected to take advantage of his financial strength to the utmost would produce the final social conflict of capitalism. Even more important, according to Marxism, is the industrial disorganization and crisis caused by the piecemeal operation of a system of private property, which cannot secure the correct proportions and smooth interlocking of the many separately managed pieces. Thus, the collapse of the system will, according to Marxism, teach people the necessity of unified all-inclusive management. The economic sphere, however, now seems to be the least dangerous for the preservation or gradual rebuilding of liberal democracy. Education and organization from below, the power of taxation from above can do, and are doing, much to correct the stratification of incomes. And pragmatic theory and experience have taught that the degree of centralization required for smooth operation is far short of the Soviet model, although it must be admitted that bureaucratic egotism tends to expand its empire far beyond the necessary minimum. Such a tendency cannot be too strongly opposed, but it is a political and social rather than an economic danger.

The gravest danger lies in the social sphere, as distinguished from the economic and the political. Of the three, it is the most fundamental but the least spectacular and also the most difficult to influence. A systematic presentation cannot be given here; only a few remarks can suggest some existing tendencies toward totalitarianism.

The great force working in this direction is modern science in all its forms and applications. This is a far cry from the days when the university taught man the relationship of things divine and human and his responsibility before God and his fellows. Modern academic science tends to be positivistic; it teaches facts, meaning tangible and measurable things or actions. It describes the action we must take if we want a tangible result of tangible causes, and calls this the scientist's responsibility within the field he studies. Whether his responsibility before God and men permits him to want that result, science does not care to inquire. Now there are plenty of such results which we desperately need and cannot be too grateful for, primarily in medicine and its ancillary industries. Modern scientific methods have worked wonders in the analysis and control of phenomena of nature; and man being nature must be treated that way too. But man is not only nature, he is a compound of nature and spirit, and the methods of natural science fail where they are applied to spiritual life. Science studies regularities and laws of behavior; the person and the community, who are unique by definition, are not only outside this kind of science but are for this reason declared non-existent, irrational, or are otherwise argued away by scientific imperialism.

Many people, in order to avoid such consequences, will naively state that one must not be too logical. Their instinct is right; but what a judgment on science, whose teachings, if thought through to the end, convey absurdity rather than truth! There is no way, naturally, of being "too logical;" logical conclusions drawn from the truth must be true. If logical conclusions are not true, then the fault is not with logic but with the scientific premises to which it is applied; they are not true. But the use of the simplified scientific methods in which students are trained to think drowns out in their minds the complex tradition of Christian liberty as a pre-scientific illusion and makes them as pliable, as manipulatable by necessity, as controllable by law as their science assumes man to be.

The loss of the sense of standards and proportions in the accumulation and utilization of scientific facts is driven home to us in daily experiences, which would be very comic if they were not tragically symbolic. The application of science in modern civilization is supposed to enrich our daily life. But already the widest highways are so overcrowded on Sundays that one car, stopping for some slight repair, stops a thousand cars stretching over several miles. At the airports planes are one or two hours late in taking off because there is "too much traffic in the air." One need not even think of the greatest triumph of technical science, the A- and H-bombs, to realize that our achievements have become self-refuting, and frustrate our lives, for lack of a sense of value and proportion.

The truth is not sought by man for its own sake; modern science is the most powerful means of control, first over nature, then over men if and inasmuch as they can be reduced to nature, standardized, atomized, depersonalized. Once you know how people will react to this or that effect applied to them, you know how to treat them in order to have them react in the manner you desire. So science teaches how to address people in order to have them buy what they do not really need; or how to influence their votes by giving them "scientific" proof that the party in which you are interested is likely to win; or by presenting facts in an objective way but choosing sub-headings in such a manner as to emphasize certain aspects and de-emphasize others. All these are scientific results, studied and taught by special departments. Inasmuch as advertising gives information, it is good and necessary; people cannot buy useful things unless they know that these things are available. But where is the line between information and insinuation in a world where all information inevitably affects some special interests positively or negatively? And where is the limit to the influence by which ambitious men try to win over our souls by developing and using those techniques? Already chemists and sociologists announce that they will soon be in a position to remake man so as to give him happiness and peace of mind. They dream themselves in the magnificent role of the builders and wielders of unlimited power and propose to use it for the salvation of mankind from ancient ills. It does not occur to the poor devils that all they do is prepare their little tricks for use by a very different type of man, the tyrant, who knows what power is and how to seize it and enlist their own services. Oswald Spengler, the prophet of fascism, has triumphantly pointed this out a generation ago.

Democracy requires independent citizens to pool their information and arrive by exchange of opinion at a common decision about the common good. Now the world is so vast, so complicated, so hard to understand that we depend on centers of information and communication and are supplied by them with a mounting flood of materials of all kinds. What we really need is not, naturally, a maximum supply of information, more than we could digest and understand, but information in proportion to relative importance. But this the lords of information are not technically in a position to give us. Daily and hourly information is driven to the sensational rather than the important and must move swiftly on the surface of events rather than be absorbed in the study of the underlying forces and tendencies which manifest themselves in such events. Day and night, the radio shouts at the listener, pretending to give information. On three or four pages the reader is taught anything and everything, or is made to believe that this is so. Men who read and review a book a day tell him what to read in the flood of publications and what not to. Others will arrogate to themselves the right to nominate the greatest living scholar in this or that field because they happen to have read part of the work of this man but nothing by his rival.

What man requires more than ever is time to think and meditate; what he needs is a full life in joy and sorrow, in success and defeat and suspense so as to be able to understand what another serious person, perhaps long dead, may have to tell him in print; what he needs is time, privacy and quiet. But the free minute in his life is a missed opportunity for all advertisers of any cause; they all are in a conspiracy to suggest to him that there still are things he should hear or see before making up his mind. Nay, while a few serious newspapers can honestly try to present all the news, leaving it to the reader to organize his reading lest he drown in the flood, the techniques of radio and, most of all, television cannot make the user hear or see everything that is happening at the same time; so the managers have necessarily to decide what is good and what not for him to see. Even if there were in these dealers in vulgarity all the good will of the world, the structure of the field would give them power over the materials— power to organize our education, standardize our knowledge, and destroy intensity and spontaneity.

V. CHRISTIAN LIBERTY AND DEMOCRATIC THINKING

It should not be concluded that the trouble is with private property and its lust for profit even at the expense of our mental and moral sanity, and that the abuses could be avoided by Communism. On the contrary, totalitarianism, of one kind or another, can be established only by the systematic use of these methods and techniques which liberal democracy develops in a haphazard way. Systematization and unification are technically superior to a haphazard way of doing things; but whether the technique is desirable at all is not for the technician to decide. If spontaneity is deterred and organic spiritual growth distorted by our scientific techniques, it is time to measure the latter, not in terms of their perfect efficiency, but of the ultimate ends around which we want to organize our lives. If we want to preserve and restore our liberty, we had better put those techniques under the control of our sense of value and proportion instead of letting them control us.

But this is not all. If the trouble seems to come to a head in the modern techniques of communication, they still are only a part of a far larger development, the development of technical science, in the wake of which the sciences of man and society are also sailing. Whatever important insights into technical aspects of human and social life we may thereby gain, the essential nature of man, which is his freedom and responsibility, is beyond the scope of the thus constituted scientific methods. That is why these scientific methods ignore or even deny man's freedom. But by denying it they destroy it. Man's freedom includes the freedom to give up his freedom. He gives it up if he believes it to be an illusion and the truth to be that man is manipulatable; this makes him manipulatable. To preserve and restore freedom, we have to restore the Christian understanding of freedom as the freedom of regeneration, the basis, context, and main problem of our scientific and technical thinking.

The job is too big for any one man, too big also for a group of scholars or even a generation of scholars. But this does not speak against the urgency of the task. The French Marshal Lyauthey, a lover of flowers, told his gardener that he had heard of a particularly precious plant and asked him to get it for him. The gardener showed a skeptical countenance; did the Marshal realize that it takes that plant a few hundred years to develop to its full glory? Said the Marshal "If it takes that long, we must start right away lest it take even longer."

Utopianism and Realism in Foreign Policy

VERNON H. HOLLOWAY

VERNON H. HOLLOWAY *is minister of the United Church (Congregational-Baptist) of Geneva, Ohio. He is a graduate of the Yale Divinity School, and was for several years a secretary of the Council for Social Action of the Congregational Christian Churches. He has taught at Ohio Wesleyan, at Denison University, and at Union Theological Seminary, and is the author of* CHRISTIANS AND THE WORLD OF NATIONS, *and* RELIGIOUS ETHICS AND THE POLITICS OF POWER.

IN THE decade now closing, both the American nation and American Christians have been sobered by the hard realities of our age. Many of the characteristic hopes and illusions of the nineteenth century have been destroyed. The contrast between optimistic hopes and ominous probabilities has developed most sharply with respect to international relations. Our Churches have lacked prophetic power and the ability to estimate the depth of evil in contemporary social structures. Our nation has lacked the maturity with which to clarify its interests and assume its obligations in the historical crisis of international society.

It is not the primary task of Christian ethics to provide estimates of the future or to sit in judgment on the past, but rather to prepare men spiritually for present duties and perennial temptations. Our present confusion in American foreign policy, however, has many roots in the attitudes and beliefs that were popular in recent generations. Therefore, a critical judgment of the past is relevant to the disillusionment and the search for new standards in the present. Likewise, some estimates of long-run trends and future probabilities, however tentatively we construe them, are essential for the guidance of contemporary policy and are integral to a Christian ethic of social responsibility.

I. THE END OF AN ERA

In many significant respects, the conflict between the United States and the Soviet Union marks the end of an era. For *international society* it reveals the ending of those conditions that characterized the eighteenth and nineteenth centuries when European powers were dominant in world politics and Britain played the role of balancer of power. Europe is no longer the center of power and Britain has ceased to be a dominant nation. There is no longer a multiplicity of powers of more or less equal strength, providing flexibility of alliances and counter-alliances, encouraging and permitting the practice of balance-of-power principles. Instead, the United States and the Soviet Union are the two dominant centers, drawing most of the other nations into their orbits with no third nation or combination of powers able to play a balancing, mediating, restraining role.

The prospects for peace have suffered not only from the redistribution of power and the emergence of a bi-polar system but from two other developments of signal importance: the tremendous advances in the technical means of waging warfare, and the absence of any community of understanding between the principal powers which oppose one another. The technological developments are epitomized in the atomic weapons, which both sides now possess. Instead of the degree of community between dominant powers, which formerly rendered plausible the concept of a "European Civilization," today we find the conflict heightened by notions of two rival communities, opposed to one another spiritually. The rise of nationalism and social revolt in Asia further complicates the quest for international peace and security, and marks indelibly the end of European and white domination of the Far East.

For the *United States* the era has ended in which public opinion and popular leadership could afford to indulge in utopian expectations of the end of power politics. Although this era has endured for approximately half a century, the objective conditions of international politics can no longer be ignored and the quest for peace and security can no longer be undertaken with the assumptions of nineteenth-century optimism. The era which has ended reached the peak of its influence on American opinion and religious bodies in the nineteen-thirties and early 'forties, and has left its mark upon the foreign policy debates of the present. A deeper understanding of our present problems may be gained by re-examining some of the principles and programs of the domestic struggle over American foreign policy in recent years, including some attention to the responses of religious groups.

The utopian spirit is displayed in a variety of forms and in alliance with various movements, a few of which are selected here because of their relevance to the continuing debate over American foreign policy. There are other climates of opinion which are also important, but it is useful in the above context to refer to the following types of response, all of which manifest in one form or another a utopian spirit: "isolationism" (both old and new) and "moralistic internationalism" in the public at large, and the "crusading spirit" and "pacifism" in the churches.

II. ISOLATIONISM

Our traditional isolationism has stressed the self-sufficiency of our nation within the Western Hemisphere, in protest against involvement in Europe's power politics. This policy, fashioned by Washington and Hamilton, made sense when the world was less interdependent, when we were not a powerful nation, and when our geographical barriers combined with the interests of British foreign policy to protect us from European aggressors. In its origin and early application isolationism was a wise response to the conditions of world politics by the "Founding Fathers," who were aware, incidentally, of the political implications of "original sin." The actions of Washington and the writings of Alexander Hamilton on matters of foreign policy reflect the same realism which provided for "checks and balances" in the American Constitution.

At the beginning of the twentieth century, however, we enjoyed a false sense of security. Our national experience when isolationism was workable had made us the more receptive to the prevailing optimism of nineteenth-century views of man and history. Two hopes were thus fostered and became popular: that the United States could continue, if it wished, to abstain from "foreign entanglements," and that power politics were diminishing as democratic governments increased and history "advanced." It is therefore not surprising that twice during the last thirty-five years we have tried to abstain from participation in global conflict by declaring our neutrality, and that following the First World War we rejected membership in the League of Nations.

The inadequacy of isolationism amidst the conditions of the twentieth century is now obvious. As a nation we learned this the hard way: by our inability to adhere to such a policy in the two global conflicts which we sought to evade. Isolationism, which began as a practical policy, was rendered impractical by the interdependence of nations in the twentieth century and by changes in the distribution of political power. The methods of travel and communication, trade relations and the modern techniques of waging war, have produced a unity in space and time which poses new problems for the security of nation-states. The involvement of the United States in the problems of security and diplomacy has been radically affected by its shift in status: from a hemispheric power with little influence on world politics, to a world power whose action or inaction is of decisive importance to the interests and destiny of the society of nations.

The isolationism of the 'twenties and 'thirties is practically dead. Its negative approach to international relations, expressed in the notion of non-participation in European and world politics, has become a utopian view irrelevant to the needs of the nation in the world politics of the twentieth century. The utopian element consists of the delusion that the non-American world is essentially what it was in the eighteenth and nineteenth centuries, and that the United States is politically self-sufficient as long as it remains aloof.

III. NEO-ISOLATIONISM

If the old isolationism is dead, its spirit has been resurrected in a new form. In 1950-1951 the nation experienced a rising tide of *neo-isolationism*. This is best illustrated, not by Joseph P. Kennedy's proposals in 1950 that we forego our overseas commitments and withdraw to the positions that we occupied in 1939, but by the arguments of several Congressmen that we reduce our European commitments and that we "go it alone" in the Far East. This spirit is evident in the minds of some who favor a "preventive war" against the Soviet Union, and in the readiness of others to disparage diplomacy and a "limited war" in Korea and to consider American intervention on the mainland of China. Ex-President Hoover has been likewise inspired to advocate the renunciation of the North Atlantic Treaty and the Military Assistance Program, while urging the revision of the United Nations so as to exclude the Soviet Union and its satellites.

Such positions and proposals have in common the following general attitude: the denial of American responsibility to the world, plus willingness to intervene wherever necessary in our own interests, but only on our own terms and without collaboration with others. The isolationism of the 'twenties and 'thirties proposed to act as if the non-American world did not exist. The neo-isolationism of the 'fifties is aware of the international world, but proposes to act without consideration for the interests of other nations and without awareness of the limitations of the United States.

The moral and political verdict against neo-isolationism can be stated briefly: it absolutizes and thereby distorts the interests and the power of the United States. In world politics we need the allies and also the international organization which the new isolationists would scorn or neglect, and we need them for two reasons which are separate and yet related. In the contest with the imperialism of the Soviet Union we need allies and we cannot afford to "go it alone." But more important, because it is more inclusive of all considerations, we need the discipline and the moral restraints upon our power that the company of the United Nations and the requirements of diplomacy help to provide.

If isolationism is inadequate because there is no return to the conditions of the late eighteenth and nineteenth centuries, neo-isolationism is equally "escapist" because it substitutes new wishes for objective reality in the mid-twentieth century. The new-style isolationists realize that we cannot ignore the rest of the world, but they fail to recognize that we are neither powerful enough to remake the world in our own image nor good enough to be trusted with such a mission. They believe that we can defeat Communism in Asia purely by military means, without consideration of the indigenous needs and interests of the peasants and patriots who are the backbone of the revolutionary movements in the Far East. The neo-isolationists are likewise tempted to force decisions on the United Nations without respect for the wisdom as well as the fears of other non-communist nations. When collective decisions are reached in the United Nations, sometimes slowly, and always by means of diplomacy and compromise, the neo-isolationists are tempted to press for unilateral action without collaboration, or for revision of the United Nations into a group of "American friends."[1]

No nation, including the United States, can afford to overestimate its political and military power in relation to the world of nations. No nation, including our own, can afford to indulge its emotions in self-righteous contemplation of its own goodness. The temptation to measure the virtues of the world solely by reference to American standards or American achievements is dangerous both to ourselves and to the world. The most dangerous element lies in the fact that a moral crusade is substituted for a discriminating approach to international politics. The crusader sees the issue in simple terms: "American Democracy versus Communism!" He thereby ignores the need for combining firmness with patience, and for employing power with moral restraint.

The Old Testament prophets were much wiser. When Israel was tempted to idolize itself, the prophets declared that the nation itself was on trial and that the real peril was not confined to the presence of an external enemy. These are sufficient reasons for concluding that Soviet imperialism and American neo-isolationism are twin threats to the prospects for peace.

IV. MORALISTIC INTERNATIONALISM

At the opposite pole from isolationism and neo-isolationism, as regards aspirations and programs, there is a stream of "internationalism" in American public opinion and in various social movements and peace organizations. It has served in some respects to counter-balance the influence of the isolationist heritage, but not without adding new

---

[1] For example the proposals of ex-President Hoover in 1949 that if the United Nations could not be reorganized without the Soviet bloc, and if the latter could not be expelled from the U. N., then a new anti-communist front should be formed, "based solely upon moral, spiritual and defense foundations." The new front would be composed of those who, without cost to the United States, would stand in opposition to Communism. (These proposals in effect would amount to the sacrifice of the U. N. as an inclusive organization for public diplomacy, and they implicitly called for U. S. withdrawal from the Marshall Plan and the North Atlantic Pact.)

elements of confusion in the definition and understanding of foreign policy.

There are elements of this "moralistic" type of internationalism in the responses of large segments of public opinion in wartime as well as in times of peace. After attempting neutrality in both world wars, we finally intervened and helped to conduct victorious military campaigns, assuming as we did so that the triumph of arms would serve to abolish power politics and the source of international disorders. It is difficult for us now to recapture and understand the utopian mood of our military effort of 1917-1918. The words of President Wilson are a discredited monument to the spirit of that crusade. The famous phrase, "a war to end wars," was destined to become a hollow mockery. So also were the thoughts which he expressed in 1918 and 1919: "National purposes have fallen more and more into the background and the common purpose of enlightened mankind has taken their place. . . . The day we have left behind us was a day of balances of power."[2]

Wilsonian internationalism declined amidst war weariness, domestic strife, and disillusionment with the conditions of the peace, but it was resurrected on the occasion of the Kellogg-Briand Pact in 1928 on the grounds that this agreement introduced a new era in international law and morality. Virtually every nation solemnly promised "to renounce war as an instrument of national policy in their relations with one another." No police measures were provided in the document, and public opinion was depended upon as the sole enforcement agency. Secretary of State Cordell Hull declared with Wilsonian hopefulness in April, 1939, that "a public opinion, the most potent of all forces for peace, is more strongly developing throughout the world."

The tragedy of this type of internationalism is that it substitutes sentiment for an awareness of political reality, and does so with the best of intentions. Wilson sought in vain to reform the world on liberal democratic lines, and Hull overestimated the effectiveness of treaties and public opinion as guarantors of peace. Neither of them was able to comprehend the limitations of international politics and

---

[2] From Wilson's address in New York City, September 27, 1918, opening the campaign for the Fourth Liberty Loan.

the relation of the United States to the world. This also applies to some of the internationalist principles of the late Franklin D. Roosevelt. If we credit him with political wisdom for initiating aid to Britain, and for helping to prepare our nation to recognize its interests and obligations in the restraint of the Axis powers, we may proceed to question his political wisdom in 1944-1945, especially in connection with the Yalta agreements.

The concept of "unconditional surrender," invoked by Roosevelt against the Axis, symbolized the attitude of the American people and the triumph of moralistic internationalism. The Axis enemy was seen as the essential and evil source of power politics and aggression, and the liquidation of the enemy was expected to herald a new world, a world in which the big-power victors would cooperate for peace. This expectation prevented American statesmen from anticipating the postwar political conflicts, and it apparently deprived them of the political shrewdness which would have been useful both during the war and at the Yalta conference of February, 1945. This popular expectation was shattered, for the American public as well as their leaders, by the Soviet violations of the Yalta terms—the domination of eastern Europe, plus new threats to southeastern and central Europe.

If we criticize our leaders, we should note above all the confusion of our own thought and action. As a people, twice we have assumed that the triumph of arms in global conflict would serve to abolish the struggle for power and the source of international disorder. After the first military triumph we rejected the League of Nations and sought a false refuge in isolationism. During and immediately after the second military triumph we were possessed, by and large, with Wilsonian optimism. We fought against the Axis nations, perhaps with more misgivings than in the great crusade of 1917-1918, yet with basic optimism for a new world of peace and security.

Our moralistic disdain for power politics and our proclivity for utopian expectations were further illustrated in our attitudes toward the United Nations.

V. MISCONCEPTIONS OF THE UNITED NATIONS

As a type of international government, composed of sovereign states, the United Nations is basically another League of Nations. In

structure and function it covers a wider range of non-political interests than its predecessor, but it is no less immune to the problems and
limitations of power politics and the nation-state system.

The United Nations is not a government over and above the
national governments that compose it. The United Nations in all of its
agencies and functions is essentially a parliamentary device, a network
of committees and forums, existing on the surface of international
politics. Below that surface lie the realities: the nation-states themselves, varying considerably in size and political power, in concepts of
justice and in type of government—seeking to preserve their independence, to strengthen their security and to improve their living
standards. The United Nations serves to bring the diplomats of sixty
nation-states more closely and more publicly together, and with a regularity which was impossible under the older style of diplomacy. But
intimacy, publicity and regularity of contact do not insure agreement.
They frequently serve to make disagreement more explosive.

The United Nations is therefore an instrument in the hands of
its members. The Charter is a legal declaration with many loopholes
and ambiguities, most of which were necessary in order to induce the
members to join; and the organization itself consists of a variety of
instruments and occasions for the public diplomacy of the delegates
of the sixty member states.

In American public opinion, however, the United Nations was
greeted as a substitute for power politics and as a threshold to a future
of permanent peace and international cooperation. We were tempted
in 1945-1946 to overestimate the solidarity of the members and the
political prospects of the organization. We wrongly assumed that the
creation of a political instrument would suffice to solve a problem,
while in reality the problem remained because the instrument could
be used or misused (in this instance, according to the interests and
capacities of numerous national governments amidst the insecurities
of the nation-state system).

The popular support which the United Nations received in this
country in 1945 appears in retrospect as the earnest hope that the
new organization would prove to be the constitutional framework for
a developing world community. The ability of the big powers to cooperate for peace, as they had for military victory against the Axis

nations, was presupposed. Indeed, another presupposition was apparently also present in the popular expectations of many Americans: the assumption that the existence of the United Nations would somehow relieve us of the burdensome responsibilities of a world power.

The social idealism of liberal Protestantism was a contributing factor to the popular misconceptions of the United Nations as a substitute for power politics. Moralistic internationalism, which is unable to recognize and to cope with the problem of balancing and ordering political power, was sustained rather than corrected by the prevailing attitudes of Protestant social idealism.

VI. THE CRUSADING SPIRIT OF LIBERAL PROTESTANTISM

If "internationalist" climates of opinion in the American public have depended too heavily upon misconceptions of the nature of international politics and have created or sustained utopian expectations of international peace and community, the Churches of the United States are partially responsible for this development. We who are Protestants may profit from re-examination of our own actions, acknowledging in repentance and faith our need for a deeper understanding of man, especially his collective relationships.

The "isolationist-internationalist" debate in American public affairs since 1914 was not ignored by the Protestant Churches. The issues were taken up and defined in a religious and moral context influenced by the religious-social idealism of the late nineteenth and early twentieth centuries.[3]

As the "Social Gospel" arose in American Protestantism from 1865 to 1914 it was primarily concerned with the problems of a domestic society which was experiencing the rise of cities and industries. Exponents of this gospel were devoted to the achievement of a "Christian social order." Influenced considerably by the evolutionary optimism of the period they sustained the belief that men could "build the Kingdom of God on earth." The Social Gospel was a creative movement,

---

[3] This analysis does not apply to Protestantism *in toto*, but to substantial portions of the religious bodies affiliated with the National Council of Churches. Although these denominations vary in their specific doctrines and approaches to social ethics, there is a substantial common denominator: the desire to influence society at large in the direction of Christian ideals. We may thus roughly distinguish between "liberal Protestantism" and numerous other bodies such as the adventist, pentecostal and holiness groups.

helping to correct the individualism of nineteenth-century Protestantism, but as a framework for the interpretation of international politics in the 'twenties and 'thirties it was seriously handicapped.

The acquisition of evolutionary optimism encouraged the Churches to think in utopian terms about the possibilities of political reform. The unpopularity of the doctrine of "original sin" had its counterpart in the responses of Protestants to the problems of international politics: the perennial and underlying problem of "power politics" and "balance-of-power" was ignored. Another factor which contributed to this utopian mood was the preoccupation of the Social Gospel, prior to 1918, with issues of domestic life. When the spokesmen of social Christianity responded to the foreign policy issues of the two world wars and the period in between, their idealism was re-enforced by the assumption that the methods of domestic life could readily be extended to control international conflict. Morality, public opinion, and international law were felt to be sufficient for the restraint of international aggression.

The First World War came as a surprise. When the nation finally became a belligerent, the Churches responded by acclaiming the war a crusade for democracy (and also for Christ), and they supported the nation in a "war to end wars." The vitality of their optimism was only temporarily impaired by the cynicism and disillusionment of the war's aftermath. A new crusade arose on the ashes of the old: a holy crusade against all war. In a mood similar to that of the Anti-Saloon League and the Prohibition movement, churchmen turned with hope to the "renunciation" and "excommunication" of war by the Churches, and to disarmament and "outlawry" of war by the State. This was a religious pacifism rooted in the modern Social Gospel belief in the possibility of radical social reconstruction by "Christian means." Resolutions which denounced war as "sin," or which demanded of the State in 1929 that it "outlaw war," and in 1939 that it "keep the United States out of war," were proclamations of a crusading temper. They expressed a popular concern for peace in which it was assumed that any military action by the United States would be unnecessary intervention or aggression. This assumption was no longer tenable after Pearl Harbor, and was a matter of serious dispute during 1940-1941.

The crusading spirit of liberal Protestant responses to the problem of world order proved to be inadequate. Idealism, sincerity, and the denunciation of war were insufficient for interpreting the meaning of national and international crises. Much of the militancy of the anti-war crusade was inspired by a combination of internationalist moral principles and isolationist political assumptions. The disorder of international society was denounced with the hope and expectation that it could be remedied without involving the United States beyond such measures as the following: more liberal economic and immigration policies, mediation of European and Asiatic conflicts, and the provision of a "good example"—a nation that was both democratic and non-aggressive.

This position was ambiguous, and it became a source of confusion. It failed to reckon with the objective reality of national interests and the conditions of order as these were affected by the imperialist policies of the Axis powers. The trend of world politics and the course of war made it difficult and finally impossible to reconcile "internationalism" as a moral requirement with isolationist political assumptions. In the Protestant Churches there remained only a small, although influential, minority who adhered to a pacifist line. Consisting of individuals and small unofficial groups, liberal Protestant pacifism regarded opposition to war as an absolute requirement of the Christian ethic. The principles and programs of this minority have never, in their entirety, been espoused by the main bodies of Protestantism. Yet the religious and political ethic of the pacifists is in many respects a symbol of the predicament of liberal Protestant idealism.

VII. PACIFISM—SYMBOL OF THE LIBERAL PROTESTANT DILEMMA

Pacifism, in the sense of conscientious objection as a duty in the event of war, is by no means novel in the Christian tradition. In modern history it was primarily a manifestation of the sectarian ethic of the historic peace churches (the Mennonites, Brethren, and Friends). For the Mennonites and the Church of the Brethren, opposition to military service was incidental to an ethic of withdrawal from civic life and from any responsibility for the ordering of power relationships in the secular community. Nonresistance was affirmed as a *duty* for the Christian, and as an *impossibility* for the world. The Friends, however, managed to combine non-resistance with affirmations of civic responsibility and concern for social reforms, with more optimistic hopes for the Christian influence of secular institutions.

In the United States during 1917-1918 three-fourths of the members of the pacifist sects who were drafted, accepted military service. But from 1940 through 1945, under the administration of the Selective Service Laws, the historic peace Churches contributed only sixty per cent of the men assigned to Civilian Public Service, while members of the historically *non*-pacifist religious bodies (Roman Catholics, Jews, and especially the liberal Protestant Churches) were far more in evidence then in 1917-1918. Liberal religious pacifism had achieved significant influence in the following religious groups: Episcopalians, Methodists, Presbyterians, Baptists, Disciples, Congregationalists, Evangelical and Reformed, and Unitarian. The principles espoused by pacifist clergymen, religious youth conferences, and by the interdenominational Fellowship of Reconciliation[4] were in sharp contrast to the otherworldly and non-resistant pacifism of the Mennonite and Church of the Brethren heritage.

The spirit of liberal religious pacifism was characterized by a two-fold appeal: (1) *religious* loyalty to the teachings and example of Jesus; and (2) the *pragmatic* value of love and of pacifist "techniques" over against the "futility of war." The existence and the employment of military power were condemned as both evil and futile. The "Cross of Christ" and the Sermon on the Mount were considered to be not only religious symbols of God's nature and love but also human possibilities and strategies for the achievement of justice and order.[5] The practical application of these principles included not only the personal duty of conscientious objection in wartime but the social obligation to work for a pacifist nation. For the liberal religious pacifist the Kingdom of God was a religious demand *and* a social-political objective. The goal was to be realized by substituting love and strategies of nonviolence for the narrower loyalties and coercive methods of national and international life.

---

[4] The Fellowship of Reconciliation had its origin in 1915, as a movement of Christian protest against war, declaring its faith "in a better way than violence" for the solution of all social conflicts. Its membership grew from 68 in 1915 to 13,800 in 1942.

[5] Consult, for example, the pamphlets or other writings of A. J. Muste, John N. Sayre, Kirby Page, John Haynes Holmes, Richard B. Gregg, Paul C. French, Harry Emerson Fosdick, Albert E. Day, John H. Lathrop, Ernest F. Tittle, Henry H. Crane, Elmore McKee.

The dilemma of this position can readily be seen. When the Fellowship of Reconciliation, the Peace Section of the American Friends Service Committee, and other religious spokesmen endeavored to apply these convictions in the domestic struggle over foreign policies, they became the victims of two incompatible principles: the absolute demands of the Sermon on the Mount, and the obligation to be "effective" in the transformation of the social order. Convinced of the evil and futility of war, they opposed American aid to the nations fighting the Axis powers and they opposed Selective Service legislation. They sought to increase the number of conscientious objectors as a means of transforming politics, they supported the Keep America Out of War Congress, and helped to provide a religious sanction for neutrality and isolationist policies. In the name of the "Christian way," neutrality was defended against international collaboration whenever the latter involved non-pacifist methods.

Liberal religious pacifism becomes a witness *against politics* when it cries "No!" to war unconditionally, and when it claims to substitute love or "Christian methods" for the coercive policies of the State. Such principles deny to the State its legitimate use of power, and refuse to accept the State as useful and meaningful in God's concern for men in a sinful world. The Sermon on the Mount plays an "ideological" role when it is employed as a sanction for isolationist political judgments or for the efficacy of non-violent methods. The rejoinder which was frequently made in pacifist speeches and literature, that Gandhian non-violent methods are the "strategy of love" and the "politics of the Cross," is misleading and deceptive. The Christ on the Cross achieved no political purpose, and the politics of Gandhi were a variety of power politics in which shrewdness and moral discipline were combined, aiming at a transfer of political power.[6]

---

[6] Gandhi should be credited for achieving a way of using non-violent coercion as an instrument of power in the pursuit of justice. American pacifist interpretations of Gandhi, however, are misleading both in their religious and in their political generalizations. The roots of Gandhi's principles lie in the Hindu and Jain beliefs, on which he bases his distinction between the physical as evil and the spiritual as good (contrary to the biblical view of man). In the light of these principles he employed the strategies of class conflict, similar to their use in British and American labor struggles. Civil disobedience meant self-withdrawal from political and economic enterprises, in order to impose Gandhi's will upon British rulers. Among the consequences were imprisonment, the shooting of crowds of unarmed rebels, and unemployment in British industries. Gandhi was wise in employing his strategies against Hindus indoctrinated in the virtues of ascetic passivity, and against British rulers

VIII. THE DANGERS OF POLITICAL MORALISM

Both the militarism of 1917-1918 and the pacifism which followed are subject to a common judgment: in the name of Christian idealism they overestimated the virtue and the relevance of their proposals. The idealism miscarried and confused the issues. No nation is good enough to conduct a "Holy War," and if it has to fight in order to defend its interests it will obscure the real issues by pretending to possess a higher virtue than it has. Self-righteousness leads to an overestimate of the evil of the opponent, and to an underestimate of one's own responsibilities in both war and peace. Furthermore, no nation can act like a community of saints, although this has been the hope of liberal religious pacifism. No nation, including our own, will resolve to sacrifice itself, or to run the risk of such sacrifice, in order to provide a "moral example" for others. Even if this were possible, it remains doubtful whether any nation, especially a powerful one, would be justified in doing so if the consequences included the encouragement of another big power to act aggressively.

Some of our past illusions persist, making it difficult for us to see where the basic issues lie in defining and formulating American foreign policy, and in relating our Protestant heritage to the decisions which the people must make. The testimonies of religious groups since 1945 suggest how difficult it is for churchmen as well as other persons or agencies to transcend the inadequate principles and expectations of the earlier decades of our century. The majority by far of denominational testimonies in Congressional hearings on aid to

---

and soldiers who were inhibited, to considerable degree, by their own democratic heritage. Nevertheless, it must be noted that non-violence was not devoid of evil consequences, and that there is little historic evidence for Gandhi's assumption that this strategy as applied by a small disciplined group can be applied by a nation against armed aggressors.

The entire matter of "non-violent strategies" should be studied in the context of social action methods which possess no inherent virtue but which are relative to the social circumstances, the discipline and aims of the actors. Within a domestic society these strategies may be highly useful for minority group purposes. But as a national policy in international politics and war, there are serious limitations: Can the *nation* be disciplined to choose and to maintain such a policy? Will an imperialist enemy be *deterred* or *encouraged* by such a response? Could non-violent resistance within *one* nation fulfill two different moral requirements: the achievement of national security *and* the strengthening of the collective security of a wider community? If pacifist numbers and influence are not proportionately distributed among the contending nations, their existence may be a liability rather than an asset for the very nations which are pursuing non-imperialist policies.

Greece and Turkey, in 1947, were in opposition to any form of military aid program. A similar response rose in 1949, against American ratification of the North Atlantic Treaty. In both instances the critics employed arguments which are reminiscent of the pacifist idealism of the 'thirties. They demanded of the United Nations what it could not do under the prevailing political conditions. They expected the protection of Greece, Turkey and the North Atlantic area from Soviet aggression by renewed "goodwill," by a diplomacy which was deprived of deterring power. They limited American responsibility to economic aid and to diplomatic efforts to persuade the Soviet bloc "without resort to power politics." These proposals were formulated according to the perfectionist principles of the 'thirties, and amounted to impossible demands upon the nation: that it rely upon "Christian methods of goodwill," "Jesus' program of the Kingdom of God," and the disavowal of the politics of power.[7] The public statement of the Fellowship of Reconciliation in July, 1950, expressed similar principles in denunciation of United Nations collective security action in Korea.[8]

These testimonies displayed little if any awareness that political action by its very nature presupposes the strife of competing interests, the conflict of nations, and the need for the balancing and ordering of power if peace with justice is in some measure to be attained.

IX. RELIGIOUS ETHICS AND POLITICAL RESPONSIBILITY

The tragedy of many American peace movements and of numerous "Christian" approaches to the problem of world order, lies in their inability to interpret the facts of life with significance and to devise relevant programs of action. The task of genuine morality, illumined by the principles of the Protestant Reformation, is to act with responsibility to God and with concern for the neighbor, and to do so with awareness of man's limitations as well as his possibilities.

Since conflicts of interest are inseparable from human life and

---

[7] The few exceptions to these statements were provided by the Federal Council of Churches, the Council for Social Action of the Congregational Christian Churches, and the Catholic Association for International Peace—all of which took positions of discriminating support.

[8] See, in contrast, the statement of the Central Committee of the World Council of Churches, meeting at Toronto, July, 1950, reported in the pamphlet, *The Churches and World Affairs* (New York: The Commission of the Churches on International Affairs, 1950).

every achievement of justice gives rise to new problems, a Christian ethic of responsibility will seek, for reasons of love, to give serious consideration to the constant achievement of the "best possible justice." The Christian ethic neither idealizes "power politics" nor provides a substitute for this aspect of human existence. All political considerations involve estimates of power: judgments concerning the use, distribution and balancing of the power which men have or seek to attain over one another.[9]

Since men are not angels, their lust for power and for imperial domination of their fellows needs to be restrained. It is significant that in spite of the eschatological outlook and the minority position of the early churchmen in the Roman Empire, the New Testament recognizes the importance of *two* approaches to this problem: (1) the need for personal *loyalties* and *religious disciplines* which strengthen the capacity of persons to love rather than to hate, to share rather than to exploit, to work with and for others rather than to dominate them; and (2) the need for *political restraints* upon evil-doers. In the context of biblical faith both the Church and the State are "divinely ordained." When *liberal religious pacifism* appeals to the "love ethic" of primitive Christianity it ignores or dismisses the eschatological outlook of the early Church, the minority and non-political role of the Christians in a pagan society, and it substitutes modern views of the inherent goodness and rationality of man. When the *historic peace Churches* appeal to the "primitive gospel" as the sanction for an other-worldly pacifism of non-resistance, they absolutize testimonies which were relative to the circumstances of the first two centuries, A.D., and destroy the basis for "Christian callings" in the political sphere.

In an age in which the political order, the risks of war and the struggle for power occupy a prominent place in the minds of men, it is imperative that we avoid two misconceptions of "power politics": the cynicism of the "realists" who think solely in terms of national security and international "balance-of-power," and the utopianism of

---

[9] "Power" is definable here as the means and methods by which men seek to influence or control the minds and actions of their fellows, regardless of what their motives or ultimate goals may be. The motives and goals vary considerably, and the desire for power is considerably broader than the "lust for power." Liberal pacifism desired the power of non-violent coerciveness for its own ends, which it identified with the good of society, when it aspired to increase the number of pacifists and to change the social order.

the "idealists" who seek to substitute ethics for politics. The only alternative for a Christian ethic of political responsibility is to seek to be obedient to God within the political and social sphere. Christian social action is action motivated by faith in God, and therefore in concern "for the neighbor." It is action in which we have to contend not only with the egoism and isolationism of our own hearts but with the practical and strategic difficulties of social movements and political programs—none of which can succeed purely on the basis of their motives.

The only motive which is ultimately acceptable to the Christian faith is the love revealed in Jesus Christ. Because of man's involvement in sin, love has to be expressed in terms of law and justice, although it never can be identified with any particular system. It is therefore the task of Christian political ethics to guide us in the achievement of social structures which limit and contain the egotistic tendencies of human nature, enabling and encouraging the highest possible achievements of justice, order and freedom. Allegiance to such principles must of necessity be combined with the practical wisdom of competent statesmanship. One must acknowledge responsibility not only for his motives but also for the consequences of his actions.

X. MORAL RESPONSIBILITY AND THE NATIONAL INTEREST

In any serious consideration of Christian responsibility for American foreign policy it is imperative to understand the nature of international politics and the interests which underlie the historic policies and conflicts of nation-states. The basic difference between domestic and international society is the fact that the latter is not "domesticated." There is no world community as there is a national community. There is no world state with central legislative or administrative bodies, nor a legal system with compulsory jurisdiction over serious disputes, nor a central police force for the restraint of aggressive individuals and groups.

Politics among nations, therefore, differ not in principle but in the conditions of their practice, when compared with domestic politics. In a stable and democratic nation, for example, the struggle for political power is held within limits, and the basic methods for waging the struggle are propaganda, pressure groups, ballots and party politics. In the international struggle for power the insecurity and incipient anarchy of the society of nation-states leads inevitably to the placing of a high premium upon national security. No responsible statesman can ignore considerations of power or neglect the national interest in security. Political relations are conducted with other nations by diplomacy, employing persuasion, economic power, and the prestige (or if need be, the threat) of military force. If the conflicting interests of two or more nations are held to be vital, and no accommodation is possible through diplomatic effort, there are but two alternatives: (1) the capitulation of the weaker party to the stronger one, or (2) the substitution of war for diplomacy.[10]

In the absence of a world community and a world state there is no substitute for the above methods of international politics. How, then, is the Christian principle of "concern for the neighbor" to be understood and implemented in this complex and impersonal sphere?

The basic moral issue for the vocational conscience of the statesman or for the attitudes of the citizen toward "foreign policy" matters might well be defined as follows: the *responsible use* of national power and the methods of international politics, in pursuit of the national interest, but with insistence that the "national interest" be defined in moral terms so as to *include* the nation's responsibility for the common welfare of international society. No nation can be expected to sacrifice its existence for the good of others, and no responsible statesman would entrust the care of his nation to other nations. Moral responsibility under these conditions consists in defining and interpreting the national interest so as to recognize the mutual needs and interests of the society of nations.[11]

---

[10] It may be argued that "appeasement" is a third alternative. But if this results in no genuine accommodation of conflicting interests it leads only to capitulation or defeat on the "installment plan."

Military alliances, in peacetime or war, are extensions of the above patterns. The United Nations is primarily an instrument of multilateral diplomacy among nation states, and does not therefore constitute a distinctively different pattern or a third alternative.

[11] The chief deficiency of the otherwise penetrating and commendable works of an outstanding political scientist, Hans J. Morgenthau, consists in his ambiguous definition of the "national interest." "National interest" is defined in terms of security, territorial integrity, and preservation of basic institutions. But no criterion is provided for judging and weighing these, for determining what is basic in the national interest. In dealing with contemporary issues he *implies* a democratic prin-

It is therefore religiously meaningful and politically relevant to insist that the real interests of the nation are not to be served by fanatical nationalism, by indifference to the plight of mankind, or by imperialist ambitions.

United States foreign policy therefore cannot be "purified" by pursuing peace without calculations of power, or without concern for national security. The principles of our basic heritage, applied to the conditions of the mid-twentieth century, require us to define the national interest with recognition of an interdependent world. The mature and enlightened use of American resources calls both for the prevention of war and the advance of the free world. A responsible foreign policy must include moral and political, economic and military exertions. The national security and the democratic heritage are involved in the outcome of the power struggle between the Soviet Union and the United States, and so are the securities and the prospects for freedom of other nations and millions of people. The traditional American interest in a balance of power in Europe and in Asia continues to be "legitimate" (whether we measure it by the national self-interest, the democratic principle of "live and let live," or the Christian norm of action with responsibility for the neighbor).[12]

Responsible action is impossible without incurring grave risks on many fronts. An outline of constructive action must weigh the importance as well as the limitations of the United Nations.

XI. THE IMPORTANCE OF THE UNITED NATIONS
TO THE UNITED STATES

The violations of the Yalta agreement by the Soviet Union were the primary factor in dispelling our utopian illusions of a new era in international relations. The necessity of American aid to Greece and Turkey and of a North Atlantic Alliance was reluctantly conceded. As the "cold war" developed, and as it turned to a "hot war" in Korea,

---

ciple: the statesman's obligation to search for the *compatible* and "legitimate" interests of other countries. See, for example, his major work, *Politics Among Nations* (New York: Knopf, 1948) and also his later volume, *In Defense of the National Interest* (New York: Knopf, 1951). I am deeply indebted to his incisive work.

[12] This is *not* to imply that national public opinions or interests are essentially inspired by Christian motivations, or by democratic convictions devoid of self-interest. It *is* to insist that the interest in balanced power is permissible and useful in the Christian conception of a just order.

our attitude toward the United Nations became cynical rather than utopian. We tended to remain consistent in but one respect: our moralistic desire to censure or punish the "criminal" rather than to take stock of our own misconceptions. Substantial portions of our people began to think in military terms alone, as General MacArthur invited them to do in 1951. It likewise became popular to search for communists or "fellow-travelers" in the State Department on the assumption that *someone* had played a treasonable role or we never would have suffered a foreign policy failure in the Far East.

Under these circumstances, we have been tempted to *under-estimate* the importance of the United Nations. Since we have learned by disillusionment that the United Nations is not and cannot be a substitute for power politics, we are inclined to disregard the values that remain in "diplomacy by conference." The membership and the instrumentalities of the United Nations are in fact exceedingly useful to the vital interests of the United States. The international organization provides us, far better than did the older forms of diplomacy, with opportunities to discover the common interests and objectives of the society of nations. This in turn is both a stimulus and an opportunity for the fashioning of American policies which serve our national interest in peace and order without ignoring or undermining the common interests of the greater society.

It is true that United Nations diplomacy is frequently the display of "power politics in disguise." But it is also true that the Security Council continues to provide a bridge of minimal contact between the dominant powers of the communist and non-communist worlds. And the General Assembly is both the symbol of an interdependent world and the instrument whereby American resources may be employed to serve the common interests and strengthen the general health of the non-communist nations. Not only does the United Nations need the United States, but the latter needs the former. If we erred in expecting the impossible of international agencies, we err no less in our neo-isolationist temptations to "write off" the international experiment as a bad investment.[13]

---

[13] If the security of the United States requires a balance of power in the Far East, and is threatened by Soviet expansion, by Russian domination of Asia, then the American interest in restraining aggression against South Korea coincides with the wider interest of the United Nations majority in discouraging and preventing such

XII. THE RESPONSIBLE USE OF AMERICAN POWER

World society has never been "domesticated." The two world wars are a symbol of the new but only technical interdependence of this society, and of the imperative need of world community and global institutions which will limit the strife of nations and reduce it to the proportions of domestic politics as they are conducted within the stabler countries. The possibility of such an achievement remains to be seen, but the goal of the World Federalists is justified—at least as a general recognition of the longrun requirement—although the movement for "world government now" can be dismissed as premature constitutionalism.[14]

Because of its position of power in world politics, the United States must play a morally dangerous role which it may be incapable of playing. Its real interests and its duties in terms of the United Nations Charter are akin to those of a "vigilante" in a "frontier" society.[15] The United States needs to be sufficiently powerful to provide a deterring influence upon the imperialist ambitions of the Kremlin. It is Russian imperialism, in the guise of Marxist "revolution," which threatens Europe and aspires to dominate Asia. American economic and military aid to Europe has proven its worth in stemming the tide

---

aggression. It is relevant to ask how successful would *unilateral* American intervention be in Korea, under which circumstances the Russian charge of "imperialism" would indeed be persuasive throughout Asia.

Likewise with respect to the giving of economic and technical aid to underdeveloped countries: United Nations agencies are in a far better position to impose conditions upon local authorities and native governments for the efficient use of economic and technical assistance than is the United States acting alone. It would be far more difficult for an irresponsible regime to cry "imperialism" if an international agency imposes the standards. The objectives of the American "Point IV" program can be more readily achieved through wider use of U. N. agencies.

[14] The *programs* espoused by "World Federalist" groups are largely irrelevant, especially when they encounter the following questions: (1) As an immediate demand, could their goal be achieved by *voluntary* methods? (Most of our modern nations have grown by conquest.) (2) Can a world state be achieved *or* maintained without *tyranny*? (The mid-twentieth century world lacks the essential forms of community: common interests and loyalties that override nationalism and provide the basis for common concepts of justice and a representative government.) (3) Is a world state *possible* under any such conditions as the bi-polar structure of world politics, the gulf between Russia and the West, etc.?

[15] This is the role designated by the U. N. Charter for the permanent members of the Security Council. Contrary to the expectations of 1945, the power of Britain has diminished, China has been engulfed in revolution, and the big power "vigilantes" are divided into two competitive blocs of power.

of internal communist threats and in deterring the expansionist aims of the Soviet Union. If the United States disarmed, as some pacifists propose, or retreated from European commitments, as some isolationists would have it do, further Soviet expansion would undoubtedly occur.

The Russian strategy in Asia has continued to be the employment of "Marxist" ideology and the promotion of native communist parties, appealing to the nationalism and to the poverty-stricken condition of patriots and peasants. The United States is involved here in the unenviable position of preventing the expansion of Soviet influence by: (1) the "limited war" of United Nations collective security measures against Soviet satellites in Korea; (2) military aid to western colonial powers against communist guerrilla forces in Southeast Asia; (3) the defense of a great perimeter extending in Asia from Japan and the Philippines to New Zealand and Australia, and westward into the Near East; and (4) a small and inadequate investment in economic and technical aid to the governments of several non-communist nations. The risks are grave, the burden is heavy, and the outcome is unpredictable.

Underlying all of the questions of strategy and tactics, of maneuvers within and outside of the United Nations, and of economic aid versus military appropriations, there exists one basic issue: *can a diplomatic settlement eventually be achieved with the Soviet Union,* or will some local or regional conflict (as in Korea or Germany) precipitate a third world war?

The only policy that has proved effective in dealing with the Kremlin is a combination of patience and power: firmness in diplomacy, backed by military strength, and implemented by American commitments for the joint defense of substantial areas of the non-communist world. But neither "cold war" nor "limited war" can go on forever. Already a serious question is emerging in diplomatic and military planning: how to distinguish between *deterrent* power and *provocative* power. An equally serious question arises domestically: can the people of the United States achieve and maintain the patience and moral nerve which are required for the twofold task of avoiding both war and appeasement, while working with other peoples for the achievement of conditions which will deprive the Soviet rulers of any opportunity for imperialist policies?

The magnitude of the task is overwhelming. But in the context of the Christian faith it has an infinite meaning. The United States as well as the Soviet Union stands under the judgment of God.

Faith and Secular Learning

WILL HERBERG

———————————————— ✳ ————————————————

WILL HERBERG *is author, editor, and lecturer in the field of theology and ethics. Educated at Columbia University, he was for many years educational and research director in a large AFL labor union. He is the author of* JUDAISM AND MODERN MAN, *and a frequent contributor to such periodicals as* CHRISTIANITY AND CRISIS, COMMENTARY, JEWISH FRONTIER, *and* COMMONWEAL. *In recent years he has lectured widely in colleges and universities throughout the United States.*

THE relation of faith to secular learning constitutes a serious and perplexing problem for the man of faith who is concerned with the wisdom of the world. The present almost total divorce and mutual suspicion seems to be the consequence of a long history to which both religion and learning have contributed. Secular learning denies the relevance of faith and insists on total self-sufficiency. Not that faith is necessarily written off as of no account—indeed, it is often highly prized for its "spiritual" and cultural value—but it is held to be a matter of purely private concern, of no relevance to such public, and far more serious affairs, as science and scholarship. Curiously enough, the outcome of prevailing religious attitudes is very much the same. In the thinking of the religious liberal, faith is identified with something called "religious experience," which may be the subject-matter of philosophic and scientific analysis but itself can have no cognitive significance. Religious liberalism thus substantially shares the attitude of the secularist on the relation of faith to learning. The fundamentalist, on the other hand, sees secular learning as vain and delusive. All the knowledge that really matters is to be found in the Bible (and tradition), and while the sciences are undeniably of some utility in certain areas of life, they are not to be taken seriously as providing knowledge relevant to human existence. The fundamentalist attitude is, indeed, very much like that attributed to the Caliph Omar at the taking of the Alexandrian library: "If it is true, it is already in the *Koran;* if it is not in the *Koran,* it cannot be true. Therefore, to the flames with these books." Thus on both sides, on the side of the "religionist" as well as on the side of the secularist, it seems to be taken for granted that faith and secular learning are properly and irretrievably divorced: faith is faith and science science, and never the twain shall meet!

In this situation, we can easily understand the nostalgic longing that has arisen in certain quarters for the good old days of the "medieval synthesis" when a genuine unity is supposed to have prevailed between faith and learning, between religion and what we would today regard as secular studies. And indeed, particularly in the high middle ages, the structure of knowledge and culture did display an impressive unity. All learning was organized into a well-integrated hierarchy, and theology was recognized as the "queen of the sciences." But if we scrutinize the picture a little more closely, we cannot fail to note its darker side as well. All too easily and all too often, as the case of Galileo so plainly shows, the hegemony of theology became in effect the dead hand of a scholastic-ecclesiastical vested interest holding thought and learning in its oppressive grip. For all its theonomous pretensions, medieval culture was basically and inescapably *heteronomous.*[1]

In any case, it was in revolt against the heteronomy of the medieval system that what is characteristic in modern culture emerged. With the Renaissance, two attempts at a new cultural synthesis were made: the humanist-classical culture developed out of the Greco-Roman literary tradition, and the scientific-scholarly culture erected largely on the foundation of the new empirical sciences. With the

---

[1] It may perhaps be desirable to define explicitly the three concepts that form the basic operative categories of this analysis:

Heteronomy is the attitude in which life, or any area, interest, or concern of life, is subjected to an outside and alien law, to outside and alien control.

Autonomy is the attitude in which life, as a whole or in any of its aspects, claims to be a law unto itself, subject to nothing above or beyond.

Theonomy is the attitude which sees life in all its aspects lived in recognition of the ever-present lordship of God and His law.

eighteenth century, the latter became predominant, and in varying combinations, the two still constitute the substance of the culture and education of the West. In both, it should be noted, religion is essentially extrinsic. Classical humanism has the "highest regard" for religion, but largely as a cultural grace and refining influence. In the scientific scheme, religion is simply irrelevant, except as an empirical subject-matter for study. Modern culture is essentially *autonomous*, and until recently it was militantly so.

It is my purpose in the following paragraphs to examine the basic presuppositions of the scientific-scholarly culture, as it forms our mind (the "modern mind") and permeates our thinking, and attempt to assess what a mature biblical faith might have to say about it. In this way, perhaps, we may be led to a more satisfactory understanding of the relations between faith and secular learning.

I. BASIC PRESUPPOSITIONS OF THE SCIENTIFIC OUTLOOK

Cultural presuppositions are notoriously hard to define; they pervade our thinking as the air pervades the physical world we live in. In fact, they constitute our cultural atmosphere. I do not think, however, that we will go far wrong if we take the following as the fundamental positions of the scientific-scholarly culture and therefore as the underlying "pre-judices" of the modern mind.

1. *Empiricism*—Basic is the affirmation that the empirical world, the world with which we come in contact through the senses, is real and important, and knowledge about it is real knowledge. This is very much what Sorokin means by the "sensate" attitude. It should be noted that, however obvious this attitude may be to us, it is by no means universal. Indeed, taking human thought, as far as we know it, as a whole it may truly be said that the "empirical" attitude is quite exceptional. The enduring tradition of western philosophy and eastern spirituality has consistently emphasized the unreality of the empirical, the temporal, the mutable, the material as against the ideal, the eternal, the timeless, and the spiritual, and has therefore consistently depreciated the reality and worth of empirical knowledge. Only since the late middle ages, and then (at least until recently) only in the western world, has the empirical-"sensate" attitude become dominant and normative.

2. *Research*—It is difficult to give a name to this presupposition, but perhaps "research" will do. What is asserted here is the value—both intrinsic and instrumental—of the acquisition of scientific-scholarly knowledge. The pursuit of such knowledge is held to be in itself a thing worthwhile, and at the same time its utility to man for a better life is strongly emphasized. This, too, is an essentially new attitude, as the merest glance at the history of thought will show.

3. *Determinism*—The behavior of things in the world, including human beings, is held to be somehow determined by antecedent factors, themselves of an empirical, usually material character. This assumption is perhaps not so radically new as the others, since determinist ideas are fairly widespread, but its exclusive emphasis on "efficient" causality and its insistence on the empirical nature of the determining factors give it its distinctive quality.

4. *Relativism*—Characteristic of the modern mind, especially in more recent times, is the assumption that human thinking is not timeless, abstract intellection achieving absolute and timeless truth, but is somehow relative to the changing social, cultural, and psychological conditions in which the thinker is involved. This, of course, immediately raises the vexing problem of the scientist's own thinking about the relative and conditioned thinking of others, but whatever the difficulties, the conviction of an all-pervading relativism seems to be a feature of the modern mind.

5. *Progressivism*—Since the eighteenth century at least, it has been the conviction of all modern-minded men that some law of progress underlies the history of mankind (and perhaps also of the cosmos), according to which there is an immanent movement towards the cumulation of values (reason, knowledge, moral sensitivity, social order) and the dissipation of "disvalues"—in other words, that there is continual change for the better and mankind is ever moving upward and onward to perfection. This conviction—expressed in such extravagant terms by Condorcet, buttressed with all the evidence of "science" by Herbert Spencer, and restated by Marx, though in variant "revolutionary" form—runs directly counter to the traditional thinking of virtually all mankind which has consistently tended to see the pattern of time either as one of endless cyclical recurrence or as one of steady corruption and retrogression. Along with commitment to the

empirical, the "progressive" outlook has been most influential in molding the modern mind.

6. *Autonomy*—The entire modern outlook can perhaps best be summarized under the rubric of autonomy. This involves a double claim, for science as a whole and for the particular fields of science. For science as a whole, autonomy involves the claim that science is a self-enclosed, self-validated, self-sufficient whole, with no dependence on anything outside or beyond itself. For the particular fields of science, autonomy implies that each field, or discipline, is properly to be cultivated as an autonomous specialty under its own laws and principles. Beyond both of these affirmations and in a sense embracing them is the feeling that science and empirical scholarship are somehow ultimate, dependent on nothing, while everything else is dependent on them. Science and empirical scholarship are held not only to be a law unto themselves but also to be quite competent to lay down the law for the whole of life. This attitude is what has come to be known as "scientism": the exaltation of an autonomous science to ultimacy and absoluteness.[2]

Lately, signs have been multiplying that modern man is beginning to find his autonomy unbearable. After three centuries of victorious struggle to establish the claim of autonomous human thought against church, state, and society, modern man seems to be rushing headlong into a new and more oppressive heteronomy, the heteronomy of an omniscient, omnipotent, omnicompetent Party-State, which reaches its ultimate development in communist and fascist totalitarianism. Autonomy is apparently easier to fight for than to sustain when won. The modern age may well be drawing to a close, and a new phase in the cycle of autonomy-heteronomy may be opening. At this point, however, the question with which we are concerned is of another kind. It is: *what can biblical faith say as to the claims and presuppositions of the modern scientific-scholarly outlook?*

II. THE "YES-NO" OF FAITH TO THE PRESUPPOSITIONS OF SCIENCE

It would undoubtedly be much more convenient all around if the attitude of biblical faith to the presuppositions of the modern scientific-

---

[2] On "scientism," and indeed on many of the topics discussed in this paper, see D. R. G. Owen, *Scientism, Man, and Religion* (Philadelphia: Westminster Press, 1952).

scholarly culture could be expressed in a simple, well-defined *yes* or *no*. The secularist, with the religious liberal in tow, can say a quite unequivocal *yes;* the fundamentalist has his *no* equally unequivocal. But for a mature biblical faith, such simple, unequivocal answers are unfortunately impossible. A faith that is both biblical and realistic, and is one because it is the other, cannot say simply *yes* or *no*. It must say first *yes,* then *no,* and then a combined *yes-no—*a *yes* of affirmation, a *no* of limitation and qualification, and finally a *yes-no* in an effort to hold the two together in dynamic balance. The biblical approach, in other words, is inescapably dialectical.

What, then, are the *yes* and the *no* that faith must say to the claims and presuppositions of the scientific-scholarly culture? Let us proceed in the order we have outlined:

1. *Empiricism—*Yes, the world of empirical actuality is real and important. It is the world created by God and the scene of the divine-human encounter. Here, as is well known, biblical faith takes an uncompromising stand against the spiritualistic devaluation of the empirical, the temporal, the many, the material. Here it takes its stand with the secular thinker in insisting that the world of empirical actuality is the context of reality for man in existence. In this respect, biblical faith is in conscious opposition to the dominant tradition in the philosophies and religions of mankind.

The world of empirical actuality is real and important, both biblical faith and the scientific-scholarly outlook agree, but biblical faith goes on to assert that *it is not ultimate or self-subsistent.* This total affirmation is necessary not merely in the interests of faith, but in the interests of experimental science as well. For the modern scientific attitude requires the world of nature to be real and important—else the entire scientific enterprise would be delusive—and yet somehow subjected to man for his questioning and experimentation. Consider the "hardboiled" disenchanted approach to nature implied in the phrase that one may regard as the baptismal formula of modern science: "put nature to the question," that is, put nature on the rack and force it to give evidence under torture (experiment). Such an approach was impossible for the Greek to whom nature was divine, "full of gods;"[3] it would

---

[3] "All things are full of gods" (Plato, *Laws,* x, 899).

have been nothing short of impious. Indeed, as Michael Foster points out:

> [The attitude of the Greek scientist was] an intellectualized form of nature worship. . . . This nature is thought of as being changeless and eternal. The idea that it could be subjected to mastery by the human will could hardly have been entertained by a Greek thinker.[4]

It is the biblical doctrine of creation that is "the source of [the] un-Greek elements in the modern theory of nature by which the peculiar character of . . . modern science . . . [is] determined."[5] For the biblical doctrine of creation sees the empirical world as real but not divine, indeed as "void of divinity,"[6] and therefore subject to man. It is this doctrine that entered into the making of modern science, and that, in however remote and secularized a form, underlies the attitude of the contemporary experimental scientist toward the nature he is constantly "forcing" to "yield its secrets."[7]

By taking its stand against the tendency of empiricism to absolutize itself and convert the world of empirical actuality into a self-subsistent ultimate, biblical faith is thus at the same time fighting in the interests of science. Naturalism and materialism, the ideologies that emerge from the self-absolutization of empiricism, are essentially a reversion to pantheistic nature-worship, the logic of which would be fatal to experimental science.

2. *Research*—Empirical, scientific knowledge is a genuine good,

---

[4] Michael Foster, "Some Remarks on the Relations of Science and Religion," *Christian News-Letter* (November 26, 1947), No. 299.

[5] M. B. Foster, "The Christian Doctrine of Creation and the Rise of Modern Natural Science," *Mind*, Vol. xliii (1934), p. 448. The entire passage reads: "The general question arises: What is the source of the un-Greek elements which were imported into philosophy by the post-Reformation philosophers, and which constitute the modernity of modern philosophy? And the particular question, which is merely part of the general question repeated: What is the source of those un-Greek elements in the modern theory of nature by which the peculiar character of the modern science of nature was to be determined? The answer to the first question is: the Christian revelation, and the answer to the second: the Christian doctrine of creation."

[6] "To Hebrew thought, nature appears void of divinity" (Henri Frankfort, *Kingship and the Gods* [Chicago: University of Chicago Press, 1948], p. 343).

[7] E. A. Burtt shows how conceptions of God and His creative work derived from biblical tradition served to provide the metaphysical foundations of early modern science; see *The Metaphysical Foundations of Modern Physical Science* (New York: Harcourt Brace, 1932). See also John Baillie, *Natural Science and the Spiritual Life* (New York: Scribners, 1952), and A. N. Whitehead, *Adventures of Ideas* (New York: Macmillan, 1933), esp. pp. 154ff.

both in itself and instrumentally as technology. Man is put into the world to know it and to use his knowledge to fulfill the needs and purposes of human life. Recognizing this as the order of creation, biblical faith cannot yield an inch to the obscurantism that believes ignorance to be indispensable to piety or to the primitivism that holds the complexities of civilization to be a barrier between man and God. The Rechabites, it will be recalled, felt that wickedness had set in when men left the tents of the nomad for the fixed habitations of an agricultural civilization. Perhaps they were right, but they did not go back far enough: they should have deplored the lapse into civilization when men left the tree tops to live in tents! This kind of "Rousseauistic" primitivism will find no comfort in realistic biblical thought, which stands much closer to the secularist insistence on the value of science, pure and applied.

The acquisition of scientific knowledge must indeed be affirmed as a good, but it is not the *ultimate* good, as the devotees of "scientism" seem to believe. If scientific knowledge were the only real or worthwhile knowledge, and its acquisition the be-all and end-all of existence, what would there be to inhibit the medical scientist, for example, from pursuing his enterprise by vivisecting human beings? Why not, if science is ultimate? Certainly a great deal of genuine scientific knowledge, otherwise virtually unobtainable, could be gained thereby. If, nevertheless, we feel that human vivisection is *not* permissible, it must be because we recognize that the whole scientific enterprise stands under a higher law, and that scientific knowledge and its acquisition do not constitute the ultimate good. That is what biblical faith here asserts with its *no*.

Very much the same is true for science taken in its practical, or technological, aspect. A century ago, most forward-looking men saw in science and technology an unmixed blessing. They interpreted human misery as due primarily to the recalcitrance of nature, so that every technological achievement appeared to them as but another step in the overcoming of evil on the way to the earthly paradise that science would ultimately create. Today, we see things rather differently. Not only do we understand that the sources of human misery are far more complex and multidimensional than the nineteenth century believed, reflecting as they do the perversity of man and his social arrangements as well as the recalcitrance of nature; we have also learned to recognize the inescapable ambiguity of every human achievement, which has potentialities for evil as well as for good, for chaos as well as for cosmos, for destruction as well as for the enhancement of human welfare. The airplane and the atom bomb are ironic symbols of this ambiguity, and we would not now be standing in terror of bacteriological warfare had it not been for the great advances in medical research during the past fifty years. Scientific progress, like all human achievement, cuts two ways, and it is the purpose of the *no* that faith pronounces to warn against the perils that are generated out of the delusion of automatic salvation through science and technology. Science and technology are useful, very useful, but useful *in their place*, as part of a larger whole that goes beyond them and their presuppositions.

3. *Determinism*—Man's creaturely dependence on the world he lives in, and his subjection to the conditioning forces of his environment, are obviously implied in the biblical view of man and the world. The doctrine of determinism, as it relates to human beings, whatever else may be said about it, does at least repudiate the idealist notion that man, because of his spirit, somehow escapes the conditioning forces of nature. Man is a natural organism, though an organism of a unique kind with a unique dimension of existence; as a natural organism, he is subject to formative and conditioning influences at every level of nature, physical, biological, social, and psychological. In this area, too, the secular-scientific view comes closer to biblical teaching than does idealism or spiritualism, according to which man is essentially a discarnate soul outside of nature.

The creaturely conditionedness of human existence is something that the scientific emphasis on determinism will not permit us to forget. But the methodological principle of causal explanation which science employs cannot be converted into a metaphysical *total* determinism without self-contradiction and without doing violence to the freedom that makes man's existence specifically human. The *no* of faith in this area is a warning against extending the exhaustive determinism of the non-human world to man and his doings, which, though subject to all the conditioning of nature, nevertheless exhibit an inexpugnable element of self-transcending freedom.

4. *Relativism*—The conditionedness of all human life, to which I have just referred, gives a measure of justification also to the relativistic stress of modern thought. An understanding of man's creatureliness, particularity, and egocentricity, which lies at the heart of biblical faith, is surely enough to convince one that human thinking can never entirely transcend its *Sitz im Leben*. Men's thoughts and judgments are indeed in a real sense relative to the changing context of conditions and interests. Here again biblical faith must say *yes* to the secular view because it too is hostile to the absolutism which some types of relativism at least are concerned to challenge.

Relativism, like determinism, bears useful witness to the creatureliness of man. But again it is valid only up to a point; beyond that, once it is tempted to make total and absolute claims for itself, it becomes quite inevitably self-defeating. Intellectually, thoroughgoing relativism, like thoroughgoing determinism, is obviously self-contradictory. "All philosophies of universal relativity," as Carl Becker points out, "must be prepared at the appropriate moment to commit hara-kiri in deference to the ceaseless change which they postulate."[8] Practically, an attitude of total relativism generally ends up in a premature and arbitrary absolutism. Since nothing can be relative except in terms of something *not* relative, what the thoroughgoing relativist always does—quite unwillingly, of course—is to take something of this world, some conception, value, ideal, or institution, which he feels to be "obviously" good and true, and make that his absolute measure of everything else. "Man is the measure of all things": this battlecry of humanism sounds relativistic enough, but repeat it with a slightly different emphasis—"*Man* is the measure of all things"—and it becomes uncomfortably clear that what it proclaims is the deification of man, his absolutization into a fixed standard and measuring-rod for everything else in the universe![9]

The biblical *no* to total relativism is a *no* against idolatry, for the premature and arbitrary absolutization which is as characteristic of the thoroughgoing relativist as of the avowed absolutist is but an aspect of what the Bible knows as idolatry: the absolutization of the relative.

---

[8] Carl Becker, "Progress," *Encyclopedia of the Social Sciences*, XII, 499a.
[9] For a more detailed critique of scientism, determinism, and relativism, see Will Herberg, *Judaism and Modern Man* (New York, Farrar, Straus and Young, 1951), Ch. 3, and D. R. G. Owen, *op. cit.*

The biblical affirmation of *God-centered* faith cuts deep in two directions: on the one hand, it affirms God as absolute and therefore is compelled to reject every *total* relativism; on the other, it affirms God *alone* as absolute and therefore insists on the relativity of everything that is not God, of every institution, idea, or value, no matter how true or precious. The theocentric relativism of biblical faith thus preserves what is significant and vital in the relativistic emphasis, without permitting it to lapse into self-destroying absolutism. Once again, the biblical *no* sets limits which are much more than merely negative.

5. *Progressivism*—The biblical outlook emphatically rejects the Greek-Oriental view of time as "circular" and history as a succession of endlessly recurring cycles. Nor is it hospitable to the once almost equally widespread notion that the world is running down and things are getting consistently worse with the passage of time. The biblical world-view, in its messianic eschatology, sees all life and history headed for a great consummation in which all human enterprises will be judged and fulfilled and all existence redeemed. This "thirst for the future," this "futuristic" orientation, bears an obvious kinship to the idea of progress, as many historians of thought have indicated.

This kinship, however, harbors some very crucial differences. For the idea of progress does not merely take time and history seriously; it makes history—progress, evolution—into the vehicle of redemption and fulfilment, and here biblical faith must say *no*. To put such trust in history, which means to put such trust in man's power to save himself by and through his works in history, is utterly unwarranted. "We delude ourselves," the historian Arthur M. Schlesinger, Jr., states, "when we think that history teaches us that evil will be 'outmoded' by progress. . . . [This] is to misconceive and grotesquely to sentimentalize the nature of history. For history is not a redeemer promising to solve all human problems; nor is man capable of transcending the limitations of his being. Man generally is entangled in insoluble problems; history is consequently a tragedy in which we are all involved, whose keynote is anxiety and frustration, not progress and fulfilment."[10] Biblical faith endorses this realistic view from its own standpoint.

---

[10] Arthur M. Schlesinger, Jr., "The Causes of the Civil War: A Note on Historical Sentimentalism," *Partisan Review*, vol. xvi (Oct. 1949), No. 10.

What the ideology of progress has done is to secularize and truncate the biblical view of history. Instead of looking forward to a fulfilment of history beyond history through a power above history, the ideologists of progress see history fulfilling itself, in and through itself. They thus transform eschatology into utopia, the "thirst for the future" into the dangerous delusion that the future can be achieved and fixed in time through human effort. They do not see that, taken in its own terms, history remains ambiguous to the very end, and so far from solving the problems of human existence, it itself emerges as the crucial problem requiring solution, a solution beyond the power and resources of men in history.[11]

The ideologists of progress are persuaded to their utopianism by a misleading extension of the pattern of development of science and technology to the entire field of human affairs. Within their limited scope, science and technology are indeed "progressive"—that is, self-correcting and cumulative. But that is manifestly not the case with other aspects of the human enterprise, or with the human enterprise as a whole. The attempt to "manage" history by subjecting all experience to the pattern of progress is, from this point of view, but another aspect of "scientism," the tendency to universalize the scientific pattern and make it cover the whole of experience. Biblical faith, which sets limits to man's pretensions on every front, warns him that despite the vast resources with which science has equipped him, he remains a creature who must look to a power beyond his own for the ultimate meaning and fulfilment of life.

6. *Autonomy*—The autonomy which modern culture is so insistent on maintaining must be recognized as in some degree indispensable to the scientific-scholarly enterprise, as indeed it is indispensable to every enterprise of the human spirit. Biblical faith, in its theocentric emphasis on the sovereignty of God, must necessarily regard any thoroughgoing heteronomous claims on the part of earthly institutions or authorities as idolatrous usurpation. Heteronomy—subjection to alien, outside control—is never the will of God.

However legitimate may be the measure of autonomy that science,

---

[11] For a profound analysis of the problem of history and of the fallacy of liberal and Marxist utopianism, see Reinhold Niebuhr, *Faith and History* (New York: Scribners, 1949) and *The Irony of American History* (New York: Scribners, 1952).

like any other human enterprise, must have for its proper development, the claim to *total* autonomy that has been made in its name cannot stand criticism. For it is simply not true that science is a self-enclosed, self-validated, self-sufficient whole, with no dependence on anything beyond or outside itself. On the contrary, it is today generally understood that the entire scientific enterprise depends on assumptions and postulates that are essentially *extra*-scientific and that science must simply accept without being able to validate. "Even the most empirical scientist cannot avoid making assumptions of a metaphysical and epistemological sort;" these assumptions, indeed, "inevitably shape the nature of the descriptive concepts he uses, the phenomena he observes, and the way he collects his data."[12] Science is thus not a closed system, entirely sufficient unto itself; it is open at both ends—in its philosophical presuppositions as well as in its implications and consequences for human life.

It is important, moreover, to note that the presuppositions of science as well as the direction of its relevance to life are themselves rooted in affirmations of faith. This is true of the natural sciences, though in a more abstract sense,[13] but of the social sciences quite concretely, for the social or "human" sciences, in addition to the metaphysical and epistemological presuppositions of science as such, require certain specific "existential" presuppositions, defining the "image of man" and the concept of the good which enter into every structure of social thought. Science, particularly social science, therefore, necessarily raises the question of faith.

> No research in the social sciences [Clark Kerr and Lloyd Fisher state] can be free of value assumptions, and the claim that is sometimes made that the social sciences must eschew values if they are ever to rise above the level of ethical exhortation is always naive.

---

[12] Dorwin Cartwright, foreword to Kurt Lewin, *Field Theory in Social Science* (New York: Harpers, 1951), p. ix.

[13] However abstract, it is of course of decisive importance. "The basic assumption in modern science 'is a widespread, instinctive conviction in the existence of an Order of Things, and, in particular, of an Order of Nature' (A. N. Whitehead, *Science and the Modern World* [New York: Macmillan, 1925], pp. 5ff). This belief, this faith, for at least since Hume it must be recognized as such, is simply 'impervious to the demand for a consistent rationality' . . . [In scientific thought] the testimony of experiment is the ultimate criterion of truth, but the very notion of experiment is ruled out without the prior assumption that nature constitutes an intelligible order . . . Hence the assumption is final and absolute." Robert K. Merton, *Social Theory and Social Structure* (Glencoe, Ill.: Free Press, 1949), p. 335.

It is seldom a difficult task to discover the implicit values held in a theoretical system. . . .

It is not, therefore, a meaningful charge that Mayo and his followers are moralists. So are the economists. What is more disturbing in economist and plant sociologist alike is the effort to disguise these moral judgments as truths objectively deduced from observation or research, and the prescriptions which follow as the inevitable consequences of a neutral set of facts. . . . The charge [of the plant sociologist] against those who do not share [his] vision cannot be, therefore, that they are blind to facts, but rather that they are of the *wrong religion* and worship *false gods* (our italics).[14]

What Kerr and Fisher, two distinguished economists and sociologists, are here saying is that at the bottom of one of the major controversies in contemporary social science lies not so much a conflict over facts as a basic difference over fundamental outlook which they themselves describe in religious terms. Faith and secular learning are here mutually involved in a very obvious way, and so they are, in one way or another, in every aspect of science. The total autonomy of science, once so axiomatic to the modern mind, is simply delusive.[15]

III. HETERONOMY—AUTONOMY—THEONOMY

The *no* of faith to the claims and pretensions of the scientific-scholarly culture is thus primarily an insistence on the limited character of these claims and a warning against the disastrous consequences, intellectual and practical, of ignoring or overpassing the proper limits. But the final word of faith cannot remain on this negative note. Faith must indeed emphasize its double negation—neither medieval heteronomy nor modern autonomy, neither subjection to an alien control nor self-absolutization—but beyond this double negation it must pass on to its essential affirmation: *theonomy*.

What does theonomy really imply in the relation between faith

---

[14] Clyde Kerr and Lloyd Fisher, *Plant Sociology: The Elite and the Aborigines* (unpublished paper).

[15] Autonomy in the narrower sense—the notion that each discipline constitutes an autonomous field to be cultivated by autonomous specialists—is equally delusive, if taken in any absolute sense. It originally emerged in early modern times on the basis of the supposition, sometimes explicitly stated, that God's "invisible hand" could be trusted to bring harmony out of the diverse and unrelated activities of specializing scholars and scientists. Some time in the late eighteenth century, God dropped out of the picture, but the implicit belief in ultimate harmony remained. The autonomy then became self-validating!

and secular learning? This question may perhaps best be answered by a brief inquiry as to the kind of service each can render to the other. What can secular learning do for faith? It obviously cannot create or even "prove" faith. It can, however, provide the intellectual material of which faith must make use in its attempt to illumine human existence, as well as the technical power it must employ in serving God in the affairs of the world. Much more difficult is the question as to what faith can do for secular learning. Negatively, it is clear that no faith, not even the purest and most mature, can serve as a substitute for science and scholarship in the sense of supplying the empirical facts about the world. Nothing can replace science and scholarship in their field of competence. Scripture and other documents of faith do indeed contain much factual information of an astronomical, geological, geographical, and historical character, but in this respect these documents constitute not the revelation of God, but rather the time-bound, culturally conditioned vehicle of revelation. Faith cannot provide us with the empirical facts; only science and scholarship can do that. What is it, then, that faith can do in relation to secular learning?

The most direct and perhaps the most important way in which faith is relevant to secular learning is by providing it with a standpoint from which the mind's tendency towards premature absolutization can be detected and resisted. Here we touch upon something fundamental in human existence. Man's creatureliness, combined with his egocentricity, tend to limit and distort the operations of his reason: his creatureliness compels him to see everything from his finite perspective; his egocentricity makes him, quite unwittingly, prone to interpret everything he sees in terms of his own ideas, desires, and interests. But being human, he is also driven to universalize his partial understanding and to claim undue validity for his inescapably relative insights. There thus arises a tendency towards idolatrous fixation in the intellectual life analogous to what we know in the moral sphere, and a tendency to make some relative standpoint absolute and to distort reality in order to suit the false perspective thus generated. We are all acquainted with some of the more familiar manifestations of this mechanism under the names of ideology and rationalization; its operations go deep and subtly affect life and thought at every level.[16] We cannot, remaining human, altogether escape its influence, but we may recognize and offer permanent resistance to it. That is what biblical faith helps us do. It helps us do this by reminding us that everything in this world is relative and stands under the judgment of God, so that we must not accept any human perspective as fixed and final. Insofar as it is operative in intellectual life, this kind of faith tends to untwist human reason and free it from its idolatrous fixations; in this sense, it helps give thought a true perspective. It is not that it eliminates the necessity for presuppositions in science; presupposition-less thinking is quite impossible. What it does rather is to place all presuppositions under criticism and judgment and refuse to grant any of them more than a limited and qualified validity. The presuppositions of science are necessary and valid in their place; but once they are converted into absolutes, valid for all reality, they become false and destructive. Not only science but every enterprise of the human spirit falls under this limitation. Here we have the first aspect of the the-onomy of biblical faith in its relation to secular learning.

At the same time, biblical faith, with its profound view of the meaning of existence, can contribute to the presuppositions that go into the making of scientific-scholarly thinking and to the formation of principles and standards to guide the application of science and schol-arship to human life. We have already seen how intimately the attitude to the empirical world defined in the biblical doctrine of creation enters into the presuppositions of the entire scientific enterprise. In the so-called "human" sciences, the relevance is more obvious, for these sciences rest on assumptions about man which are plainly related to questions of ultimate *Weltanschauung*. Thinking that is theonomous will always strive to see the world in both its reality and its contingency, and man in the tension of his self-transcending existence as creature who is yet in some sense creator and therefore ever prone to forget his creaturely limitations. An entire philosophical anthropology is implied in this formulation, and some sort of philosophical anthro-pology is implied in every science of man. Biblical faith offers one that

---

[16] "All human knowledge is tainted with an 'ideological' taint. It pretends to be more than it is. It is finite knowledge gained from a particular perspective, but it pre-tends to be final and ultimate knowledge" (Reinhold Niebuhr, *The Nature and Destiny of Man* [New York: Scribners, 1941], vol. i, p. 194).

is both comprehensive and profoundly realistic in its grasp of human existence in all its dimensions.[17]

The interpretation of the results of science and their relation to human life is obviously something that goes beyond science itself. Science defines no structure of meaning and yields no scale of values. It is, as Bertrand Russell points out, "ethically neutral; it assures men that they can perform wonders, but it does not tell them what wonders to perform."[18] What "wonders" to perform, what to do with the vast power science gives us, is a matter of moral responsibility, and moral responsibility points directly to faith. On this level, theonomy implies a God-centered ethic, grounded in the prophetic vision of divine vocation and judgment.[19]

As long as culture and learning remain unanchored in theonomous faith, they will oscillate endlessly between the two poles of autonomy and heteronomy. Only theonomy can break the vicious circle and save human thought from forever stumbling from a heteronomy against which it revolts to an autonomy which it cannot bear, and back again. Only theonomy can provide a standpoint from which this false alternative can in principle be transcended, and the valid insights of both reconciled. Every human interest, every form of human creativity, must be granted its proper freedom and its immunity from alien domination: this is the truth in autonomy. But if it is to realize itself, it must come to recognize the inherent limitations and relativities of its position and renounce all pretensions to ultimacy, totality, and absoluteness. It cannot, therefore, be a law unto itself, but must somehow recognize a higher regulative principle: this is the truth of heteronomy. The two may be reconciled only if this higher regulative principle is

---

[17] The classical statement for our time of the biblical understanding of man is Reinhold Niebuhr's Gifford lectures, *The Nature and Destiny of Man* (New York: Scribners, 1941, 1943), 2 vols. Of this work, Arthur M. Schlesinger, Jr., has declared: "[Reinhold Niebuhr succeeds] in restating Christian insights with such irresistible relevance to contemporary experience that even those who have no decisive faith in the supernatural find their reading of experience and of history given new and significant dimensions." *Christianity and Society*, vol. xiv (1949), No. 3.

[18] Bertrand Russell, *A History of Western Philosophy* (New York: Simon and Schuster, 1945), p. 494.

[19] A statement of a realistic biblical ethic of responsibility, with particular relevance to politics and social life, will be found in Reinhold Niebuhr, *An Interpretation of Christian Ethics* (New York: Harpers, 1935) and *Moral Man and Immoral Society* (New York: Scribners, 1932); also John C. Bennett, *Christian Ethics and Social Policy* (New York: Scribners, 1946).

seen to be the divine law, transcending every human formulation of it, but ultimately identical with the true law of man's own being. In acknowledging the sovereignity of God, man acknowledges no alien law and subjects himself to no outside control, but he knows, nevertheless, that he is not his own master, that he thinks, as he lives, by the grace of God and under His continuing judgment. In the last analysis, the theonomous principle means the recognition that in our intellectual life, too, we are saved by faith.

Theonomy cannot be institutionalized, for the moment theonomy is embodied in an institution which pretends to proclaim the divine law, it becomes heteronomy. But just as the constitutionalism of the democratic state is, in effect, an institutional recognition of the sovereignty of God and an institutional barrier to the usurping claims of men,[20] so it is conceivable that the theonomous claim may be given some sort of indirect but nonetheless effective institutional expression in the structuring of culture and the organization of higher education. But when all is said and done, theonomy remains a transcendent principle, not a third option to autonomy and heteronomy, but standing over all cultural forms and systems as an eternal assertion of the will, judgment, and redeeming grace of God.

---

[20] For a development of this conception of constitutional democracy, see Reinhold Niebuhr, *The Children of Light and the Children of Darkness* (New York: Scribners, 1944), and Will Herberg, *op. cit.*, Ch. 14, "Society, State, and the Individual."

Can Social Problems Be Solved?

LISTON POPE

---------------------------- ✳ ----------------------------

LISTON POPE *is Dean and Professor of Social Ethics at the Yale Divinity School. A graduate of Duke University and Yale University, he has for many years been a leader in the field of social action. He has also written widely, including the volumes* MILLHANDS AND PREACHERS *and* LABOR'S RELATION TO CHURCH AND COMMUNITY, *as well as numerous essays.*

To QUESTION whether social problems can be solved would have seemed a strange and defeatist procedure to many of our forebears at the beginning of the twentieth century. For the most part, the new century was greeted with enthusiasm and unbounded social hope. Technological and industrial achievements were visibly improving the material basis of life. Autocratic government was on the defensive and freedom was in the air. The age-old dreams of peace and prosperity were coming true. The three greatest social philosophers of the nineteenth century—Comte, Marx, and Herbert Spencer—had agreed in their various ways that war was anachronistic and that an ultimate form of human community would soon be realized. Progress was regarded as inevitable and social evolution would bring the solution of all important social problems.

The general optimism was widely shared and promulgated by religious leaders. The editor of a religious journal looked to the new era with such confidence that in 1900 he renamed his periodical *The Christian Century*. Horace Bushnell and his colleagues had challenged the doctrine of human depravity and had inculcated faith in man's possibilities, though seldom so unreservedly as had their philosophical predecessors of the eighteenth century. The spokesmen of the Social Gospel movement rejoiced in the social prospects, often without reservations. Washington Gladden declared in 1893:

Our laws are to be christianized; the time is coming when they will express the perfect justice and the perfect beneficence of the Christian law. . . . The administration of justice is to be christianized. . . . Doubtless this millennial perfection of state is a great way off, but it is the goal toward which we are journeying. . . .[1]

Two years later the Reverend George D. Herron was even more confident:

The political appearing of Christ is . . . more than a vision, and no dream, but the accomplished fact with which nations and institutions must begin to reckon, and the distinction and glory of our age.[2]

Walter Rauschenbusch was generally more cautious than other spokesmen for the Social Gospel, but he shared the basic optimism about social possibilities:

Even a Christian social order cannot mean perfection. As long as men are flesh and blood the world can be neither sinless nor painless. . . . But within the limitations of human nature I believe that the constitutional structure of the social order can be squared with the demands of Christian morality.[3]

Rauschenbusch considered that many spheres of society in the United States had already been christianized: the family, the Church, education, and the political life. The economic order was the principal citadel still uncaptured but it was under heavy assault from the working class: "If the banner of the Kingdom of God is to enter through the gates of the future, it will have to be carried by the tramping hosts of labor."[4]

The social expectations of the Social Gospel leaders were not untypical of the age. Francis G. Peabody summarized the outlook in America during the first decade of this century in saying that "never before were so many people concerned with the amelioration of social conditions and the realization of social dreams."[5] The organization of the Methodist Federation for Social Service in 1907 and the Federal

---

[1] Washington Gladden, *Tools and the Man* (Boston and New York: 1893), p. 17.
[2] George D. Herron, *The Christian State* (New York: 1895), p. 32.
[3] Walter Rauschenbusch, *Christianizing the Social Order* (New York: 1912), pp. 126, 127.
[4] Walter Rauschenbusch, *op. cit.*, p. 449.
[5] Francis G. Peabody, *The Approach to the Social Question* (New York: 1909), p. 2.

Council of Churches in 1908 reflected these purposes and gave institutional form to efforts for their realization.

Social optimism surmounted the shock of the First World War, which was quickly interpreted as a war to end wars. It persisted through the intoxication of the Twenties, and was only somewhat benumbed and muted by the depression of the Thirties—which produced a major crop of panaceas.

The Second World War and the postwar legacy of confusion and uncertainty have dispelled the dreams and dimmed the hopes. Most acute social diagnosticians now are cynics of one stripe or another. Egregious blunders in high places are accepted apathetically. Corruption and venality are campaign issues and front-page stories, but there seems to be little expectation that they can be eliminated. Polls indicate that a majority of the American people believe there will always be wars. Solutions for social ills are viewed skeptically and programs of social action in the churches are generally on the defensive. There appears to be widespread acceptance of the "ninth beatitude" of Alexander Pope: "Blessed is he who expects nothing, for he shall never be disappointed."

The climate of hope has changed likewise in religious circles. A soberer estimate of man and of social possibilities has replaced the buoyant expectations at the turn of the century. The humanist, anti-theological mood of the Social Gospel movement has been shattered by the reiterated assertion that man is a sinner. Utopianism and perfectionism are in theological disrepute. Hope is defined in eschatological rather than sociological terms.

Belief in progress toward perfection has been reduced to the more modest hope for proximate justice. Use of the phrase "the Kingdom of God on earth" betrays the fact that the user is an outmoded liberal, either uninformed about recent trends or else stiff-necked and incurable. The Kingdom of God is not an ideal social structure; rather, it is the reign of God despite man's sin or the power of God over all things. Jesus was not an ethical teacher or the architect of a new society; He was One Sent, He is the Christ.

In part the more cautious estimate of social possibilities is derived from the revival of interest in theology and the recapture of ancient

Christian insights that had been largely discarded between 1850 and 1930. In part it has resulted from the collapse of a number of fond crusades such as prohibition, pacifism, and socialism, and from complete disenchantment about "the significant Russian experiment." Forms and vitalities of social injustice are seen to be more intransigent and perennial than had been assumed, and the complexities of social problems at the present time are baffling. The explanations of social evil by Rousseau (bad institutions) and Marx (the one institution of private property) are rejected as oversimple, and reliance on good will and love as social solvents is regarded as naive. All social movements and reforms are designated as ambivalent and each social achievement is hailed with the suspicion that it contains within itself the seeds of new problems.

No person has been more influential than Reinhold Niebuhr in changing the climate of opinion regarding social possibilities. Combining in a rather unique way the heritage of the American Social Gospel movement and the more recent insights of European theology, he has recalled the churches to their Christian foundations and has challenged them to social responsibility. He has warned that every human achievement is tentative and ambiguous but has insisted (as against Barth in particular) that:

> The certainty of the final inadequacy of every form of human justice must not lead to defeatism in our approach to the perplexing problems of social justice in our day. The possibilities as well as the limits of every scheme of justice must be explored.[6]

Professor Niebuhr clearly holds that social problems are not capable of ultimate solution. This conviction appears in many of his writings; it has been stated with special clarity in a discussion of the problem of race prejudice:

> A democratic society must . . . seek proximate solutions for this problem in indeterminate creative ventures. But the solutions will be more, rather than less, creative if democratic idealists understand the depth of the problem with which they are dealing . . . There is no unprejudiced mind and no judgment which is not, at least partially, corrupted by pride . . . Upon the basis of such a presupposition we could work indeterminately on many proximate

---

[6] Reinhold Niebuhr, "We Are Men and Not God," in *The Christian Century*, October 27, 1948, p. 1140.

solutions for the problem of ethnic pluralism. Our knowledge that there is no complete solution for the problem would save us from resting in some proximate solution under the illusion that it is an ultimate one.[7]

Choice of this particular quotation from Professor Niebuhr poses the issue of the solubility of social problems at one of the most serious and difficult levels, since no social problem (with the exception of war) is so elusive and deep-seated as that of racial discrimination. A great deal depends in this matter on careful definition of terms. Ethnocentrism has been a perennial feature of inter-group relations. But racial prejudice, in the sense of pride in the superior physical and intellectual quality of one's own breed and scorn of a different breed, has not been. Much ethnocentrism appears in the biblical narratives, especially in the Old Testament, but the concept of "race" is so lacking that the Bible contains no specific teaching on the question. Group differences were conceived in terms of accent (shibboleth) or other cultural characteristics and most profoundly in terms of the relation of the group to its God or gods. The few references in the Bible to "race" pertain to a course to be run and the concept of "blood" is not equivalent to the latter-day definition of race.

As a matter of fact, the notion of "race" is relatively recent and patterns of discrimination simply on grounds of race are only a few centuries old. *Race* discrimination as such belongs principally to the last century. Racial differences probably were not chronologically primitive, and there is little warrant for making the conception of race ontologically primitive and sociologically ineradicable.

Even when the idea of race is prevalent in a society, its definition varies from group to group and from time to time, and the patterns of social behavior associated with it assume highly diverse forms. Comparative studies of racial segregation and interaction, now only in their infancy, will illuminate the vast differences in definition and behavior associated with the idea, and will seriously challenge the doctrine that the phenomenon is intrinsically and permanently embedded in nature or human nature and that there is therefore no ultimate solution for it.

The race problem has not been solved in the United States. But

[7] Reinhold Niebuhr, *The Children of Light and the Children of Darkness* (New York: Scribners, 1944), pp. 144, 145.

the problem of exclusion of Negroes from state universities is hastening toward solution. The problem of segregation based on color is disappearing rapidly in the United States as decades of inter-racial mating blur the color spectrum. The problem of admitting Negro baseball players to the big leagues has been virtually solved. Many other such examples might be given, as a virtual revolution is currently taking place in American race relations. It may be that "solutions" are precarious and that the old abuses will return in the future; one can only speculate—and rather idly—about contingencies as yet unrevealed. Meanwhile, certain problems appear to have been disposed of rather effectively.

A comparable analysis could be made of various other social problems. Slavery, once regarded as an evil of the first magnitude, has been eliminated from most nations of the world. The reëmergence of forced labor poses a fresh problem, but it can hardly be designated as identical in structure or content with the former institution of legalized slavery.

The problem of the colonial system is rapidly being solved. According to Ralph Bunche, a dozen years ago there were 750,000,000 people in the world under colonial rule, but today there are barely 200,000,000. The problem of foreign domination of less-developed peoples is by no means solved for the world; it has been disposed of, and probably for good, in many particular instances. For the emancipated peoples, this problem has been solved; other problems have arisen, and the joys of freedom are always precarious in the world, but the old problem has been put behind. To be sure, new imperialisms have emerged during the last decade as Communism has built its own system of satellite peoples. But the questions posed by the new forms of dominion are not identical with those of the colonial period.

As these examples illustrate, a social problem, when recognized as such, is always defined in cultural and relative terms and these terms are often capable of resolution and disposition. A social problem is not to be equated with the basic stuff of human nature or despaired of because man is a sinner. It may result from sin or be a manifestation of sin, but it is recognizable as a *social* problem only when it emerges as social behavior and accumulates social form and content with all the relativities and impermanence of any social structure. The traits of man, viewed psychologically or theologically, may or may not be comparatively fixed and uniform. But social problems manifest pluralism and wide fluctuation, and close study of their endless variety discourages monolithic and deductive interpretations of them.

Sin is perennial but it is not a social problem. It emerges into many diverse social problems, each of which may in itself be capable of final solution or of transformation beyond recognition. Efforts to explain particular social problems in terms of sin are generally fruitless, as it is a *tour de force* to describe a transitory and sporadic form of social behavior (for example, war) in terms of a presumably continual and permanent human characteristic or perversity. If sin inevitably causes war, why do we not have continual war?

War as socially organized violence appeared rather late in the evolution of culture, at the stage loosely called barbarism; it has by no means been a universal aspect of human existence. Have there then been men without sin? The Dutch were once very warlike; in recent centuries they have been comparatively peaceful; has their sinfulness been overcome or lessened? If war be defined as only a special organization of violence, and it be argued that there has always been violence, it can be replied that particular forms of violence have been overcome in human affairs and war in its present form may at length be subject to a similar outcome—though the vast complexities and impersonalities involved in it render this prospect implausible in the foreseeable future.

Probably both the unbounded optimism of 1900 and the limited pessimism at mid-century should be discounted. Neither progress nor problems should be accepted as absolute. The recent reaction against the superficial utopianism and perfectionism of fifty years ago has produced a more realistic and sober attitude toward human possibilities. It may provoke a counter-reaction if it despairs of human tasks and opportunities.

There is no support from history or from scrutiny of human nature for the hope that *all* social problems will ultimately be solved, in the sense that a society without problems will emerge. But there are adequate grounds for the belief that particular social problems can be solved once and for all. Society is a fluid, ever-changing realm; new problems generally resemble former ones but they are never quite the same. To lose heart about an immediate problem is defeatist; to suppose that it will have no successor is fatuous.

Words from Professor Gilbert Murray, addressed to a different question, may provide a proper charter for the mid-century Christian who faces the perplexing social problems of his day:

> There is no royal road in these matters. . . . It is as much a failure of nerve to reject blindly for fear of being a fool, as to believe blindly for fear of missing some emotional stimulus. . . . The uncharted surrounds us on every side and we must needs have some relation towards it . . . careful not to neglect the real needs of men and women through basing our life on dreams; and remembering above all to walk gently in a world where the lights are dim and the very stars wander.[8]

[8] Gilbert Murray, *Four Stages of Greek Religion* (New York: Columbia University Press, 1912), pp. 152-153.

Christian Faith and Social Action

REINHOLD NIEBUHR

———————————————— ✳ ————————————————

REINHOLD NIEBUHR, *to whom this volume is dedicated, has since 1930*
been Professor of Applied Christianity at Union Seminary. After studying
at Elmhurst College, Eden Theological Seminary, and Yale Divinity
School, he was for many years pastor of a church in Detroit. Through his
writing, speaking and teaching, he has exercised wide influence upon
American social thought, and upon religious thought throughout the
world. Important among his innumerable articles and books are MORAL
MAN AND IMMORAL SOCIETY, AN INTERPRETATION OF CHRISTIAN ETHICS,
THE NATURE AND DESTINY OF MAN, FAITH AND HISTORY, *and* THE IRONY
OF AMERICAN HISTORY.

THE essays of this volume are all written by members of a small group,
the Frontier Fellowship, which has since been absorbed into a larger
organization, Christian Action. The main concern of the smaller, as of
the larger, group was to find the most effective way of bringing testimony to the Christian faith in the affairs of human society, for the
achievement of economic and political justice.

A history of this group, as excellently portrayed by Professor
Hutchison in the initial chapter of this volume, will serve as a telling
parable of the basic problem. The parable lies in the relation of the
original convictions of the group and in the development of those
convictions in the two decades of its life.

The group was originally concerned to establish a viable Christian
social ethic. It conceived its task to require refutation of four alternative positions. These positions were 1) The standpoint of Protestant
pietistic individualism, according to which there is no obligation or
necessity to change the social and political structures in the interest
of a higher justice. It was regarded as unnecessary partly because these

structures were interpreted as eternal "laws of nature" which make for justice, and partly because right individual conduct is supposed to be more important than any social structure. This position was judged the most indefensible of all allegedly Christian positions because it combined a naturalistic version of human society with a highly individualistic version of the Christian faith. It was, nevertheless, the dominant attitude of American Protestantism until the Social Gospel rescued the Church from its influence. It has achieved a new relevance in this latter day, in which war and post-war armament expenditures have been able to obscure the inherent problems of a free economy and thus encouraged the American business community to a new complacency. Yet it does not hold this position with a completely good conscience and it seeks whatever support, religious and otherwise, it can find for it. 2) The second position which the Fellowship challenged was a vague Christian or secular moralism, which was uneasy about the social realities of an industrial society but assumed that any injustices could be cured by persuading the society to govern its relations by the "ideals of love." This position was really the moralistic wing of the Social Gospel and was not very distinct from secular moralism. Frequently it expressed itself in terms of pacifistic socialism. It hoped to achieve collectivism without the class struggle or without any serious dislocations and conflicts. It was against this position that the Fellowship emphasized the Christian doctrine of original sin. In terms of social theory, this implied the inevitability of tensions of interest and conflict in human affairs. The idea of the progressive perfectability of man was rejected as a secular corruption of the Christian faith and as in manifest conflict with the realities of history. 3) The third Christian position in which the Fellowship felt itself in conflict was that of historic Catholicism's idea of a "Christian civilization" and of "Christian politics." According to this position, the Christian Church, though one among other political forces in the world, made the pretension that it was, not one among other forces, but a redemptive overarching force. The Fellowship felt that such a pretension was theologically and religiously unsound, for it created an idolatrous force in the name of Christianity. We also believed that its political unsoundness was proved by the realities of Latin politics whether in Italy or Argentine. 4) A fourth position deserves special consideration for thereby hangs our tale. It was the position which the Fellowship espoused and from which it gradually retreated, though the degree of the retreat is still a matter of debate. It is, broadly speaking, the socialist alternative in politics. In an original statement of principles the Fellowship declared that it was "committed to the belief that the social ownership of the natural resources and the basic means of production is a primary requisite of justice in a technical age." It justified this conviction by the fairly orthodox Marxist analysis that "capitalism in its inevitable contracting phase subordinates the needs of the masses to the preservation and enhancement of a steadily narrowing class of owners." Those words were written twenty years ago and give a fairly accurate picture of the convictions of the socially sensitive part of the Christian Church of the early days of the New Deal.

It must be added immediately that the Fellowship did not espouse Marxism or even socialism without reservation. It called itself a Fellowship of Socialist Christians to emphasize by its use of adjective and noun the primacy of its Christian, rather than socialist, convictions. And it insisted that it objected to socialist philosophies on "empirical grounds as well as on Christian grounds because of the danger of collectivism, mutilating organic forms of social life by coercing them into mechanical moulds." It also repudiated the optimism of the Marxist belief "that a new mechanism of ownership will eliminate all conflict in the world and solve all the problems of the human spirit." In short, it rejected Marxism as a guaranteed solution of the socio-ethical problem and objected even more to the religious pretensions of Marxism. These reservations could be regarded as fairly shrewd anticipations of what history actually proved to be the monstrous errors of Marxism. Yet the anticipations were not too profound, and the Christian understanding of the relativity of all socio-political systems not too discerning. The depth and degree of corruption which Communism would create on the basis of orthodox Marxism was not fully anticipated, though the Fellowship followed this disillusioning development with clear eyes and challenged the poor deluded Christian Stalinists who confused the conscience of the Church with their loyalty to the tortuous processes of Stalinist politics, step by step.

More significantly, however, the weaknesses of parliamentary or democratic socialism were not fully understood. It was not realized that even a democratic socialism might face problems of preserving incentives in a completely collectivist economy and would betray the perils of the concentration of economic and political power in the hands of a bureaucracy even when held in a democratic framework.

In a revision of its Statement, issued in 1946, the Fellowship declared: "Our understanding of socialism has undergone progressive modification due to a deepening of our theological convictions, a gradual assimilation of European experience through our émigré members, a close observation of the Soviet development, and our experience with the American communist party." While still believing that "most strategic centers of economic power must be socialized," it nevertheless expressed fear of too great concentration of power "through state intervention" and therefore asked for the creation of autonomous public agencies such as the TVA. "We are deeply aware," the statement continues, "that economic collectivism may be achieved at the price of losing democracy in the social and political sphere." Here we have the consequence of our tragic contemporary history upon the Christian conscience, as indeed upon the conscience of the modern world. What seemed to be a fairly clear alternative to the injustices of a free economy has turned out to be not only worse than the disease for which it was meant to be the cure; but a disease of such virulent proportions as to threaten our whole world with disaster.

Thus the fact that socialism could not be unequivocally espoused, which the Fellowship hinted at even in its earliest years, became a certainty in the present situation. This certainty has not only called any intimate relation between Christianity and socialism into question. It has also made the whole question of a Christian social ethics more problematic. We cannot doubt that Christians must make their decisions about political and economic alternatives with a sense of responsibility to the divine Will as revealed in Christ. But the question is whether there are any criteria whereby we can judge between alternative movements. The love which is the final criteria is obviously a principle of criticism upon all political and economic realities, since it reveals the sinful element of self-seeking and of coercive restraint in all forms of human community. But does it help us to arrive at discriminate choices between alternative systems since all of them have morally ambiguous elements in them? In the field of economic life, self-seeking, about which one must have an ultimate scruple, must be immediately used and harnessed for proximate purposes. In the field of politics, power which may be provisionally useful in establishing tolerable harmonies of life may become, if unrestrained, the instrument of tyranny and oppression.

Since there is moral ambiguity in every possible political and economic position (derived from the fact that self-interest and power must be used and manipulated despite the perils to justice and to order which they may bear within themselves under certain conditions) it would seem that the first duty of Christian faith is to preserve a certain distance between the sanctities of faith and the ambiguities of politics. This is to say that it is the duty of a Christian in politics to have no specific "Christian politics." The Christian politics based upon concepts of justice derived from an eternal natural law have been a source of error because relative historical judgments, prompted by interest and passion have been insinuated into the sanctity of eternal law. The Christian politics of Protestant individualism is even more unsatisfactory because it regarded the competitive struggle in a modern bourgeois-capitalistic society as a simple instrument of justice and obscured the disproportions of power and resulting injustices in the system. The Christian politics of a moralistic socialism, on the other hand, hid the power-realities of a collectivist state behind the concept of "cooperation" interpreted as Christian love. In every case religious sanctities confused rather than clarified the picture. Sometimes they are the screen for particular interests, as, for instance, when a feudal nobility or a modern business oligarchy appeal to the eternal standards of natural law or natural rights to justify their power and privilege. Sometimes they are meant to hide the tension between the purity of the ultimate and the complexity of the immediate situation, as, for instance, when a coercive political arrangement is pictured as an embodiment of the principle of love.

I. THE POSITIVE ANSWER

But this exclusion of the religious element from pragmatic decisions is only a negative determinant of a Christian approach to the economic and political order. How shall we find a positive answer?

The basic presupposition of a positive answer must lie in a Christian understanding of the realities of man's social life. It is wrong to interpret these realities in purely cynical terms or in purely idealistic ones. It is important to recognize an admixture of self-seeking in every form of human togetherness and also in every strategy of government required to prevent competitive self-seeking from degenerating into anarchy. We cannot (as does classical liberalism) regard the self-seeking which a bourgeois-liberal economy permits as completely harmless; and we cannot, as does orthodox Protestantism, particularly Lutheranism, be uncritical toward the coercive power of government on the ground that God ordained it to prevent anarchy. For both the economic power which competes in the market place and the political power, which sets restraints upon the competition, are tainted by motives other than the desire for justice. On the other hand, it would be wrong to be too cynical about this admixture of self-interest in all the vital forces of society. Men do have a residual capacity for justice. Government does express the desire of a community for order and justice; and not merely the will-to-power of the oligarchy which controls the engines of power in government. An attitude which avoids both sentimentality and cynicism must obviously be grounded in a Christian view of human nature which is schooled by the Gospel not to take the pretensions of men at their face value, on the one hand, and, on the other, not to deny the residual capacity for justice among even sinful men.

If this be the general attitude of circumspection it follows that no political decision can be reached in terms of merely broad principles, whether of "freedom" or "justice" or "planning." The evils which have developed from communist pretensions are a reminder and proof of the fact that the worst evils of history are derived not from pure selfishness but from self-interest clothed in the pretensions of ideals. Western society has been in virtual civil war between the middle-class proponents of free economy and the proletarian proponents of a collectivist one. Each creed obviously contains a mixture of truth and error. Property is not as simply the servant of justice as the liberal creed assumes and not as simply the basis of all evil as the Marxist creed avers. The power of the state is not as dangerous as the liberal creed imagines and not as beneficent as collectivist theory assumes. The damage to society is being done by general programs, serving as weapons of warring groups and classes.

It is important to understand this baneful effect of general and abstract programs upon the social life of man. Two reasons may be given why evil flows from these too inclusive and abstract programs. 1) These generalizations fail to take the endless contingencies of history into account. 2) General programs and panaceas are stubbornly held and not easily amended by empirical data for two reasons: (a) They tend to be a screen for particular interests in society and as their weapons in social controversy. Thus medieval conceptions of natural law were used by the aristocratic classes to put the rising middle class at a moral disadvantage; and modern "natural rights" concepts were used with similar purpose by the bourgeois classes to prove that a system of "natural liberty," which would be to their advantage, was in accord with the "laws of nature" and of "nature's God;" and the modern industrial classes are generally inclined to view processes, defined as "historical dialectic," as giving a kind of cosmic support to their particular struggle in society. (b) Panaceas do not, however, merely hide special economic or social interests. They may have another purpose which is of particular concern for students of morals and religion. They tend to obscure the tension between individual and social morality. This tension is a serious problem for all religiously sensitive individuals. The social order is involved in collective forms of egotism, in injustices, in conflicts of self-interest, and in subordinations of life to life which are an affront to the sensitive conscience. There is, therefore, a strong tendency to develop "ideologies of conscience" as well as ideologies of interest. The middle classes eased their conscience by the conviction that the "natural system of liberty" would make for justice in the long run even if in the short run it manifested obvious injustices. When this failed to materialize it was a natural inclination of the religious conscience to invest a collectivist alternative with more moral capital that it did not deserve. This was done primarily by contrasting the "motives of service" which were supposed to rule the collectivist order as against the "motives of profit" in the old order. A certain taint of this moral ideology is evident in the earlier pronouncements of our Fellowship, and indeed in all pronouncements of the Christian left. The ideology obscured the fact that no form of social organization could eliminate the "profit motive" insofar as it stood for particular interest as opposed to "general" or universal interest. What was defined as the profit motive was, as a matter of fact, not purely individual interest but usually concern for the family. Not only were particular interests likely to include concern for the family rather than the self but they were also not purely economic since they might express desire for prestige and power rather than gain. Furthermore, the "general" interest is not simply universal. It is most generally national. Certainly the Marxist doctrine that the socialization of property would destroy national self-interest has been refuted not only by Russian nationalistic-imperialism but by the display of national self-interest in the mildest social European states. Thus it is obvious that this moralistic ideology of the Christian as well as the secular left, tended to obscure moral perplexities in man's social life which are perennial and not merely the fruit of capitalism or any other form of social organization.

II. THE NECESSITY OF DECISION

The rational, moral, and religious defects of general political and social and economic programs, does not justify the conclusion that no moral choice between general programs is possible and that only pragmatic approaches to detailed problems of justice are legitimate. General decisions must be made at particular points in history. It was, for instance, morally right as well as historically inevitable that the rising middle classes should have challenged the organic cohesions and the traditional authorities of monarchial absolutism in the early part of the modern period. The bourgeois movement destroyed the monopoly of political power by espousing democracy against monarchism. And it released vast new energies by supporting a system of "natural liberty" against mercantilism and other forms of political restraint upon economic life.

It is just as right and inevitable that the sensitive conscience should now support programs for bringing economic power under state control and for insisting upon certain minimal welfare standards in housing, social security, education. The fact that it has been necessary to shift from the emphasis upon liberty to the emphasis upon mutual responsibility and political restraint upon economic power, proves the historical relativity of all socio-moral choices. The "sweetest things turn sourest by their deeds" and the virtues of one era become the vices of the next. The shift in emphasis was necessary because justice did not flow as inevitably from liberty as the earlier bourgeois creed assumed. It did not do so because modern industrial society develops more serious disproportions of power in the economic sphere than had been anticipated; and these disproportions of power are more destructive of justice than had been assumed by a creed which understood the relation of power to interest and justice so little. But by the same token the creed by which this shift in emphasis was accomplished must also be re-examined in the light of historical experience. Nothing is more important and tragic in contemporary history than that the Marxist alternative to capitalistic injustice should have generated so much more terrible evils than Capitalism itself. But these communist evils are only vivid revelations of a general defect in collectivist theories. If the libertarian creed failed to anticipate the disproportions of power in modern economic society, the collectivist creeds failed to anticipate the moral perils in a system which compounded political and economic power in a single oligarchy. It also failed to provide for sufficient local and immediate centers of initiative in both the economic and political life of the community.

Thus it is clear that significant decisions between competing systems and political philosophies must be made; but also that they must be constantly reviewed empirically and amended in the light of new evidence. Some of the resources for these procedures have nothing to do with our Christian faith, at least not directly. They are the resources of an inductive rather than a deductive social science. Such a science will not speak vaguely about general concepts such as property or planning. It will ask what the institution of property is in an agrarian as against an industrial situation. It will recognize that a peasant's relation to the soil is of a different order than the relation of either an owner or a worker to a factory. It will study the effects of socialization of property and will probably conclude that there were important economic as well as social reasons for Britain's socialization of coal which do not necessarily justify the plan for socializing steel. It will recognize the necessity of guaranteeing human welfare in areas in which a market economy does not satisfy human wants as, for instance, in housing and medical services. But it will not assume that human desires are naturally ordinate and that they can be satisfied by government agencies without the necessity of some restraint upon inordinate, or at least disproportionate, demands. It will not assume that all government interference in economic process is either good or bad; but it will study the effect of each type of interference.

In Professor Tillich's brilliant chapter, in which he analyzes the conflicts between human personality and the realities of a technical civilization, we have evidence of another ironic historic transmutation of good into evil which must be pragmatically analyzed. For technics originally came as an emancipating force, creating flexible and mobile forms of property, and individual forms of skill by which men were freed of the dead weight of a traditional society as well as from the slavery of poverty. But gradually the elaboration of technics has created a mass society in which men are held together mechanically, and in which their tastes are standardized and vulgarized by mass means of communication. There could be no better symbol than this of the meat of one generation turning into the poison of the next. We need not elaborate upon the spiritual strategies required to counteract the deleterious effects of a technical society, particularly not since that is done so ably by Professor Tillich. It is worth observing, however, as he himself points out, that some of the spiritual animus directed against an allegedly capitalist society by modern reformers was really more applicable to the growing dangers of technics as such. The elimination of the property system, which was intended to cure the evils, actually accentuated them in modern totalitarian regimes. Nothing could be more ironic than the contrast between Marx's early visions of creative personality in an ideal society and the sorry realities of a totalitarian community.

III. THE CRITICISM OF ABSTRACT IDEALISM

But the problems of social ethics are not solved merely by an empirical and pragmatic approach to the complex issues. Or perhaps it would be more accurate to say that something more than wrong traditions of science prevent men from applying their intelligence empirically to the problems of their common life. The real fact is that a religious problem underlies this persistence with which general ideals, laws and systems are used either as weapons of special interest or as efforts to hide the hiatus between the demands of a sensitive conscience and the morally ambiguous realities of man's social life. There can, therefore, be no genuine empiricism without a religious correction of this tendency.

The relevance of a genuine and vital Christian faith is that it unmasks the errors of a false and abstract idealism by two forces, one negative and one positive. The negative force is the contrite recognition in the Christian faith, as expounded in the New Testament, that the law is not redemptive but may be the servant of sin. This recognition belongs to the radical Christian understanding of the persistence of sin in the life of man. It is able, as Kant recognized in a rare moment of evangelical insight, to corrupt the standards themselves. The laws and ideals which we regard as guarantors of justice and bearers of our goodness can be persistently used as instruments of the ego. The knowledge of this fact is withheld from all secular idealism, and this ignorance is responsible for the fact that an age which prides itself on its humanity becomes so inhumane, and not merely among the exponents of a totalitarian creed. It is also withheld from Christian idealists. Its absence is always proved by the complacency with which Christian business men or labor leaders or any other group in society hold to and propound their ideals without fear and trembling, that is, without a contrite recognition of the ambiguity of all human laws and ideals. It must be observed that democracy at its best rests upon a recognition of this truth because it provides that no laws, ideals, structures and systems should exist without the criticism which may disclose their ambiguous character and thereby prevent the evil in them from destroying the good. Without this contrite recognition of the double character of all human ideals even a democracy can degenerate into a tyranny of the majority. The weakness of what is now generally defined as "liberal Christianity" is that it does not rigorously subject the admixture of interest in ideals to religious criticism on the one hand, and does not, on the other, detect the moralistic effort of men to close the gap between individual sensitivity and social ambiguity on the other. That is why one type of liberal can lend himself to a religious support of the *status quo*, while another type can be uncritical toward Communism under the illusion that it establishes a community based upon the "service motive."

We must consider this "ideology of conscience" rather than of interest more carefully. If one form of ideology is meant to hide the force of self-interest in human life, the other form is meant to obscure the deep tension between the individual conscience and the moral realities of man's collective life with their bewildering confusion of coercion, conflict of self-interest, domination and subordination. The one is meant to hide particular sins of particular groups. The other is meant to hide the moral precariousness of all human striving. For the collective life of man is a reminder to individual man of the moral ambiguity in all human virtue.

This second form of ideology is the most fruitful source of confusion in the relation of the Christian faith to the political order. Thus Augustine sees the realities of the political order very clearly and describes them accurately in defining the character of "civitas terrena." But he wrongly assumes that the force of a self-love does not exist in the "civitas dei." The Church is for him a "societas perfectas." Luther describes them with equal realism in his doctrine of the two realms; but he underestimates the residual capacity for justice among ordinary men, and the involvement of Christians in evil. Liberal Christianity thinks that collective self-seeking can be easily overcome by the spirit of love; and Calvinism falsely imagines that the "Rule of the Saints" can banish evil from the political order. This is another version of the Catholic error which imagines that the Church is a "societas perfectas" which can simply redeem the social order by claiming ultimate sovereignty over it.

It is instructive to note how the ideology which seeks to hide the moral ambiguity of the social order is almost as fruitful of evil as the ideology which hides the admixture of interest in particular ideals. Both forms of ideology are guilty of being so busy establishing human righteousness that no one submits human actions to the righteousness of God (Romans 10:2). The real problem of a Christian social ethic is to derive from the Gospel a clear view of the realities with which we must deal in our common or social life, and also to preserve a sense of responsibility for achieving the highest measure of order, freedom and justice despite the hazards of man's collective life.

IV. THE RELEVANCE OF THE LAW OF LOVE

If the Christian humility which has no illusions about our ideals and structures or about any of the realities of the community is the negative precondition of a Christian social ethic, the positive form of it is the application of the law of love to man's collective relations. The problem of the application of the law of love to the collective relationships of mankind contains within itself the whole question of the possibility of a Christian social ethic. When Catholic thought embodies the law of love into counsels of perfection and relegates these to the realm of ultimate possibilities of the "supernatural" life in the individual, and when it seeks to regulate the collective relations of mankind by the standards of "justice" which are given in the natural law, it is seeking to come to terms with the realities of the social order which seem to make the law of love inapplicable. This is also behind the logic of the thought of Protestant theologians who, following Luther, relegate love and forgiveness to the heavenly kingdom, as distinguished from the "earthly" one, where "the sword and the law" that is power and coercion, prevail.

On the other hand, we have long since learned to recognize the sentimentality of Christian liberalism and other forms of liberalism which regard the establishment of "motives of service" in contrast to the "profit motive" as a simple possibility. The question is therefore how, if love is not a simple possibility, it may yet be relevant to our political decisions. This question really involves the relevance of our final Christian insights as individuals to our actions as members of a group. It is as individuals that we know about love as the final law of life, although in our political actions we act as members of the group. As individuals we know the law of love to be final, if we view life through the revelation of Christ. From the standpoint of that illumination we can see the self-destructive character of every form of self-seeking and the redemptive possibility of minding not our own things but those of another (I Corinthians 10:24). It is thus possible to condemn and to guard against national egotism and other forms of collective pride even though we know that they can not be eradicated. It is equally possible to guard against the corruption of individual self-interest in establishing social institutions even though one does not expect it to be eliminated. The law of love is thus not something extra to be added to whatever morality we establish in our social relations. It is the guiding principle of them.

Thus, when the issue is raised whether one's own nation should adhere to alliance of nations, one may well know that it is not possible for any nation to do this if it means sacrificing its own interest to the interests of the whole. In that sense the law of love is remote, if not irrelevant. But one also knows that it is wrong for a nation to prefer its own welfare to the welfare of a larger community. Therefore every form of political activity which exalts a class, nation or group absolutely stands under condemnation. This is, of course, a fairly simple application of the law of love. It is more difficult when, as is usually the case, the conflict is between two groups, the family and the nation, or between two families or two nations or two classes. The simplest application of the law of love is to ask the question: are we doing this for ourselves? But this simple question does not always suffice, for it invariably gives the advantage to the other group which may not deserve it. We cannot, for instance, solve the problem of our conflict with Communism by yielding to it as "the other," to the disadvantage of our civilization because it is our own. We have to ask what universal values are embodied in our several collective efforts and then use the question to check the undue advantage which we give our own cause. This is the strategy which Professor Bennett follows in his admirable essay on the relations between East and West, and which Professor Heimann follows in his critical attitude toward values of a liberal society, which he generally affirms. We must try to do justice both to the general values which our cause embodies beyond our own interest and to our tendency to value these too highly because our cause embodies them. In very specific terms it would require that in the social struggle the business community should learn from the Gospel a certain uneasiness about its uncritical devotion to freedom, and that the industrial workers should learn to be less confident of the consequence of a policy of planning. It would not mean judging issues in terms of general principles but learning to understand the limit and ambiguity of every general principle and the taint of self-interest in every devotion to general principle. It would mean, in short, that insights into the mixture of motives in the espousal of ideals which can only be learned, as it were, in the final wrestling of the soul with God, should be incorporated into institutions which can know nothing of such wrestling. In that sense the Christian faith must be a "leaven" which leavens the lump. It must derive, as the prophets did, insights for collective action which are drawn only from individual religious experience. They are applicable because the collective life of mankind conforms to the ultimate laws of God, as surely as does individual life. But they are not ascertained by the collective conscience, if indeed there is such an entity. They are mediated by the individual conscience to the collectivity.

V. LOVE AND DISCRIMINATE JUDGMENT

In one sense, the applicability of the law of love to the complex problem of social ethics could be defined as the question how the heedlessness of perfect love can be related to the discriminate judgments which are required to weigh competing values and interests in the field of social relations. Perfect love is sacrificial love, making no careful calculations between the interests of the self and the other. Perfect justice is discriminate and calculating, carefully measuring the limits of interests and the relation between the interests of the self and the other. The spirit of justice is particularly well served if reason finds the points of coincidence between the interests of the self and those of the other, and if not, if it makes careful and discriminate judgments between them. What can this heedlessness of Agape have to do with discrimination? It would have nothing to do at all, if there were such a thing as pure reason which could arbitrate between interests, and if there were recurring patterns of life so analogous as to reveal structures of justice which reason could discern. Actually, the human situation lacks both of these elements upon which rationalistic ethical judgments depend so much. The reason with which we reason about each other's affairs and interests is not "pure" reason and it cannot be made "objective and impartial" by any rational discipline or scientific method. The self, whether individual or collective, is too deeply involved in its processes. Furthermore, the historic encounters between individuals and groups in which rights and interests must be adjudicated and arbitrated always contain so many novel and contingent elements that it is not wise to trust general rules and principles too much. There is, in short, no guarantee of justice in man's reason. There is a possibility of justice only in the self, provided it is not too sure of itself. The heedlessness of love, which sacrifices the interests of the self, enters into the calculations of justice by becoming the spirit of contrition which issues from the self's encounter with God. In that encounter it is made aware of the contingent character of all human claims and the tainted character of all human pretensions and ideals. This contrition is the socially relevant counterpart of love. It breaks the pride of the implacable contestants and competitors in all human encounters and persuades them to be "kindly affectioned one with another, forgiving one another, even also as God in Christ has forgiven you" (Ephesians 4:32). This spirit lies at the foundation of what we define as democracy. For democracy cannot exist if there is no recognition of the fragmentary character of all systems of thought and value which are allowed to exist together within the democratic frame. Thus the Agape of forgiveness as well as the Agape of sacrificial love become a leaven in the lump of the spirit of justice. Or rather it would be better to use the other Gospel symbol and define them as the "salt" which arrests the decay in the spirit of justice.

The relevance of these forms of love, which transcend justice, to the spirit of justice will become apparent whenever communal life is analyzed, not as Aristotle and Stoic rationalists analyzed it, as an order of vitalities which is prevented from falling into chaos by its conformity to particular structures which reason must ascertain. It is recognized rather as a vast series of encounters between human selves and their interests. The encounters are indeed regularized into patterns and stabilities, and the habit of conformity to these stabilities mitigate the encounters. But these social patterns are not "eternal laws" and they cannot hide the essential character of social life as an encounter between myself and another, whether individually or collectively. Whether the encounter is creative or destructive, cooperative or competitive, depends not so much upon the rule of justice which is finally found to compose an incipient conflict but upon the humility with which the pretensions of the self, particularly the collective self, are laid bare and the contrition with which its dishonesties in conflict are acknowledged. The law of love is, in short, always relevant to the field of social ethics whenever it is recognized that this field has to deal primarily with human selves and not with either mind, on the one hand, or sub-rational vitalities, on the other.

VI. LOVE AND SELF-LOVE

The relevance of the law of love to the field of social institutions and collective relations is established whenever the religious awareness of the individual, in conscious relation to the divine, is related to the intricacies and complexities of social relations. In that sense, a Christian social ethic requires competent technical judgments. But the relevance of the law of love rests upon a more basic religious consideration. It is established whenever religious experience bears testimony both to the law of love and to that of self-love. For to understand the law of love as a final imperative, but not to know about the persistence of the power of self-love in all of life but particularly in the collective relations of mankind, results in an idealistic ethic with no relevance to the hard realities of life. To know about the power of self-love but not to know that its power does not make it normative is to dispense with ethical standards and fall into cynicism. But to know both the law of love as the final standard and the law of self-love as a persistent force is to enable Christians to have a foundation for a pragmatic ethic in which power and self-interest are used, beguiled, harnessed and deflected for the ultimate end of establishing the highest and most inclusive possible community of justice and order. This is the very heart of the problem of Christian politics: the readiness to use power and interest in the service of an end dictated by love and yet an absence of complacency about the evil inherent in them. No definitions or structures of justice can prevent these forces from getting out of hand if they are not handled with a sense of their peril.

Naturally, the justice and harmony which is achieved in this way is not the harmony of the kingdom of God, nor yet identical with the highest possible harmony between individuals in their personal evaluations. For this reason, there must always be a final distinction between what the Gospel demands of us in our individual and spontaneous relations and what is demanded in the institutions and structures of society. It is equally idle to expect any system of law or any codified relationship to exhaust the possibilities of grace and freedom which can be expressed by individuals above and beyond the law, or to expect such spontaneous and gracious relations to take the place of law. Professor Miller's discussion of the doctrine of vocation is a good illustration of the double attitude which is required for this problem. For, on the one hand, Christians must seek to serve God, that is, consider the ultimate purpose of their toil, no matter how inadequate may be the structure of justice in which they are forced to toil. But, on the other hand, they must always reconsider the organizations and arrangements through which the toil of men is organized so that impediments to life's more ultimate purposes may be removed.

Usually Christian sensitivity becomes becalmed and isolated in the realm of personal relations and sheds no light and offers no creative contribution to the political and economic problems of life. The liberal Christian form of sensitivity overestimates the moral possibilities of man's collective life while the more orthodox Protestant versions are usually overcome by a pessimistic overemphasis on the evils in collective life, thus consigning it to the devil.

The task of any movement devoted to "social Christianity" must be, therefore, not so much to advocate a particular nostrum for the solution of various economic and social evils, but to bring a full testimony of a gospel of judgment and grace to bear upon all of human life: Upon the individual in the final heights of individual self-consciousness, where it transcends all social institutions and historic situations, and upon human communities which do, on their own level, make contact with the kingdom of God, whenever individuals recognize that judgment and mercy of God are relevant to their collective as well as to their individual actions, and to the actions by which they order their common life as well as to actions in which they express themselves above and beyond every particular order or system.

Index

✳

243

HN31 .H85   c.1
Hutchison, John
Christian faith and social act

9310 00014957 3

GOSHEN COLLEGE-GOOD LIBRARY

Date Due